The Rule of the Land

GARRETT CARR

The Rule of the Land

Walking Ireland's Border

FABER & FABER

First published in 2017
by Faber & Faber Ltd
Bloomsbury House
74–77 Great Russell Street
London WC1B 3DA

First published in the USA in 2017

Typeset by Faber & Faber Ltd
Printed in the UK by CPI Group (UK) Ltd, Croydon, CR0 4YY

A CIP record for this book
is available from the British Library

ISBN 978–0–571–31335–8

FSC
www.fsc.org
MIX
Paper from
responsible sources
FSC® C020471

2 4 6 8 10 9 7 5 3 1

For Caroline, for everything

Contents

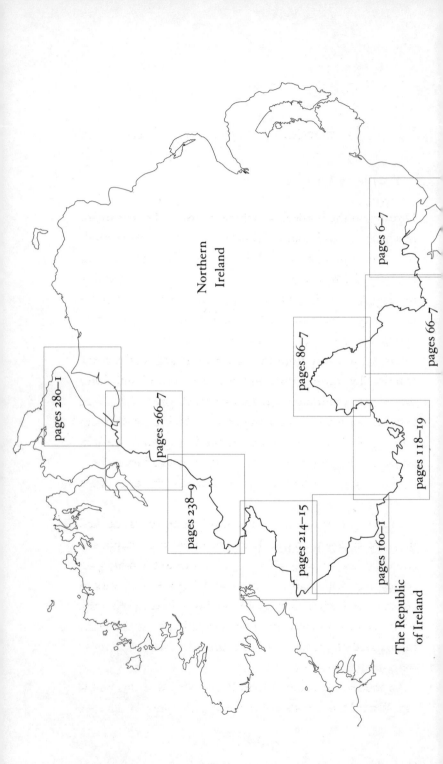

pages 6–7

pages 66–7

pages 86–7

pages 118–19

pages 280–1

pages 266–7

pages 238–9

pages 214–15

pages 160–1

Northern
Ireland

The Republic
of Ireland

The Border Interpretive Centre

Directly on the borderline, where it crosses the first major north–south road, stands a child's drawing of a house made real. Four walls, one doorway, two windows and a roof, it could hardly be a simpler structure. No door and nothing inside but a single small room. Housemartins have made mud nests in the rafters. I step in, look out of the windows and then step out. There is nothing else to do.

Only a few feet from the doorway an articulated truck trundles by, raising dust and making the roadside litter dance. Every minute or so another truck goes by, straight over the border. I am standing between Ireland's north and south, a place now set to become the European Union's in and out. This tiny house is the only structure here. There are no immigration checkpoints to delay the drivers, at least not yet.

Once a grocery shop stood on this spot but it was burned down in an arson attack. The owners did not rebuild the shop but they knew that leaving the site vacant would mean reapplying for planning permission if they ever did want to construct something here again. So this was quickly put up, a placeholder, just enough to ensure a building lineage is maintained on the site. This is a structure with no purpose other than to simply *be*.

In 2000 an artist called John Byrne borrowed this building. What he did with it was the manifestation of an idea

born on the fly, in the middle of delivering a standup comedy routine. Suppose, John wondered aloud, we actually encouraged people to visit Ireland's border? People go to see stranger things – tombs, bridges, old walls. Couldn't the border be a tourist attraction? John Byrne had an idea: put an interpretive centre on it. A proper tourist attraction always has one of those.

No one else was going to do it, so Byrne did. He set up and staffed the Interpretive Centre himself. It was an information bureau and shop. You could buy T-shirts and badges saying 'Good Luck from the Border'. Byrne sold postcards featuring photographs of military forts. But these were not the ruins of Norman or Elizabethan castles normally found on postcards, their bloody aspects now safely historicised. Byrne's postcards featured modern military watchtowers, installations built by the British army in response to a terrorist threat on the borderland, a threat that was still ongoing. This zone was militarised at the time. The watchtowers were still staffed and operational, steel structures bristling with cameras, aerials and spotlights. From any- where along this stretch of the border, the eastern end, you could see at least one of them. And its cameras could see you, watch you cross the border, read your car's number plate.

The border was a troubled place when Byrne opened the Border Interpretive Centre, and had been contested for all its existence. The borderland itself is thinly populated, often tranquil, but the twisty line that divides the island on the map is a symbol that divides opinion. The line on the map offers no space to meet so it was smart of John Byrne to make room here on the ground. The Border Interpretive Centre stood directly on the borderline, proving it was not just a symbol, it was also a patch of earth, a living place where things happened. A busload of people came to the official opening of the Border Interpretive Centre. They stood around, remarking on the weirdness of what they were doing. Rather than driving over the line they had stopped to look at it, to take it in. They were pioneers of a sort, they were visiting the border. They could take some home with them; sods of border soil were for sale in ziplock bags. A Northern Irish comedian gave a speech at the event. He noted that although Ireland's border was small, and despite having viewed many other borders, he still felt it to be 'the best', 'something that unites the whole country'.

I meet John Byrne long after his time on the border. I walk up to him in a Belfast bar, introduce myself, and we get chatting about the Border Interpretive Centre. The pub is overcrowded and I suggest we go out with the other drinkers who have flowed out into an alley but John refuses as that would mean drinking from plastic cups instead of proper pint glasses. I like this commitment to doing things correctly. John says he was a 'border worrier' – not meaning he actually fretted about it, but that he couldn't leave it alone. He felt compelled to poke at the border, get under it or look at it from original angles.

I too, I realise, am a border worrier, and I'm glad to meet another. I tell Byrne my plan. I am about to begin a long walk, travelling Ireland's border from end to end. I want to see the entire line, following it no matter where it brings me. Some of the border is water, so I'll have to borrow a boat occasionally. Most travellers are only on the border for the blink of an eye; it is something to go over on the way to a destination in the north or south. But the border itself is my destination and I will follow it east to west, come what may.

'Will you record it?' he asks.

'Yes,' I say, 'I'm going to make a map of it.'

John goes on to tell me about an idea of his own. 'Do you know, on TV nature documentaries, the landscape fly-over footage that they use, if they've got the budget?'

I know the sort of thing, and can imagine it's expensive to capture. Headlands, peaks or savannah seen from above in smooth tracking shots, filmed with a Steadicam slung under a helicopter.

'I want to make a film with footage like that,' he tells me, 'make a film featuring a fly-over of the border.' His eyes drift to the ceiling as he describes the idea. He wants to get a camera and a helicopter and cruise the borderline, filming it from high above. Perhaps fly on summer evenings, catch it in golden light, give the border an epic sheen. I love the idea immediately. Such footage is often shot of coastlines, there is drama in the clash of land and sea, but John wants to capture the drama of two countries striking against each other. Instead of land and sea it will be land and land, think of it as two edges for the price of one.

But if John ever raises the large amount of money it will take, watching the film will still not be a substitute for my walk. I want to see the line up close. I want to see how the land and its people have reacted to the border, and the ways in which the line is made manifest. First it just demarcated counties, then countries and will next be where the United Kingdom and the European Union touch – this line has a lot of responsibilities. In 2016 the UK voted to disentangle itself from the EU, while the Republic of Ireland remained a committed member. It was striking how little the possible effect on Ireland was discussed in the lead-up to the referendum on EU membership. You might have thought the border between the UK and the EU was going to be the English Channel. But it won't be, it's here, and it's as thin as wire. It turns out that I will see the border in a peaceful yet fragile moment. Looking at the border will also require thinking back in time, charting its past. So far my map is just a large sheet of paper with nothing on it but the border's crooked course and an X representing the Border Interpretive Centre. I'm not sure what else I'll find. As a symbol the border divides, but I'm going to see what it is doing on the ground, and in the water.

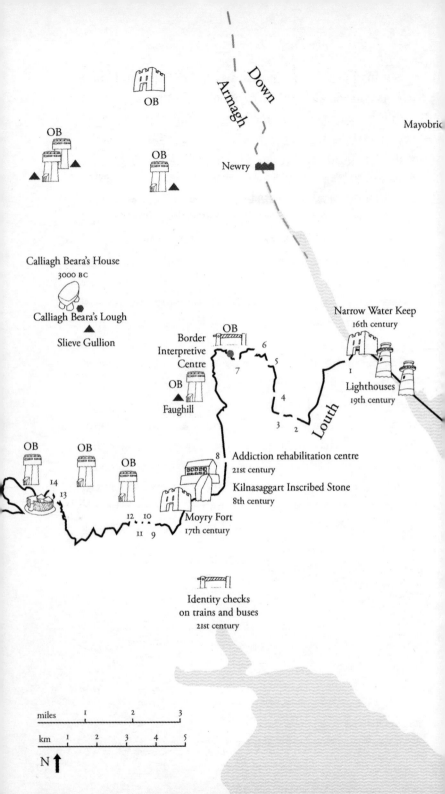

Down

Armagh

OB

OB

OB

OB

Newry

Mayobric

Calliagh Beara's House
3000 BC

Calliagh Beara's Lough

Slieve Gullion

Narrow Water Keep
16th century

Border
Interpretive
Centre

OB

7

6

5

4

3   2

Louth

OB

Faughill

Lighthouses
19th century

1

OB

OB

OB

14

13

12 10

11   9

8

Addiction rehabilitation centre
21st century

Kilnasaggart Inscribed Stone
8th century

Moyry Fort
17th century

Identity checks
on trains and buses
21st century

miles   1   2   3

km   1   2   3   4   5

N

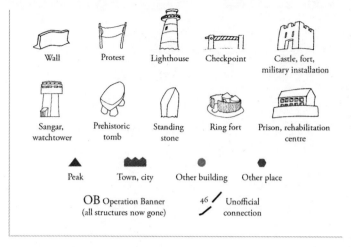

Wall   Protest   Lighthouse   Checkpoint   Castle, fort, military installation

Sangar, watchtower   Prehistoric tomb   Standing stone   Ring fort   Prison, rehabilitation centre

▲ Peak   Town, city   Other building   Other place

OB Operation Banner (all structures now gone)   46 Unofficial connection

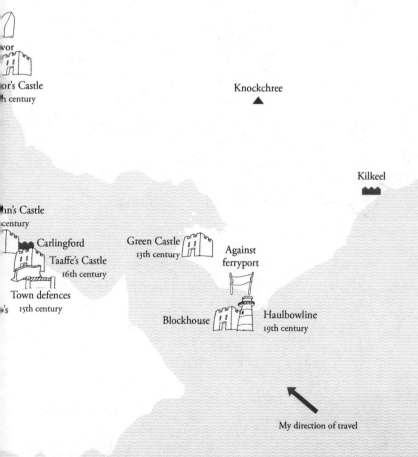

...vor
...or's Castle
...h century

Knockchree
▲

Kilkeel

...hn's Castle
...century

Carlingford

Taaffe's Castle
16th century

Town defences
...'s   15th century

Green Castle
13th century

Against ferryport

Blockhouse

Haulbowline
19th century

My direction of travel

Lighthouses, Vikings

We pick up the border from the open sea, approaching it in a twelve-foot canoe. Rain is coming down so hard it seems there are no individual drops, just thick cold saturation. I am accompanied by Paddy Bloomer. He will journey with me a few times, wherever the border travels open water like it does here on Carlingford Lough. I am kneeling in the bow, pulling us forward with a paddle. He is sitting to stern, at the tricky business of steering and keeping us right with the waves. Paddy is an artist, engineer, barn-raiser and recycler. His practice involves taking junk and transforming it into things of beauty and usefulness. He is also a canoeist, this vessel and the knowledge to handle it belong to him. I've never been in one before, I just do what I am told, the mindless engine, pulling us forward – reach, dip, tug, reach, dip, tug . . .

'The oar is cutting into my hand,' I complain.

'It's called a paddle,' says Paddy.

Ahead, tall and grey in the sodden atmosphere, is the border's first monument. Haulbowline Lighthouse stands off shore. Waves crash at it from all sides. I think of it as the beginning because this lighthouse – smooth stone, seamless from a distance – is a fine spool from which to unwind the border. I imagine the line as three hundred miles of oily black cable, wrapped around the lighthouse, waiting to be drawn out.

When Ireland's lighthouses were staffed, the keepers were usually relieved every fortnight but Haulbowline was so grim a confine that its staff were relieved twice a week. You can't stroll around Haulbowline, you can barely take a step. The tower completely smothers the rock it stands on. Paddy and I slip into the lighthouse's orbit. Currents slap about unpredictably but we paddle closer and experience its immensity. I am soaked, rainwater runs from my wrists and down my sleeves, but I feel no hurry. There is something comforting about the lighthouse, something paternal about the way it dominates our small craft. There is elegance here too, Haulbowline's body tapers out smoothly, granite made graceful. As the foundation is out of sight it is easy to imagine the lighthouse's body continuing to curve under the water, an upside-down funnel, getting wider and wider, until it might slide against the sea floor in a disc the size of a racetrack. Above the water, the structure is nothing but solid blocks for at least twenty courses, a mighty stump giving the lighthouse a low centre of gravity. Each block is wedge-shaped and a perfect fit to its neighbours, so tightly packed not even damp can enter. Haulbowline was designed to deny the sea any bite because even a tiny space between blocks would have been eaten at and widened, weakening the structure, eventually pulling the lighthouse down. Without a nook or cranny for waves to pick at, Haulbowline has been standing since 1824.

A short distance away, on one of Carlingford Lough's tiny islands, we see what waves can do. The island is all black rock slabs and seaweed, the highest point only a few feet above water level. Paddy and I pull the canoe up onto it and tramp about for a few minutes. Waves of seaweed cling to our ankles. A bunker-like fort was built here in the sixteenth

century, or maybe it was later, nobody knows for sure, so it might have been to defend against Spaniards or Scots, Cromwell or Napoleon. Someone was always threatening the land and Carlingford is a deep inlet, a good way in. The fort walls are four feet thick, an attempt to stand up against the sea by means of simple heft. The attempt failed. The fort is in pieces now, two-ton chunks scattered wide.

'When we were kids we were told an escaped prisoner hid out in the blockhouse for weeks,' Paddy tells me. 'He survived by creeping out after dark to eat mussels and seaweed.'

We walk from one lump of masonry to another. Some are hard to distinguish from the island rocks. It stops raining and the breeze whips the damp from our clothes. I walk down to the shore, take my camera from its ziplock bag and photograph Haulbowline.

The need to create an impervious structure is what gave

Haulbowline its curve. This design was perfected in Scotland, where Haulbowline's closest relatives are found. Scotland is only a few wet miles away; at night the flash of several Scottish lighthouses can be seen from here. It was an engineer named Robert Stevenson who began building these curved towers. He was the founder of a lighthouse-building dynasty although one grandson turned away from engineering and became a writer instead. Think of the salt water washing around Robert Louis Stevenson's paternal line and you understand something of where *Treasure Island* and *Kidnapped* came from. He also held his grandfather in high regard, writing: 'He was above all things a projector of works in the face of nature, and a modifier of nature itself . . . The rains, the winds and the waves, the complexity and the fitfulness of nature, are always before him.'

Thank you Robert Louis, you've put your finger on it. A lighthouse is the product of optimism, applied with cold rationality. Haulbowline is built on rock and the belief that technology will make our lives fuller and longer. We need not be shoved around by nature; we can build things to help us hold a place in it. I realise that, just like a castle or a fort, a lighthouse is defensive architecture. Haulbowline defends cargo against fog, fishermen from heavy weather and, in some broader way, lighthouses stand against general chaos, the violence tossed up by a world at spin. Haulbowline guards a different border than the one on the map, it holds the line between order and chaos.

The lighthouse got its name from the rock it is built on. The rock got its name from Viking raiders, *Aale-bolig*; Place of Eels. So the name's nautical feel is not from its etymology, but nor is it coincidence. The Vikings left the name *Aale-bolig* behind but no one here understood it so it began to drift about, a foreign word that needed to be made to fit. A process of Chinese Whispers gradually drew the name closer and closer to the language used around it, a language fixated on boats, tackle and rigging. *Aale-bolig* . . . *Haul-bowline.*

This entire inlet got its name from Vikings. They sailed in and saw that although the waters were relatively narrow they extended far into the country. This made them feel at home – it was a *fjord*. Working their way around the coast, Vikings put the *ford* into the names of many Irish bays. But unlike many others, Carlingford truly is a fjord; carved by a glacier, it fits the typical geological definition. As glaciers slid out to sea their undersides melted and released tons of sand. Now Carlingford's bed is a layer of sand many feet thick. Paddy and I see it below us later as the weather improves and the sun comes out. We are paddling along the southern shore towards a village and the white sand below makes the water glow turquoise, a colour I associate with the equator, not the border. I almost expect to see nut-brown children splashing about. Instead, on a jetty, are a bunch of pasty boys in fluorescent lifejackets waiting for a kayak lesson.

'Lunch?' I say to Paddy.

'Food, aye,' he says, surveying the settlement.

It could be the steady work of the paddle, or it could be Paddy's beard, but as we clamber ashore at the village I feel like we're Viking raiders, here to pillage. We want carbohydrates, lots. Carlingford town is full of picturesque ruins, the streets are tidy and postcardish. The cafes are too cutesy for Paddy and me, our wellington boots and raw needs, but we have to choose one. It has tablecloths, and amateur watercolours of the town's ruins on the wall. Paddy eyes the paintings wearily but concedes they've done a good job on the framing. We order food, gobble it down, then order coffee. It comes in china receptacles only slightly bigger than egg cups. Perhaps they were egg cups. They're gone in a gulp. Luckily for the cafe's owners, we have left our axes in the boat.

Back on the water, back to the border. As we paddle inland, mountains rise to port and starboard. South are the Cooleys. North, the Mountains of Mourne sweep down to the sea. The Cooleys are ruffled and pitted, the Mournes taller and polished smooth by glaciers. Mountain ranges of differing personalities and this wide band of water between; I sense the edge of kingdoms.

'It's a good place to put a border,' says Paddy. 'I mean, if you have a border and need a place for it.'

Carlingford Lough's deep chink brought Viking raiders far inland before they had to leave their vessels. The landscape would have been greener with trees then, and would have looked promising. The people here were raised on milk and steak. There were plenty of broad-backed slaves to be had and maybe fine metalwork too if the raiders found one of the new monasteries. I picture them as spirited freebooters, laughing, goading each other, becoming increasingly excited as they get deeper inland and finally disembark. They are like a bunch of boys loose in an orchard.

Twelve hundred years later, the Danish culture minister will visit Ireland and apologise on their behalf.

*

The lough narrows into the mouth of a canal, the border goes with it. I look out for a good campsite along the shore.

'Trees, ferns, it's all gorgeous,' says Paddy. He doesn't care, he's going home.

Just before landing, Paddy and I encounter two more lighthouses. Neither of us has seen anything like them before. Very different from Haulbowline, these lights are low to the water and the stonework is crude. There is no need for watertight masonry here, we have travelled away from the open sea, big waves will not trouble these towers. The designer was free to do whatever they wanted and they decided to borrow from Ireland's medieval architecture. The lighthouses have been styled like monastic refuge towers, complete with limpet-shell roofs.

The structures that inspired the style of these lighthouses predate them by over a thousand years. They stood in the grounds of monasteries and are often simply called round towers. When I was in school we were taught that monks built the towers as a place of retreat during Viking raids. Hence a single doorway high on the side; at the approach of

trouble the monks would gather armfuls of valuables and withdraw inside the tower, pulling the ladder up behind them. I drew such scenes with colouring pencils in my exercise books, but this conjecture is now doubted. No raider would row all the way from Dublin or Denmark then give up on slaves and a silver crozier just because a door was inconveniently high. Some archaeologists now think round towers were simply predecessors of today's church spires; a statement of power, a marker, and useful for projecting the clang of a bell.

But in 1887 round towers were believed to have been refuges from Viking raids, and that was when these lighthouses were built. So, given Carlingford's Viking history, designing them to look like round towers creates a pleasant echo. Raiders rowing in, like a fog rolling in, required the construction of defences. Paddy points out the solar panels on their roofs; these lighthouses are still functional. Their war is ongoing.

Since encountering his lighthouses, I have spent time among archives trying to learn something of their designer, Allan MacDonnell. He is a very different case from the Stevensons. He left no writings and there is little to go on. I'm not even sure how he spelled his name, the records contradict. A museum curator sent me an email that amounted to a shrug; 'It seems MacDonnell is one of history's forgotten.' The few things I can say about him were pieced together by American genealogists who worked from tombstone inscriptions, newspaper mentions and MacDonnell's patents. There are many of these; MacDonnell was an inventive man.

I can place Allan MacDonnell walking through the town of Newry one day in February 1875. The pavements are

busy. This soon-to-be-border town is a hub of manufactur-
ing and trade, producing flax, linen, iron goods, mineral
water, furniture and carriages, all exported by sea, via the
canal to Carlingford Lough. Newry is one of the first places
in Ireland to have street lighting. Visitors note the town's
clean streets and comfortable coffee houses. There are a few
beggars but they aren't excessively 'coaxing and wheedling
in their talk'. MacDonnell is now forty-seven. I picture him
in a coat heavier than most, with fur on the lapels. Ships
from all over the world dock at Newry, so you might think
he had bought the unusual coat from a sailor. But no,
MacDonnell lived in Russia for many years and has just
returned to Ireland, land of his birth. In Russia he worked
with Alfred Nobel – inventor of dynamite, progenitor of
the Nobel Prize – and, by the time he left, had patented a
few compounds of his own. MacDonnell is a chemist and an
engineer. He is on his way to deliver a public lecture entitled
The Chemistry of Water and Carbon.

How would he seem as he walked? Abstracted perhaps,
a scientist, he is calculating displacement as he walks to the
town hall. Or he may have cut a much more political figure,
engaged with the street, greeting people, tipping his hat . . .
We don't know. But, introvert or extrovert, he walked pur-
posefully. MacDonnell was certainly a doer. He has just
filed another patent, a machine for filling and corking bottles. Soon he will oversee improvements to Newry's most
vital artery, its canal link to the sea, widening and deepen-
ing it to accommodate the future's bigger vessels. To see
boats safely into the canal from the lough he will build two
new lighthouses. Another designer might place them left
and right of the canal's entrance: beacons were commonly
arranged like this, like goalposts. But MacDonnell thought

there was a better way. Goalposts, even when placed close together, can be approached from any angle along a wide arc. MacDonnell will position the towers so the canal will be approached one way, the fastest way, the safest way, the best way.

Learning that Allan MacDonnell was an engineer and inventor reminds us that the evocation of monastic history is only the outer style of these lighthouses. Primarily, they were sensible technology. Travelling up the lough from the sea, a pilot steers so as to keep both lights aligned straight ahead. The tower further back has been built taller to enable this. Following this line of sight leads the vessel straight into the canal system. The lighthouses were styled with some antiquarian amusement but were really shaped by Enlightenment optimism meeting nineteenth-century entrepreneurialism and commerce. They are machines for letting trade flow.

Paddy and I paddle the recommended way, the towers lined up ahead of us. There is something satisfying in this; slotting ourselves into the groove of a fastidious mind. The border too, has fallen into line. MacDonnell's lights guide the border in.

In MacDonnell's time Newry reaches its limits. In the last decade of the nineteenth century the town had all the business its infrastructure could handle. Belfast, which Newry once rivalled, now steams ahead. Allan MacDonnell leaves, never to return, going to Texas and making a new home on the plains. His next mention in the historical record is in 1906, filing a patent for a new kind of land roller and furrower. Four years later he dies.

MacDonnell's lighthouses on Carlingford Lough are hardly famous but they have survived, and are his only remaining statement. They still fulfil their role but these lighthouses also have a sculptural quality that, I think, is sweetened by knowing a little about MacDonnell. The trajectory of his life suggests ambition arranged, like these lighthouses, in a westerly direction. Russia, Ireland, America. It is as if MacDonnell put a coded message into these towers: Go West. They certainly advise us to keep moving. You might call it progress or just momentum, but we definitely need to keep moving.

Loving, Killing

Tonight in a border pub a young man and young woman get talking. They are not strangers, they grew up in the same area but, slowly, things are going to a new level. They have, in local lingo, 'a notion' of each other. He has a notion of her. She has a notion of him. To have a notion of someone is to see potential in them, to see potential in the idea of you together. I'm talking about love.

Or perhaps that's old news, they became a couple months ago. They are not in a pub. They are at her kitchen table eating dinner with her parents. There is polite intergenerational conversation. They all agree that reinstating border controls will be bad for business. He has just gotten a job with a wholesale supplier, delivering animal feed to farms both sides of the border. Her mother asks about this, she approves. It's all quite pleasant but there are sideways glances between the young couple. She lives with her parents and he lives with his, this is limiting, as you can imagine. Their toes tap soundlessly inside their shoes.

When they get a moment alone she says to him or perhaps he says to her, 'Do you fancy a spin to Narrow Water?' Their pulses hop. 'Yes,' she replies. Or maybe, 'Aye,' or 'Alright so,' or 'Go on then.'

They get in his van and drive, following Carlingford Lough's southern shore. A stony lane leads off the road. It's after dark, most people would miss the turn-off, but the couple know the area. The lane leads through woods to the waterside and a slipway that is broken up and disused, no boat has tied up here in years. They park overlooking the canal. They can see Ireland's border slipping by on the surface. He turns off the engine. The van has been unloaded and swept but there is still the odour of cattle feed. They turn to each other. They kiss. They kiss some more. They fumble at buttons. They begin to probe each other's boundaries.

Suddenly a man emerges from the trees, right by the windscreen. His appearance is a shock but the couple can tell he is harmless because of how he is dressed; boots, mismatched walking gear. He is holding a map in his hand. No danger, but his arrival embarrasses everyone. The walker can't help but catch sight of peeled-back clothing and exposed skin. Then the van's front seat is busy with the readjusting of garments. The couple keep their faces turned down and away. The walker scuttles on past, making sure to see no more. The driver starts the engine and they reverse away, leaving the man alone by the border.

Dear couple in the van, let me take this opportunity to apologise. This is obviously a spot for lovers, for 'courting'. It suits the role, secluded and quiet, with the breeze in the branches and darkening water sliding out to the lough. You can be sure of privacy here, nobody visits the border, especially after dark. But tonight, unfortunately for the lovers, some fool is visiting. I'm even going to spend the night.

Under my boots, beneath matted leaves, I can feel the rounded stones of the old slipway. They make it impossible to pitch my tent and the undergrowth is too thick to pitch under the trees. It is a dry night so I will make do with my tarpaulin, getting in my sleeping bag and wrapping myself in the tarp until I look like a blue burrito. Across the canal, in Northern Ireland, a dual carriageway runs parallel to the water. Big lorries cruise along it, decked in yellow lights that blink out for a moment as they pass behind a black patch. This is the robust and boxy Narrow Water Keep, built out over the water, across the canal but this side of the dual carriageway.

The waterway is just wide enough for no traffic sound to reach me. I lie wrapped up in the dark and silence. It might be because of the passing vehicles, the hard stones or the couple in the van but I feel lonely. When my mobile phone chimes I grab for it, eager for a friend, but it's an automatic text from my service provider, telling me that I have roamed into another country. I will be getting a lot of these texts from now on. There is a splash. A seal parts the water and looks at me with its wet pebble eyes. Three seconds later it goes back under.

*

Next morning I make an expedition into the trees. Wading through ferns, I can hear drinks cans crunching under my boots. I emerge where a railway once ran; the sleepers and rails are gone but the route remains, readable in the flattened earth and a pair of hedgerows, parallel and close together. I stop and study the ground, like a detective searching for clues, but there are only the hoof marks of sheep. I look across the water, across the border. Lorries are still motoring along the dual carriageway, sunlight glinting off their taillights as they approach Narrow Water Keep.

One day in 1979 soldiers were travelling that road in a convoy, two trucks and a jeep. The British armed forces had been deployed to hold Northern Ireland together against escalating violence. Moving among the general citizenry, hard to distinguish, was the Irish Republican Army. Their aim was to forcefully erase the border, making the island one united and independent country. The IRA was the most recent version of physical force nationalism, an ideology that can be traced at least as far back as the 1790s. The IRA was organised along military lines but fought with guerrilla tactics and the British army was its primary foe. Road journeys were risky for the army and this route particularly so as it runs along the border; IRA snipers sometimes operated from the south. The soldiers knew it was dangerous but they were also determined not to be predictable in their choice of routes, so even this border-hugging road was used occasionally. I picture soldiers in the back of one of the trucks. Moustaches, cigarettes and pecking orders. Even in a society as small as the back of a truck there are social alliances and exclusions. Perhaps there were one or two quiet ones, not getting involved, looking at the water through gaps in the canvas.

A bomb exploded on the roadside. The convoy's last truck was enveloped in a fireball. The bomb had been detonated from where I am now standing, a few dozen feet south of the border. Two members of the IRA were crouched on the railway embankment. I see now what they would have seen and I'd like to report some sharp insight but there is just a vaguely cold sense of having stepped into the ghost of an event. Exploding the bomb at the precise moment to catch a fast-moving vehicle was difficult. The IRA members had positioned themselves where they could use one of two nineteenth-century lighthouses, out on the water, as a marker. When the truck passed behind the smaller tower they triggered the bomb. This was a line of sight that Allan MacDonnell did not predict. Dare to erect a tall structure on this landscape and you never know what alignments it could get drawn into. Seven people died in the blast.

A survivor later recalled being knocked to the ground by the blast. When he sat up he could see wreckage and burning body parts all around, and was aware of the stillness and silence in the aftermath of the explosion. Then he realised that he too was on fire. The bomb had been packed with cans of petrol.

The sound of the explosion reverberated across the water. Hearing it, other soldiers raced to the spot and a quick reaction force was dropped in by helicopter. The first thing they did was set up a control point in the gateway of a country house a little up the road. Choosing that spot was logical: granite walls gave some cover and it was close to the bomb-site. However, there was danger in logic. This choice of control point was predictable, so it was where the IRA had hidden the second bomb.

It went off thirty minutes after the first. Instead of petrol, coal had been packed around the bomb. I can't imagine what effect coal would have had in the explosion itself but, even decades later, it makes the blast somehow tangible – gives the killing a mineral ferocity. One solider was vaporised so completely that he was initially listed as missing. Now eighteen people had died.

There was confusion among the surviving soldiers, dazed, staggering about. A popping noise went off and off and off. Cases of bullets were igniting in a burning jeep but the soldiers thought they were being fired upon. They shot over a hundred rounds into the trees by the slipway across the water. But there was that unlikely thing – someone was visiting the border. A man had walked down to where I slept last night. He was hit and killed. Now nineteen people had died.

I have started counting and I don't know how to stop. This is a problem with counting, you never find the end. You can always add the next person and the next. Five other people were killed in political violence that day. In the following week two more died. Within a month, another four. Different armed groups killed thirty more in the months to the end of 1979. With most of these killings, as with the Narrow Water bombs, no one was ever convicted.

*

I lie on my back on the grassy embankment. The land is warming in the new sun, the grass is tickling my ears. Six or seven swifts swoosh over me, inches from my nose. I stand up and watch the birds glide down the centre of the waterway. I can see where the border comes ashore, becoming the United Kingdom's only land border. I retrieve my gear and go after it, into the Cooley Mountains. There is no black line painted up the slopes but the border is not invisible either, something always hosts it. It travels along a hedgerow, then a stone wall, then a fence. These boundaries are no different from the other hedgerows, stone walls and fences nearby. You need local knowledge or, like me, a detailed Ordnance Survey map to know which is the border. I find an apple tree growing straight out of the line. A coincidence, I wonder, that the tree took root in the borderline, or did someone plant it here as a marker? There is no one to ask on these unpopulated slopes, I will not see a single person all morning. I pick a day's supply of fruit and keep climbing.

The last road before the peak is a lane, too narrow for carriageway markings but a speed limit sign stands facing into Northern Ireland, 80 it says. It also tells drivers that they have crossed the border, the only way to know exactly when the transition occurs. Read the sign a little closer and more can be gleaned. The figure is in kilometres, like on the continent. The Republic of Ireland has looked to mainland Europe in issues of network cohesion, away from the UK's imperial values and use of miles. Commitment to the European Union always felt stronger south of the line. Part of a historical connection that might go all the way back to the French Revolution, an event that was a vital inspiration to Ireland's early Republicans. This sign reminds drivers that they are crossing into a place still securely linked to Europe: *Liberté, Fraternité, Métrique*.

Upwards, onwards. The air is cold and gusts occasionally, driven off the Irish Sea. The border is woven among the rocks in dry-stone walls. Here and there chunks of stonework have fallen in and channels of flattened grass either side of the broken sections indicate that they are the highways of badgers, deer, foxes; international foragers. A track pulls close to the border and I use it, glad to get off the spongy earth. It brings me up into a forestry plantation. Weatherbeaten spruces are dotted about, grass growing in tufts around their trunks. The trees struggle in soil already drained of nutrients by previous crops. In an open area the land has been torn, prepping it for more saplings, but the job has been abandoned. A bundle of fenceposts held together with steel hoops is turning green. A rock pile has waited so long to be shifted that thistles have grown up through it. An oily jacket is hanging on a branch, it looks like someone meant to return for it, after lunch perhaps, but never did. For how long has it hung here? Weeks, months, it might even be years. Here, away from farms, houses, walkers' routes, nothing can happen for a long time. Only for the breeze and the creaking trees the place would seem in complete suspension.

It is surprising to remember that this part of the border is the setting for an ancient tale of heroes and pride. In the Cooley Mountains a superman called Cúchulainn took a stand, defending Ireland's north from raiders. His story is recounted in the *Táin Bó Cúailnge*, *The Cattle Raid of Cooley*. The earliest version we have dates from the twelfth century, transcribed in Irish, though it certainly had a long life before being written down. No one knows how deep the story goes. Strip it back to its dramatic foundations and it is still solid, based on the themes of land, frontiers and invasion. It is the oldest expression of Ireland's borderland and it is also Ireland's epic, the island's answer to classical mythology. The *Táin Bó Cúailnge* is not an epic because it is written in verse; most of it is not. Nor is the *Táin* an epic because it is a foundation myth, a story that traces a culture's beginnings. No, it describes a conflict in an already established society. The *Táin* is an epic because its men and women are archetypal, as are their clashes. It is an epic because it binds its characters with their landscape, making their ructions seem almost geological, driven from deep down. Also, in the *Táin Bó Cúailnge*, there is a lot of killing.

First we get the hero's back story, meeting him as a talented child soldier called Setanta. He is crossing land when a ferocious guard dog attacks. Setanta kills the dog. The boy was entitled to be on the land so will not be punished; it was self-defence. But Culann, the landowner, is now worried for his security. Setanta – an honourable lad – offers to take the place of the dog until a new pup is reared and trained. Boy becomes guard dog and he gets a new name: the Hound of Culann, Cúchulainn. He is seven years old at the time. He grows up hard, arrogant, gruff and singular.

The main action kicks off with regional bragging. Medb, the queen of Connaught, wishes to borrow a famous bull from the Ulstermen in the north. She sends some of her men to ask for it and the loan is agreed. However, staying over that night and drinking too much, the Connaught men boast that had they not been lent the bull they would have taken it by force. Regional bragging is a familiar thing. An area's local pride and half-joking sense of superiority over other areas can be found in any region on earth, no matter how small. Even a street's width is probably enough to instil a sense of regional identity. The creators of the *Táin* understood this ridiculous aspect of humanity, they rooted their story in it. The northern hosts are offended and withdraw the loan. The big-mouthed Connaught men return to their queen without the bull.

Queen Medb wants that bull. She goes on the offensive, leading her army north to steal it. Just when they are most needed Ulster's warriors are struck by a curse called the pangs, agonising pains that leave them helpless, writhing on the ground. With the older men immobilised only one person can defend Ulster, Cúchulainn. He is now seventeen. He goes to the frontier and leaves a spancel hoop on the trail where the invaders will see it before entering Ulster, somewhere near where I am now. A spancel hoop is a simple piece of farm kit, a ring attached to the legs of a cow to hobble it, keep it from roaming. There is real poetry in this symbol, sprung from a culture based around livestock. The invaders see the hoop and understand that they are being told to go no further. It speaks of the ritualistic importance of boundaries in ancient Ireland that the warriors do not mock this humble sign or simply ignore it. They stop and ponder its demand.

One of Queen Medb's roles in the *Táin* is to tread all over such delicacy. She does not understand the hoop. Unlike her generals, she has never heard of Cúchulainn. A disregard for tradition and bad comportment are perhaps the most serious personal failings in the *Táin*, and they are traits of this queen. She avoids the challenge represented by the spancel hoop in a sneaky way, ordering her army to hack a new path through the forest, going around the hoop. This becomes known as Slechta, the Hewn Place. Cutting a new path into the kingdom of Ulster is an unforgivable insult. Things are bound to get nasty now.

The next boundary marker Cúchulainn leaves is the heads of four of Medb's warriors, thrust on spikes. Medb still doesn't catch on. 'Let us not make too much of it,' she says. 'He has only one body. He can suffer wounding. He is not beyond being taken.' She'll learn.

In keeping with protocol, warriors are sent up against Cúchulainn one at a time. In battle Cúchulainn is gripped by a bloodlust that transforms him into a kind of monster, a condition that translator Winifred Faraday describes as a *contortion*, Thomas Kinsella as a *warp spasm* and Ciaran Carson as a *torque*. In this state Cúchulainn kills everyone sent against him. Sometimes – as modern translations of the *Táin* are blends of several surviving versions – he kills the same people twice. Whole pages are devoted to listing the dead.

I hike south from the borderline to a high gap. From a distance it looks like a molar, two crags and a rounded trough in between. It is a natural channel curving up over the mountaintop, a strip of clingy bogland about the width of a motorway. Today the gap acts as a wind tunnel; I lean further and further into the wind as I climb. It's also an amplifier, the howl getting incrementally louder until, in the middle of the gully, it is an even, continuous roar. But the roar sneaks up on me, I will not register the way it filled my ears until it is gone.

The first people I have seen all day are approaching the gap from the other side, both in bright orange-and-pink jackets and using hiking poles. The man is up ahead. A GPS device dangles around his neck. He might be in his thirties, it is hard to tell as he has pulled his neck warmer up over his mouth. This also makes him hard to understand when he speaks.

'Is this Medb's Gap?' he repeats.

'Yes it is.'

'Grand,' he says and pushes on by without another word. He is annoyed. He's not as fit as he thought he was, or there's a hole in his boot, or maybe his problem is with me. He was annoyed to see me in the gap when he arrived, it was like I'd got here ahead of him. I did get here ahead of him, but hardly in a meaningful way. I probably smiled too much when answering him. Medb's Gap is a very gappy-looking gap, a deep notch in the mountaintop, with black rocky walls. I didn't feel the question was necessary. The woman passes by next. She is barefaced, damp hair clinging to her cheeks. 'There's not much easy,' she says to me with a laugh, following after the man.

Medb's Gap is the site of the *Táin*'s final battle. After killing warrior upon warrior the strength is finally leaving Cúchulainn's limbs. He ties himself to a rock to keep upright and fool the invaders into thinking he is still fighting fit. Cúchulainn's dedication to his role as defender makes sense when we remember he was trained in childhood to be a guard dog, defending boundaries is what he is for. Just as the invaders realise Cúchulainn is fading the Ulstermen recover from their pangs and go to join the fight. There is a huge clash. Thousands are slain and the invaders are repelled. Cúchulainn finally faces Medb but lets her retreat alive.

Places like Medb's Gap are more than just a setting for the *Táin Bó Cúailnge*. How places got their names is a central preoccupation of the story, adding up to something that is more significant than the raid itself. Many events unimportant to the main narrative are described because they explain the name of a hill, glen or tear in the land. The *Táin* was born in a culture without paper maps; the maps were in people's heads. If you were a bard then it was part of your profession to be able to recite long itineraries, one place-name after another, and it is natural that such mental route maps took story form, helping people remember places in the correct order. The telling of the final battle is rushed compared to the description of what follows. There's a fight between Ulster's bull, the prize of the *Táin*, and an equally matched Connaught bull. Their thrashing takes place on a gigantic scale, all across the Cooley Mountains and beyond. The battle tosses place-names right and left. Sliab nAdarca, the Mountain of the Horn; Finnlethe, the White One's Shoulder Blade. The Connaught bull is eventually mauled to death but Ulster's is mortally wounded as well. It staggers home, leaving a trail of innards along the way. Ath Luain, the Ford of the Loins; Tromma, the Liver; Etan Tairb, the Bull's Brow. When it gets back to the frontier, it falls dead at Druim Tairb, Ridge of the Bull.

So the *Táin* closes with no great victory, just two dead bulls and lots of place-names. There is a sense of exhaustion. Medb goes home. Cúchulainn goes home. A landscape has been hammered from both sides and a frontier forged.

*

I return to the borderline but can't tell if I'm rejoining it at exactly the same spot. These look like the same spruces, but spruces are hard to tell apart. The border runs along the same buckled wire fence. No living thing would be impeded by it, it merely demarcates nations. The brightest things in the landscape are empty white sacks that have been blown onto the wires; I'm sure some have been hanging there for years. They are turf sacks, made from a plastic material too thick to rustle, they can only flap. I see nothing heroic about this landscape. It feels more blunt and oppressive than anything else, rather like Cúchulainn might be if you encountered him. The border went on to see a lot more hard men, he was not so unusual.

I move on. The border begins to descend and a run-down cottage comes into view. It has a corrugated-iron roof and cardboard taped over a broken window. Way up beyond the highest road, only a rough path leads to the door. There is no sign of life; no smoke; no television aerial. Abandoned, I imagine. Then the door swings open and a man is standing there in an old jumper and jeans. He has a mug of tea in one hand and he is waving at me with the other. An excited border collie is making figures of eight around his legs.

A Pass, a Chair, a Fort

The border flows with a narrow river through lowland farms. Planks have been hammered together to build small bridges so people can visit neighbours on the other side. I cross one when an aggressive goat chases me from its jurisdiction. These footbridges are not on the Ordnance Survey map, they are too small, no roads lead to them. Not many people will ever see these bridges, just the natives and me, but they are international links. I stop and photograph them, enjoying these small statements of human irrepressibility. On my map I start to number them.

The Ordnance Survey does mark many older constructions. I go to seek a souterrain close to the border. These are medieval hidey-holes, dug under the ground and lined with stones to be used as storerooms and also as hiding places when Vikings were raiding for slaves. The souterrain is close to a bungalow and a man emerges from the back door. He is large and red-faced. 'Howya!' His bellow could cross six fields.

Together we look at the souterrain. He hasn't considered it before, he didn't know it was the work of human hands. An easy mistake to make: the souterrain's roof slabs have collapsed and, peering in, it is just a jumble of rocks and roots, easily mistaken for a natural cavity. I lie on the ground and lower my head in. My torch makes little impact on the darkness.

'There bes foxes in it,' he tells me.

I pull my head out again.

'Old is it?' the man asks. He is open and curious.

'Yes, very,' I reply.

'Pre-war is it?'

'Yes,' I say. 'If by war you mean the Norman invasion.'

That amuses him, and helps him get the measure of me. He seems to decide that I'll bring variety to his day. For my part, I enjoy how much he is enjoying my appearance. I think we connect over how unlikely we are to each other. He invites me in and at his kitchen table gives me tea in a cup so big that it is basically a mixing bowl with a handle. He talks a lot and asks a lot of questions, all loudly. Impassioned in the way a bulldozer could be called impassioned.

'Following the border?'

'I am.'

'Good on you. The whole thing?'

'The whole thing.'

'Good on you.'

He tries various foodstuffs on me, as if I'm a visitor from another planet and he is experimenting to see what my species eats. It turns out that border walkers will eat everything. He gives me a bag of crisps, a hot cross bun, a slice of Swiss roll. He ransacks his cupboards. 'A banana!' he shouts, pushing a bunch at me. 'There's great energy in a banana!'

*

The border cuts across a narrow valley which is the busiest cross-frontier route. The distance of six stone throws covers a minor road, a major road and a dual carriageway. On the

[33]

minor road the border surfaces, I can see the borderline between my feet as it worms through the tar, a thin, dark ripple left when materials of slightly different consistencies were poured side by side, by two teams of road workers. I cross that road then a field to the major road. Here stands the Border Interpretive Centre, empty now, waiting for something else to happen to it. There is always a lorry approaching or passing, swirling up dust. Their cast-offs lie about on the roadside, red plastic reflectors and rubber clasps fallen from curtain sides.

There is something of the American Mid-West about this route. The truckers wear check shirts; Country and Western singers smile from advertising placards on telegraph poles; there's an off-licence called the Last Chance. I find a crushed poker chip on the roadside and it feels appropriate. The Mid-West can also be felt in the way businesses stand one deep in strips along the road. Garages, architectural salvage, currency conversion, they are lined up both sides of the road and both sides of the border, small businesses with big car parks, taking advantage of frontier opportunities. Their signs are large but cheap, bold words on sheets of plastic – petrol, cigarettes, coffee. They don't lull you into buying, drivers either want what they've got or they don't. Just inside the north fireworks dealers operate out of shipping containers: fireworks are illegal in the south so people nip across the border for them. The shops seem impermanent, sheds and portacabins propped up on bricks, but I have been crossing the border on this road for fifteen years and most have been here all that time.

Any sort of restrictions on the border will certainly hit these roadside businesses, although they are obviously resilient. They have survived the dual carriageway laid recently two fields away. Today lots more people are crossing the border on that, travelling at a confident 120 kilometres per hour before converting to sixty miles per hour, or vice versa. Campaigners for the UK's exit from the EU often spoke of taking control of its borders, but what would control look like? I wouldn't like to be the one to stop these drivers and ask to see their passports.

I approach the road and climb over the crash barrier. The verge is untrodden and coated in dust. Standing here feels like a subversive act. A peril of following a border: I will always cut across routes; approach them, traverse them, leave them behind. I'm always in the wrong place. I'm attempting to turn the border itself into a route but this is not a role to which it is naturally suited. I'm always walking perpendicular to the sensible.

I dash across the first carriageway. In the five-foot breathing space before the next, I stop to take in the big sky and far horizons, north and south. A little further on I tramp along a narrow lane to pass under the north–south railway and then enter another valley that is wide and shallow. There are small farms, a truck depot and a religious retreat. I see no drama in this sleepy and rural place but this valley was for centuries one of the only negotiable routes in and out of Ulster. The rest of the frontier was filled with woodland, dense and disorientating, and bogs clingy enough to impede an army. This place, known still as the Gap of the North, was passable in all seasons and far from other routes, so a strategic site in Ireland's wars. I can see why confrontations here became locked in stalemate. Anyone holding the high ground each side would be hard to prise off, while a force that fails to pass can quickly retreat, regroup and take another run at it. The landscape itself tends against the possibility of a decisive moment. Elizabethan poet Edmund Spenser wrote about such places in a book of tactical advice for English soldiers going to fight the Irish: 'It is well-known that he is a flying enemy, hiding himself in woods and bogs, from whence he will not draw forth but into some strait passage or perilous ford where he knows the army must needs pass – there will he lie in wait . . .'

Queen Elizabeth's troops marched this way a few years after Spenser's warning. They were tasked with subduing the Gaelic earls of Ulster. Ulster, the northern part of the island, was the least anglicised of the provinces, and England's power had not found much traction here. Officials in Dublin called Ulster the Great Irishry. The province was also a security risk; effectively an independent realm, it was unpredictable and too friendly with continental powers, especially the dreaded Spanish. Now, in 1600, it was in open revolt. Breaking the rebellion would mean taking control of Ulster and that meant controlling the Gap of the North.

This area was Hugh O'Neill country, as was all of mid-Ulster. His was the ruling family and he was the key figure of the revolt. Legally, he was subservient to the Crown; the Earl of Tyrone, his title, was a royal grant. He had been educated among the English and spent some of his youth in London. But now he was fifty years of age, back in his homeland and the Crown's power over him had faded to something between nominal and notional. In this land he was 'The O'Neill', a title that sounds wonderfully strident to me; more than just leader of the clan, he was the embodiment of its people and territory. We have a sketch of the moment Hugh was transformed into the O'Neill, not an eyewitness report but probably based on accounts. We see a group of men with thick beards and equally thick woollen cloaks. One holds a pike. They are standing around a seated figure who is mop-haired and also bearded, Hugh O'Neill. There is no crown but a man on the right is holding up a slipper, about to throw it over O'Neill's head, a pagan sign for good luck. It is a wild, earthy sort of ritual. The inauguration chair is not in a hall or castle, but on an open hillside, a throne of rough slabs.

The Earl of Tyrone and the O'Neill; perhaps being both at once was the source of the duality that seems to hang about this man. It is very hard to know what O'Neill is thinking as he attempts to run the rebellion. He is an intriguing figure, inhabitant of two cultures, and powerful enough that his decisions will resonate for centuries. Constantly on the move, sometimes he is up for the fight, at other times he tries to seek terms for peace. The same duality could be called shiftiness. He was certainly an opportunist. To Lord Mountjoy and his lieutenants, O'Neill was the Archtraitor.

Lord Mountjoy led the English troops to Ireland. When he was appointed his fitness for the job had been doubted; he had limited experience in warfare and was suspiciously bookish. He liked playing shuffleboard and cards; his outdoor activity was limited to pond fishing. Even his secretary, and greatest fan, Fynes Moryson, describes Mountjoy as dainty, gentle and sensitive to the cold. Moryson was on the frontier with him and wrote a history of the campaign. He enjoys saying his employer was underestimated by his foes, especially the brute Hugh O'Neill. Moryson has a dim view of their enemy's character; he claimed that O'Neill had taken three wives – he had suppressed his blunt side among the English but back in Ulster had reverted to type. Moryson says that O'Neill laughed when he heard it was Lord

Mountjoy who was on the way to put manners on him.

We don't have to believe Moryson. He was a supporter of Mountjoy and committed to the subjugation of Ireland. We could as well trust Peter Lombard's writings in order to find the real Hugh O'Neill. Lombard was the Archbishop of Armagh at the time. According to him Hugh O'Neill was a pious man, a defender of faith, an upholder of law, brave, temperate, patient and prudent. His fight with the Crown was noble, based on a desire to liberate Ireland and defend the native religion. Yes, okay, Lombard concedes, Hugh O'Neill had three wives, 'but each was joined to him in lawful matrimony'. There is no mention of laughter when he heard that Lord Mountjoy was on his way, he was no fool; he did not underestimate his foes.

Of course, Lombard's account is no more reliable than Moryson's. He was an ally to O'Neill. Even if we exclude loyalties, the two descriptions were written by men with wholly different backgrounds and worldviews. I am as likely to find a truth in Brian Friel's play *Making History*. Friel was a Northern Irish playwright who often portrayed divided characters; he wrote about O'Neill three centuries after his death but I'm inclined to take his version into account too. After all, people and their complexities are the dramatist's subjects. And what is this version of Hugh O'Neill doing when the curtain rises? He is busy putting vases of flowers around his chamber. 'They really transform the room,' he says. He still has the English accent he picked up in his youth, though stage directions tell the actor to modulate to an Ulster accent sometimes. The flowers are to impress his new English wife – the only wife he has at this point. In *Making History* it is his wife who warns Hugh O'Neill about the approach of Lord Mountjoy, saying he is a meticulous and ruthless strategist. O'Neill does not laugh; he does not respond directly to his wife's news at all. In this play O'Neill is politically nimble but sometimes thoughtful to the point of distraction. His monologues go to and fro. Wondering if he should assist a rebel chief he says, 'Maguire is a fool. He's determined to rise up . . .' Then, moments later, 'Maguire's no fool. Maguire has no choice.' The audience can't miss the conflict inside Hugh O'Neill and it is bound to have consequences.

In October 1600 the Gap of the North was the theatre of war. Mountjoy's sensitivity to the cold was unfortunate; he was going to have a cold couple of weeks here. An attempt to push through the gap came under fire. Trenches had been dug and earth ramparts thrown up, reinforced with large wooden spikes. Mountjoy directed his men up the hillsides but they were forced back. Bushes and brambles had been tied and woven together, confounding Mountjoy's horsemen. O'Neill himself had overseen the creation of the defences, telling his troops that the safety of their wives and children depended on holding the pass. The English troops were hard and experienced but did not know the boggy terrain and O'Neill's men could pour fire on them from behind their defences. I'm sure bones of the dead are here still, sealed away under the truck depot's concrete yard.

Mountjoy had decided there was no task in Ireland more important than taking this pass, but each push failed. There were days of rain; when the wet was too intense for muskets, the soldiers would jeer at each other. The rivers flooded, the ground churned, tents blew away, powder and food were ruined. Many of Mountjoy's troops deserted. Dysentery broke out and may have killed more than the O'Neill's troops. O'Neill was in a position of strength, yet on

13 October he withdrew from the gap. This was unexpect-ed. Cautiously Mountjoy's troops picked their way forward, gaining confidence as they got beyond the ramparts. Looking at O'Neill's defences from behind, one English officer reported, 'I vow unto God that I did never see a more villainous piece of work . . .'

It is hard to say why O'Neill gave up the Gap of the North but it was a significant withdrawal. Mountjoy could begin to consolidate in the north by building a fort and leav-ing a garrison to defend it. He was in the ascendant now. In the pass Mountjoy did not just have O'Neill's villainous works razed, he had the forests on both sides chopped down; he would not be impeded here again. After a major defeat in the south, the Gaelic chieftains were queuing up to sur-render. Hugh O'Neill held out in Ulster woods but he too would surrender in the end, kneeling before Mountjoy for an hour in a ritual self-abasement. The old chieftain system had been overthrown in the north of Ireland, clearing the land for the Plantation and the beginnings of a new Protestant culture focused in Ireland's north. A generation later another rebellion would attempt to break the Plantation but it would be crushed, clearing the land even further and reinforcing Ulster's distinction from the rest of the island.

It is striking how forgiving Mountjoy and the queen were to their Archtraitor. Hugh O'Neill was pardoned and kept his original lands. Although he had to drop 'The O'Neill', he retained his earldom. Moryson and Lombard offer very different views of O'Neill's character, but neither explains his desire or his ability to pull off these terms. Lombard's O'Neill would be too principled, Moryson's too gruff and graceless. It is Brian Friel's telling of O'Neill that seems to fit best. *Making History* shows us a man who is divided but also, you could say, double-powered. This is an O'Neill who, when it suited, can exploit both English and Irish political systems. He can feast and whoop it up with any cattle raider, but is also able to seduce a highborn English lady and sweet-talk her back to his castle. It is not just his accent that spans the distance between England and Ireland, it is his abilities.

As the north gave way, Lord Mountjoy and his army made a point of visiting a certain small hill in mid-Ulster. Not an imposing place, the mound could be climbed in moments, but, surrounded by lowlands, it did offer good views of the land. On it was a stone throne, an unshowy chair, no trimmings or carvings, nothing but thick slabs of rock, a back and sides, arranged around a boulder. The chair was not even at the hill's peak but halfway down one side, probably because that was where the base boulder happened naturally to lie; left behind at the end of the last ice age. This was the inauguration chair of the chieftainate, where men of the bloodline were transformed into the O'Neill.

I wonder what Mountjoy made of this crude throne. I imagine him circling it, examining it, an eyebrow raised. He is well fed but neat, wearing four layers of silk stockings and a tailored coat. Several dozen of his soldiers are watching, also wondering what he will do. Their tents are pitched around the base of the hill, flags fluttering; a scarlet cross on a white background. Did Mountjoy sit in the throne? Surely anyone with a sense of humour would have sat in it. Perhaps he let all his soldiers have a go at being the O'Neill. Then he ordered them to smash the throne to pieces.

Destroying the throne was not merely vitriolic, it was a meaningful action in Mountjoy's mission to claim Ulster for his queen. Stones have power, narratives gather around them. Castles, forts, towers, they are all pegs to hold down a landscape, not just because you can watch or shoot from a fort's high window, but because the structure becomes a point of orientation to everyone who lives around it. If a fort stands long enough, it will become the embodiment of power to a whole generation, to many generations perhaps. A boulder and a few slabs can play this role too. For Mountjoy's takeover to be complete, the old network of markers and signs had to be cleared from the land. Obliterating this chair was as practical an act as deforesting the Gap of the North. When the throne was erased the very idea of the O'Neill went with it. The age of the chieftains was over, no one would have the gumption to call himself the O'Neill again. Mountjoy's next step was to deploy new points of orientation, making the landscape face new directions. A fort was built to claim and forever control the pass that had caused Mountjoy so much trouble.

I approach Moyry Fort as evening draws in. I have already set camp a little back along the line and have walked here unburdened, rolling my shoulders, enjoying the ease. The fort overlooks the pass and now the borderline too, where it runs alongside a quarter of a mile of flowering gorse.

You might say only the shell of Moyry remains but it was built almost entirely of stone so its shell is a substantial thing, with walls four feet thick. It is a single tower, square in plan but with rounded corners that soften its profile. I wonder if the corners are rounded for the same reason Haulbowline Lighthouse is all curves. Sharp corners on Moyry Fort would mean exposing a corner block from two sides, making it easier to wrench out. Then another could be pulled

out, and another; even a gang of children could have niggled at the fort's corners until the walls fell. But history, with the help of rounded corners, has let Moyry stand. I walk around it, sense the mighty weight of it, its unshiftability. Fynes Moryson commented on the usefulness of forts, writing that they 'keep the Irish in awe'.

I follow a lane back to my campsite. There are a few houses, television light flickering against the insides of the curtains. Gorse flower and the pale surface of the lane are picking up moonlight and emitting a low gleam. I meet two children walking the opposite way, a boy and a girl. It is strange for all of us, an encounter on a silent road after dark, although strangest for them: they are at home, one of these houses is theirs, but I'm a mystery. I've frightened them, they stop dead.

'Hello, I was just visiting the castle.'

They don't move. I'm not sure if I should keep approaching them, but stopping might pressurise them as well. I slow down but don't quite stop. 'It's good up there, isn't it?' I say.

'Yeah,' says the boy quietly, watchful but remembering that one should be polite. The girl is holding her hands clasped together in front of her stomach.

'Do you know who built the castle?' I ask them.

'It was a bad man,' says the boy. They both remain straight-faced but this hint of engagement allows me to stop walking.

'Do you mean Lord Mountjoy?'

They both nod vigorously a couple of times but suddenly stop, realising that they don't know what they're agreeing to. Carefully the girl asks, 'Was he a wizard?'

This gives me pause. After all, Mountjoy understood the power of stones, but I don't want to mislead children. 'He wasn't,' I say.

'Then no,' says the girl, 'a different man.'

'A wizard?' I say.

'He could cast evil spells,' she says.

I must have seemed concerned because the boy quickly chips in, 'But don't worry, he doesn't live there any more.'

'It's just a ruin,' says the girl.

Camera Mountains, Slieve Gullion

I walk one field away from the border to a grey hill, the site of a twentieth-century military installation, gone now, removed with the rest during Northern Ireland's peace process. I am climbing to see if there is any trace of it left. The hill has no name on the Ordnance Survey, which is surprising; in Ireland it often seems every rock and bend in the road has a name, yet this substantial hill has not gained an official one. I have read interviews in which people from the area referred to it as a Camera Mountain. This was because the base at the top was used for observation.

When Ireland's border was created some said it should be drawn north of here, but instead the traditional county boundary was used and this largely nationalist area was netted by Northern Ireland. In the 1970s the IRA moved quietly through these lowlands and along these laneways, mingling with the general population. Also moving among the general population, but easily distinguished by bright red berets, was the British army. Their steel-clad towers stood on hills, a chain of installations stretching across South Armagh. They were built as part of a military deployment called Operation Banner. Locals glad of the watchtowers called them Security Posts, their haters called them Spy Posts and the soldiers crammed inside called them sangars. This word entered the army's lexicon in nineteenth-century Afghanistan, where it meant defensive walls. Recently the

British army returned to Afghanistan. Soldiers who served in Northern Ireland were sent there and carried the term back with them, back to where it originated. It might have travelled with new linguistic cargo collected on the Irish border. Afghan men and women might be, at this moment, learning to accommodate their new arrivals: *glen*, *drumlin*, *bandit country*.

Both conflicts shared a vocabulary that we all learned through news reports; *insurgency*, *Improvised Explosive Device*, *roadside bomb*. There were few open battles in either Northern Ireland or Afghanistan. In both the army was sent to back up a police force. A soldier's daily routine was similar in both: go out and patrol for a few hours; be a target for snipers or bombs; experience the stress of low-intensity conflict; take it out on the locals sometimes; return to barracks. In the 1970s, along Ireland's border, soldiers on patrol became the target of attacks they were attempting to stop by going on patrol. It was a particularly vicious circle. Why not just stay in barracks? 'It is an argument which is difficult to fault but it runs diametrically against one's military instincts,' wrote Brigadier Peter Morton. He headed up the 3rd Battalion of the Parachute Regiment, or 3 Para, here in 1976. He thought no army presence on the streets and lanes would mean handing the territory to the IRA, who could then run border smuggling operations and mount attacks further north. Morton had decided that 'Many of the people of South Armagh, and their associates immediately across the border, were a tightly-knit and interbred group of law-breakers.' Sending his soldiers among them was dangerous, but they needed to be watched. Sangars were the answer.

Their design rejected everything but utility. Much exo-skeleton was visible, cubes of scaffolding to which the corrugated sheeting was attached, set at right angles, with narrow slots for windows. The only curves to relieve the eye were the cylindrical water tanks bolted on top. Everything was painted murky green, matching the land around it. Each part was standardised, prefabricated; towers came in preset elevations, six, nine, twelve or fifteen metres tall. The installations looked like they could be dismantled and all the same pieces clipped back together in a wholly different arrangement. This could have been done quickly. The first sangar, built in 1977, was up and functioning in less than three hours. They had to be fast: hostiles were circling during construction, these installations were targets before they were even built. Materials were transported under heavy guard every time a new one was erected.

From almost everywhere in South Armagh you could see a tower and a tower could see you. Their fields of vision overlapped, everything was covered, each tower had line of sight with at least one other. Driving home or working your land it was possible that you were being watched through a 500 mm telescopic lens, or maybe the soldiers were looking in another direction, or nowhere at all. Maybe they were snoozing up there on their hilltops, you never knew. The towers gave South Armagh the feel of an open prison. Inside them, the soldiers felt a similar constriction. 'It is just like being in prison, but being let out to patrol the area,' wrote Morton. The sangars were ugly and enclosed, the cell-like rooms wallpapered in soft porn. The soldiers spent interminable hours watching tractors ploughing, cattle wandering and locals making minor smuggling trips across the border. One constant task was noting car licence plate numbers and radioing them in to the central intelligence base. There a soldier entered the numbers into a computer the size of a washing machine, checking them against a database, but the database did not include cars from south of the border and it did not take long for the IRA to work this out.

The IRA were shifting and mobile, in control of the lanes, at home on the ground. The British army were bunkered down in border checkpoints or perched on hilltops, their supplies brought in by helicopter. It was risky for them to be on the fields and roads; we saw what happened at Narrow Water. This was deadlock, no victory was likely for anyone. The army had retreated up hills and were now stuck there, as if on islands, while the dangerous lowlands surged around below them.

I find a track, rough but wide, that leads me along the foot of the hill. Tattered bits of tubing lie along the way, military remnants perhaps. Skinny sheep take fright and dash away from me. One ram, a troublemaker, has had its horns cut off with a hacksaw leaving two dark voids in its head. I pass above a bungalow. Three cars are parked on a concrete drive, neatly slotted amongst each other in a way that is practised and familiar. The bungalow's windows are open, I can hear cutlery clacking against plates and lots of male voices. I imagine big grown-up sons eating eggs and bacon. As I walk further along, the house's washing line comes into view and I am startled by four sets of army fatigues hanging up to dry. Combat-style trousers are common, I would hardly have noticed them, but these are full suits, neck to ankle, made entirely of camouflage material. There is no way soldiers live here, the peace process has not settled in that much, yet this is certainly military gear. It is not until later in the day that I discover an explanation. Pinned to a fence, I see an advertising banner: 'Watchtower Adventures – Experience the blood pumping action!' I realise the family runs a paintballing business: customers dress in fatigues and run about shooting paintballs at their friends. Growing up under a sangar, you might have thought the household had seen enough fatigues. I wonder if, when the army had a base on the hilltop, the boys were of an age to find it, in a way, exhilarating. I remember these emotions from childhood, crossing the border into Northern Ireland with my father. There was a thrill in seeing toy soldiers made real. Perhaps these paintballers are still drawing energy from that excitement.

Looking at the advertisement I realise that I don't have to wonder, there's a phone number on the banner. I get speaking to Mark, the owner, and ask about Watchtower Adventures. He explains that his family owns the hill; his father bulldozed the track to the top, not knowing the aggravation it would bring. The base was perhaps the biggest hilltop complex on the border, three sangars with elevated walkways, forty-foot storage containers, sleeping quarters, a helipad, banks of spotlights and cameras. 'It was always Faughill to us, we never called it Camera Mountain,' says Mark when I ask him about the name, 'but there were certainly cameras on it. You could see the glint off the lenses, they looked to be the size of car tyres.'

'You would have been a small boy when the base was operational,' I remark. 'Did you ever go up for a peek?'

'We stayed away,' says Mark. 'If you went near the soldiers would be out to you.'

'Was it exciting in a way, having them up there?'

'Are you joking? It was more like torture. Helicopters were flying low over our house day and night. You'd be having your breakfast and soldiers would be crossing the garden. Sometimes you'd find them hunkered down in ditches. I was a wee boy, they'd try to be friendly, but I knew they were here on a mission and it wasn't for the good of me. I'd run home, bawling my eyes out.'

Mark tells me once he and his father were pouring hard fill for gateposts on their land when five or six soldiers came charging down the hill towards them. 'Nearly falling down the mountain they were. They stopped a bit above us and I heard one of them say to his mates, "Told you it was a cement mixer." They thought we'd a mortar pointed up at them.'

'Despite all this you've named your business Watchtower Adventures,' I say.

'We were all sitting around trying to think up a name,' says Mark. 'We thought maybe Bandit Country Paintball, but that was pushing it too far. We just wanted something quirky. We do get a few lads paintballing who think they're reliving history – not many. Those days are gone now and they're not coming back. We can poke fun at it all.'

*

The high slopes are coated in ferns and foxgloves, giving way to a stony cap. The hilltop offers no great reward for my climb. Buckled and pitted, it dips in the middle and refuses to give the satisfaction of an obvious peak. Walking around the rim I can see many miles of border. The dual carriageway is to the east, the west is dominated by a mountain called Slieve Gullion. I find an iron stake stuck in the ground and a few short wooden planks, all that remains of the sangars. So much of the borderland's history is still here to be read in ruins but there is almost nothing left from the most recent conflict.

Ruins on Ireland's border are still active things, the loose ends of an unfinished history, still too meaningful to settle into the background. Knowing this, the army decided to erase the sangars completely; leaving them here might have fuelled resentments for another century. When the process of dismantling the installations began, a nationalist politician argued that one should be kept as a monument. He intuited that he was about to lose some powerful propaganda; a tower isolated on a high hill was the perfect symbol of a rule that was unjust and artificially maintained. But few people agreed with him, and the towers are gone.

I notice a patch of hard aggregate under my boots. I realise I'm standing on a concrete pool about three feet across. It was poured to create a load-bearing point, a base on which to plant a sangar's pillar. So the installation is not gone entirely. The flat top of the concrete lump is flush to the ground, the base of an inverse pyramid pointing towards the centre of the hill. This might be the kind of monument

a peace process makes, not standing off the earth but bored down, without profile, a kind of anti-monument. It has resilience though. Buried and immensely heavy, this load-bearing point could be here for millennia.

*

The author Colm Tóibín travelled Ireland's border in 1986 when the towers were still up and active. Near here, on the front steps of a hall, he witnessed a raw love of the area's hills and mountains, a thing I too have found in South Armagh. He could see Slieve Gullion from where he stood. A local man was standing there too, rapt in his observation of the mountain, loving the way the light made its colours change. He told Tóibín it was the most wonderful place in the world. This love might have been a stronger cohesive force among the people here than nationalism ever was, even during the Troubles, but it had its own politics too. The man went on to tell Tóibín that he would not be responsible for what he would do if the British army put a base or a lookout tower on its peak.

I can picture the expression on the man's face as he looked at Slieve Gullion, a fixed gleam, but vulnerable too. We should probably envy them really, people convinced of the world-beating splendour of their own patch, able to lose themselves in the fragrance of their home turf. I see the same look on a terse roadworker I encounter later in the day, struggling with a trailer load of signposts. He softens when I compliment the landscape, lets his arms fall to his sides and adopts the gleam. 'It's mighty,' he says. 'People didn't know about it. It was locked away for so long, but they're coming now. It's mighty.' I met the roadworker by an empty, potholed car park, just yards from some of the ugliest industrial sheds I have ever seen in my life. However, over the roofs we could see Slieve Gullion's broad back. This mountain, more than any other feature, fuels this fervency. Slieve Gullion gives shape to the place's identity, it is something to revolve around, a local focal point. *Slieve Gullion View* was the name of a newspaper once serving this area. The mountain is used to gauge approaching weather, to work out one's orientation or simply as a place to rest one's gaze. It is a squat lumpy cone with a changing personality. Under the sun and seasons it can shimmer green, brown or an earthy red.

Slieve Gullion needs to be climbed. I follow the straight path up through conifer plantations on the lower slopes. Every step I take is a step up, the path taking on the mountain like a staircase takes on a house. Insects buzz and drone about my face but they soon meet their ceiling, the cooler, higher air. After an hour I pass above the trees, then slog through bands of heather to get to the peak. I walk around, taking in the view. To the south lies a wide plain; I am surprised by the flatness of the horizon, although I cannot see much distance today, everything hazes to blue in only a few dozen miles. Directly below, visible in every direction, are fields, their hedgerow boundaries making squares and rectangles, joined at the corners and creating the impression of a dark green net. Here and there rocky hills – including Faughill – bulge up through the net, spreading sections of it wide.

Slieve Gullion is the highest peak in this area. In addition, it stands alone while most of its neighbours are in ranges. This individuality is part of Gullion's appeal, getting the mountain starring roles in many Ulster myths and ensuring it was used as a setting for the local versions of myths that are found Ireland-wide. Slieve Gullion is associated with Culann the Smith, the man for whom young Setanta becomes guard dog. It was also home to the wicked Calliagh Beara, who cursed a lake near the peak so that any man who swims in it ages decades in an instant. It is called the Lake of Sorrows but it is harmless when I dip my hand in. The water has been stained yellow by peat and rocks beneath the shallow rim glow amber. I take a few steps into the water and peer into the centre. Yellow stones peer back at me.

Overlooking the lake is a large pile of rocks with a single passageway leading into its heart. Crouched down, I get to the middle of the mound in a few wriggles. These stones are Calliagh Beara's house, where she dragged her weakened and white-haired victims. It is in fact an ancient tomb, of a sort called a passage tomb. It is about five thousand years old.

I ought really to be awestruck by this message from the

past. Instead, I wiggle out again and am able to turn my back on the tomb to look at the countryside. This is because there is some kind of shortfall in the experience, coming from a sense of exclusion I think. The people who built these things were wholly different from us; even if someone could explain the exact workings of their faith, we could never experience the earth and the sun the way they did. Watching a few documentaries about the solar system and seeing pictures of the earth viewed from the moon has probably been enough to cut off our experience from theirs. At the top of Slieve Gullion I feel the divide again. It is almost impossible to take on this tomb and all it might signify, so it is surprisingly easy to be drawn away and think about other things. What can be said about the tomb is that the builders packed stones together to ritualise, to organise, the way we vanish into death. In the arrangement of this and other relics one can sense the importance of networks, alignments and lines of sight; from here other tombs can be seen on other peaks, although not on a hazy summer day like this. Perhaps haze is the reason the stony passageway into the tomb was built to align with the setting sun on the winter solstice, not summer. It is easy to imagine how the tomb became associated with Calliagh Beara. At some point treasure-seekers dug into the rocks, found human bones and that inspired stories; the tomb became the lonely home of a cruel goddess.

Slieve Gullion continued making myths. In 1842 William Makepeace Thackeray travelled by in a carriage heading south. 'The car-boy pointed out one hill – that of Slievegullion, which kept us company all the way – as the highest hill in Ireland.' Thackeray knew this was untrue. 'Ignorant or deceiving car-boy!' he remarks. 'I have seen a dozen hills, each the highest in Ireland, in my way through the country.' But the author admits that this attitude is not the preserve of Armagh car-boys. 'The world is full of car-boys,' he writes. 'Has not every mother a Slievegullion of a son, who, according to her measurement, towers above all other sons?'

Slieve Gullion is an extinct volcano, a cone that rose and fell cyclically in geological time. One cataclysmic thump, about fifty million years ago, sent surges of magma radiating out through the earth around it. Great spouts of this molten rock vented around Slieve Gullion and hardened into hills. So it is not completely true to say that Slieve Gullion stands alone. It is surrounded by a ring of attendant hills, smaller, subordinate hills of its own making. Come forward again through time to the Troubles and all of these lower hills had military installations built on top of them, they were all Camera Mountains. The towers stood north, south, east and west of Slieve Gullion, keeping the population under observation, but Gullion itself had no tower built upon it.

What might be Slieve Gullion's greatest distinction is hidden, an underearth remnant of its original volcanic creation. It is, to use the language of geologists, a prominent anomaly. It does not just have a strong pull on myths, stories and local pride. Gravity itself finds this mountain attractive and clings to it with a particular intensity. The gravitational force an object experiences, the strength of its desire to rush to the centre of the earth, is not the same everywhere. A gravitational anomaly is the difference between what the force of gravity ought to be at a given location and what it actually turns out to be when measured. The strength of Slieve Gullion's anomaly suggests there is a high-density mass concealed under the mountain. A massive clot of volcano-baked rock, dense enough to gather its own gravity. Look at a map of gravitational fields and you will see Slieve Gullion is wrapped in contours so closely packed that individual lines are hard to distinguish, markedly different from the widely-spaced wavy lines that drift elsewhere across the country. Gravity is drawn to the mountain and as I come back down I wonder if I can feel it in my footfalls.

Heading back to the border I encounter a local man on a lane. He has just parked and released his dog from the car. Both man and dog are fidgety, a six-legged walk waiting to happen, but he stops to talk to me. He is interested in the route I took to the peak and he nods with approval as I describe it to him. That gleam takes over. 'I'll tell you now,' he says, 'that's the best walk in the world.'

Who could blame him for feeling this way? How could he feel any other way? It was almost inevitable, having been born and raised within the tight contours of Slieve Gullion's powerful attractions.

Farmers

A thick drizzle makes the landscape one wet smear of farm-land. A fox breaks cover ahead of me, a streak of rust across dark green. This stretch of the border is all small dairy operations. Cows, perhaps related but valued in different currencies, look at each other across streams. Most farms here are part-time, cattle do not make a livelihood at this scale. These are typical border fields, small, only taking a minute to cross so I am always looking ahead for the gap in the hedgerow that will allow me onwards. Satellite images give an overview of these border fields; innumerable crook-ed rectangles and irregular shapes in one of a dozen shades of green. The fields are arranged in a shatter pattern, like reinforced glass splintered in the collision of two countries. Studying these satellite images is dizzying. Actually being down there, walking the fields, is hypnotic. A day walking the border is often a process of eating up fields, one after the other, from morning until night. When I close my eyes and attempt to remember the border, its most characteristic form emerges. I do not see water, stone, forest or mountain. I see fields. Lots of fields. From now on, if I don't specifi-cally mention that I'm walking across a bogland, or that I'm on road, lane or a mountainside, or that I'm in Paddy's canoe, then you can assume I'm in a field.

When you've seen a few dozen fields they all look the same, but once you've seen a hundred or so, every field starts to take on unique characteristics, minor differences seem major. A clump of hawthorn that has been worked around but itself remains untouched; a bathtub being used as a drinking trough; a corral built from railway sleepers; a stack of hay bales wrapped in black plastic. When a field lacks obvious features, there is always the lie of the land to look at; every field has its own undulations, swells and dips.

However, a long walk makes it possible to average out the experience. With the passing days and distance all the different fields I cross can be morphed into one archetype and the description of this field will save us from the description of hundreds. So you can assume the field I am crossing is in order but not neat. Assume the grass is healthy but not lush. Assume the field is roughly rectangular but contorted, rhomboid, or somehow possesses a fifth side. Assume there is at least one galvanised-steel gate and that the breeze is blowing a wheezy tune over the holes in its tubular design. Assume the field is churned up in one section; around the gate or a drinking trough the grass has been obliterated under hooves and tractor tyres. Assume the field is not flat but sloping at a twenty-degree angle. Assume the lower end is the border. Assume the field abuts the border with its shortest side. And assume, by the time you've assumed all this, that I have already crossed this field and am in the next.

*

There is a border native that I see more often than foxes, although not as much as rabbits or pheasants. They are farmers. I see them doing rounds of their fields, usually in the middle distance. They are checking their land to make sure that nothing has changed. If they find something has, then they'll attend to it until it is put right. We speak sometimes, if our paths cross. Unflappable, restrained, no farmers I meet are surprised by the task I have set myself. Moreover, they often seem to know what I am doing and tell me about it as I approach. 'You're following the border,' they tell me as I emerge from a hedgerow. 'You're walking the border.' 'You're mapping out the border.' All this, as if they see people like me all the time, as if I'm the fifth border worrier to pass since lunch. This is an element of rural banter, favoured by a particular kind of gentleman; making sure you know you're not anything special. I am tramping across their land, the power dynamic favours them, I must bow to their wisdom. Some farmers have walked their fields so long and know them so minutely that, in some mental conflation, they believe they have earned a special insight into everything. To them the world's most shocking events are merely scaled-up versions of something that happened on their land at some point. They have stopped registering surprises as surprising, they're certainly never troubled or impressed by me, I'm a pigeon feather drifting by on the breeze. Walking these fields, leaning on these gates, the sky pouring by, the seasons rolling over them, farmers have built up immunity to the unpredicted. They no longer see it. People occasionally go by but none have yet said anything that was able to break this spell.

One day the border brings me through a farm that I might never forget. It is at the end of a pretty lane, dry-stone walls and mature trees both sides and a thick grass mohawk running up the middle. There is a bungalow, outhouses, a shed, interconnected yards and small fields. In the gardens are dozens of ornaments and plant pots, an old plough, horseshoes hung on doors. There are little cottages built for children as Wendy houses but now perhaps the children have grown up and moved away so gnomes have been put standing in the doorways. Spare planks have been set up as benches or waddle-ways for geese. Ducks and chickens are wandering about too. Everywhere you look, time has been spent instead of money; hoses patched with puncture repair kits; breaks in chicken-wire fencing closed with careful string work. If I had driven here it would not have seemed so special but having walked across miles of repetitive fields this farm is incredible. Recalling it now is like remembering a dream – I wonder if I might have dreamed it. I find it in my notebook: 'Rabbits in handmade hutches; colourful gnomes; clumps of yellow flowers grow in plastic buckets; birdhouses on wooden poles; a hand-cut weathervane shaped like a hen; ducks lean into each other and snooze.'

I find the farmer on a deckchair, nestled among plaster-cast animals and potted flowers. He is talking with another man and I get the impression they have not seen each other in a while and are catching up, so I don't want to interrupt. I regret not interrupting now. But I do ask: 'Can I go through this way? I'm following the border.'

'Go anywhere you like,' he says, 'and enjoy it.'

'Does it cause hassle, living right on the border?'

'Put it this way,' says the farmer. 'I wish you'd take it away with you.'

And I get a picture in my head. Me, not just walking the border but coiling it up as I go, looping it around my arm like I'm gathering a lawnmower cable.

Another day I meet a farmer sitting in his parked tractor, taking his ease with a cigarette. Both doors are wide open and a local newspaper is spread open across the steering wheel. I am passing close by but on the other side of the fence.

'You could be looking at me from outside Europe,' he

says, pleased either with the situation or with himself for putting it so deftly.

'Do you think they'll harden the border?' I ask him. I am referring to the anxiety that a British exit from the EU will mean returning to a secured frontier. A situation grim enough to damage the peace process.

'You wait a long while for things to happen around here,' he says. 'And then nothing much happens. There's always a lot of talk.'

On a day further along the border I meet a farmer lugging a hay bale down one of her fields. She is trimly dressed, sensible body warmer and wellington boots that are hosed down every evening. She gives me a few minutes, pointing out features on her land, including the border. Here it is woven through a tall hedgerow. She tells me to look out for the Domees.

'Who are they?' I ask, thinking they might be a local family with a bad reputation.

She looks away, realising I lack even the most basic education. This is a challenge to her, she must now put words on things that she has never needed to before. After a pause she says, 'They are stones that people put up long ago.'

'Ah, dolmens!'

Domees. A piece of borderland vernacular, a name for these prehistoric tombs.

One morning I crawl out of my tent to see a farmer standing at the top of the field, drawn from his bungalow by the sight of my campsite. He is keeping back, hovering, not wanting to force his way into my presence, despite the fact that I have spent the night on his land without permission. He makes a broad sweeping gesture with his arm, I am being invited in for breakfast. On the way to his house he looks at everything but me, making rapid, insect-like moves. Quick head twists, right and left, arms go in and out for no obvious reason. Each gesture is sharp and would seem decisive if viewed in isolation, but taken together it seems he might fling himself apart.

I sit at his kitchen table but he does not sit. He makes me porridge and tea. He stands leaning at the sink looking out the window over his fields. He asks me about my walk and the things I have seen. He tells me about his son, killed in the Troubles twenty years ago. He doesn't give details. He fries me a slice of bacon, gives it to me on a plate, then returns to the window, leaning with his fingers wrapped around his worktop. I get the feeling he stands there a lot.

When he finally sits down he lights a cigarette and offers me one. I decline and, surprised, he makes a sharp shake of the head. His eyes rove off towards the window again. I think he's lost interest in me. 'Young ones,' he says, 'you do everything right.'

*

The hilly terrain seems to encourage small fields and small farms, none of the generosity of scale that open plains might foster in a land and economy. I have the thread of the border to lead me on but there is always the feel of impediment. The horizon is usually just a few minutes ahead, I am in the landscape rather than on it. This is because the border often follows streams and water always takes the low way, keeping the border low with it. But this evening the border is winding up into higher country and I escape the valleys for a while. The horizon is now hours away and I can see mountains that are days distant. The breeze is fresher. According to my Ordnance Survey map, I have ascended through the green contours and into the browns but the land around me is actually still green, though hardy and sun-bleached. From this elevation I can read the land itself like a map, fields unfolding all around me. I can see many miles of hedgerows, fences, ditches, boundaries of all sorts. Zigzagging among them is the border.

There is a bungalow near the highest point. Two brothers are standing by the door, watching me. They both wear wellington boots and curious expressions. I am sure they are brothers before we speak and not just because they look alike. It is a common arrangement – all over Ireland are lanes that end at little farmhouses and they often contain brothers. Their parents will have died long ago and now the brothers keep a house together and work the land and live a long time. The shy one goes indoors but the other walks with me. He is sixty-five years old. These small fields belong to him. According to my map this area is called Mile Hill but the farmer doesn't recognise that name and offers me others instead. Side by side we look at the view. We can see lakes, the curved roofs of barns and vehicles creeping along faraway roads.

The farmer has no wrinkles, a lifetime in high breezes has dried him out smoothly, shrinking his skin to his skull. His eyes are bright. They seem to belong in the head of a younger man. 'How's your eyesight?' I ask him.

'Strong,' he tells me.

We talk a while; the farmer developing a theory that looking far every day is a powerful exercise for eyes. Living up here in the constant presence of distance keeps his vision strong. City people live in perpetual foreground; buildings surround them so closely that they forget they are on landscape at all. You might think this is how the world is, close-packed and vertical rather than round and endlessly receding. Living in shallow focus means city people don't often exercise their eyes beyond a close limit.

'Ah, but in the country you might be living down among the hills,' I point out, 'and in a city you might live in a tower block, with a far view from your window.'

'I'm not sure that matters,' he says, in an indulgent tone and with a quick sideways dip of the head that means *you've missed the point entirely.*

The farmer says you could have all the view in the world but just treat it as a backdrop. It's his interest in his area and its people that really exercises his eyesight. He looks harder at his surroundings than a person in a high-rise looks at distant buildings. He seeks country gossip, wants to know the work rates of other farmers, who is building what and where. Every day he studies the faraway, giving his eyes a workout. A red car is moving along a distant road and he points to it. From here the car is about the size of a fingernail at the end of your outstretched arm. 'I don't just see the car going along,' he says. 'I want to know which family it belongs to. And when I know that, I'll want to know which of them is driving it.'

Starting at the closest hedgerow, the farmer shows me where the border passes his land. His fields are in the south, arranged around a particularly sharp point of Northern Ireland, an oblique angle elbowing into the south along rows of bramble. It isn't the southernmost point of Northern Ireland but it is the southernmost point around here, so I understand him when he calls it 'the end of the north'. The farmer then raises his hand and narrates the border's route further ahead along hedgerows and fences; right here, left there. Trying to keep up, I draw the borderline with my eyes. When I blink, I lose it but I don't interrupt as I'm enjoying the farmer's litany of names and features. Somewhere a few miles off he reaches the limit of his knowledge and lowers his hand. 'So, that's it,' he says in summation, 'that's the rule of the land.'

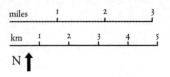

miles   1   2   3

km   1   2   3   4   5

N ↑

Mully

Clontibret ▰▰▰

28
27
26   25
    24
Crossbane
The Fairy Cave
Dumb Hole

Annyalla ▰▰▰

Castlebla

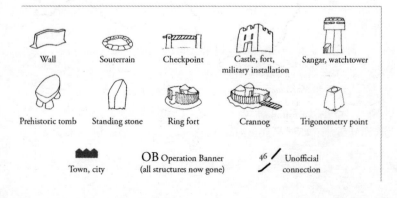

Wall	Souterrain	Checkpoint	Castle, fort, military installation	Sangar, watchtower
Prehistoric tomb	Standing stone	Ring fort	Crannog	Trigonometry point

Town, city   **OB** Operation Banner (all structures now gone)   46 / Unofficial connection

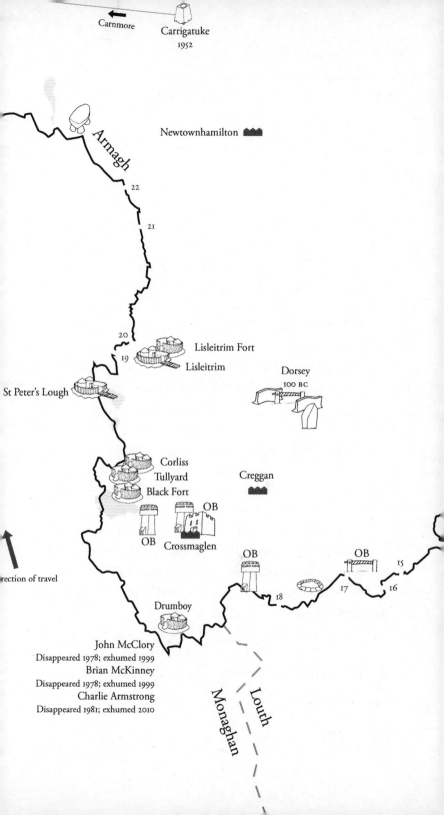

Carnmore ←   Carrigatuke
                    1952

Armagh   Newtownhamilton

22

21

20   Lisleitrim Fort
19   Lisleitrim   Dorsey
                                            100 BC
St Peter's Lough

                Corliss
                Tullyard   Creggan
                Black Fort

                        OB
                OB   Crossmaglen

                                OB   OB
                                                        15
                                        18   17   16

                Drumboy

John McClory
Disappeared 1978; exhumed 1999
Brian McKinney
Disappeared 1978; exhumed 1999
Charlie Armstrong
Disappeared 1981; exhumed 2010

                Louth
        Monaghan

rection of travel

Checkpoints, Customs

I am standing at the site of a border checkpoint. There was an installation here during the Troubles, walls, bollards and a pillbox that guarded this lane, an official in/out route, one of only about fifteen approved crossing points along the whole border. There is no sign of the installation now. The only structure I can see belongs to a farm; the ubiquitous corrugated shed, oxblood red. There is a bucolic atmosphere: fuchsia hedging, emerald green dashed with pink; swallows flitting overhead; pastureland; the smell of manure cut with the tang of diesel. The lane passes seamlessly over the border. I pace back and forth over it a few times, feeling like an archaeologist of the recent. A Royal Engineer probably paced here too. He had a selection of restrictors to work with, three-ton concrete blocks and steel walls, all placed to make crossing the border into a slow wriggle. I kneel down and touch the road, examining the mundane in a way I haven't done since I was aged about seven. Compacted aggregate encased in tar. I find no trace of the checkpoint; the lane has been resurfaced and not a dent remains.

I grew up close to the border. Goods were cheaper in the north and as a child I went over the border with my parents when they were purchasing an audio cassette player, curtains or lino. The things that caught my eye in the north were different. I understood from a young age that supplies

– biscuits, toys, everything important – weren't just cheaper in the north, but better. At home we bought sweets by weight, an old shopkeeper scooping them out from big jars stacked behind the counter, but across the border there were pick 'n' mix stalls in the shopping centres, freestanding islands where you scooped your own. By taking just two of a certain sweet, three of another, I could optimise my experience while staying within the ninety or so pence I had to spend. In the south you could only get one kind of Monster Munch. I'd thought the yellow pack, with the Cyclops on the back, was the only sort. In the aisles of northern supermarkets I discovered two other varieties; I remember standing wonderstruck before them.

The border was gateway to this excitement and also an excitement in itself. The checkpoint fortresses towered over our car, the barrels of guns poking out of dark slots. There was barbed wire, spotlights and English accents on CB radios. The guns cradled in the soldiers' arms were black and heavy, I could have touched them had I rolled down my window. In our car we would have to wait in queues, between soldiers and blast walls. I have since read that there were hidden microphones listening to us during those minutes. The mics were placed to catch the words of people waiting in line or, perhaps more usefully, to register heavy silences. I was queuing once with my father as two soldiers walked up and down the line with their automatic rifles pointed to the ground. We were returning south but had not moved in five minutes. I was in the front passenger seat and my father had his hands on the steering wheel, looking ahead blankly, a state of suspension he always slipped into when held up at checkpoints. Both soldiers saw me at the same time, my hands in movement but down out of sight.

Concealed activity was a thing they watched for. One soldier stepped forward and peered in at me. I held up my bag of Monster Munch.

There was tax to be paid on goods transported south, so approaching the border my father might shove a bottle of gin under his seat or even under me. For a few moments I would play smuggler. Our concern was not the soldiers — they did not care about contraband alcohol. Our concern was the customs official stationed just inside the south. Their bases were called *customs posts* in legal language but *huts* in the multitude of situations that, taken together, constitute reality. Huts was the best word for them: some were the size of an outdoor toilet, made of wood and corrugated steel, painted green so you knew what country you were in. Most were built in the decade or two after partition. In their early years they would have seen very little traffic as there was very little, just bicycles and rattling tractors.

I can imagine the snoozy harmlessness of a hut's day-to-day operations throughout the 1930s, forties and fifties, before the Troubles gave cover to organised crime and the countryside developed a thirst for diesel. In those days smuggling was mainly about butter, tea leaves and the occasional cow. Oral history projects have gathered hundreds of small-scale smuggling tales; I'm quite worn out reading them. They are recounted with the mischievousness and enjoyment that comes from outsmarting a system. Smuggler is hero in these mini-epics, the treasure is an untaxed can of heating oil or a piglet. These anecdotes could be the makings of a Sunday evening entertainment series. I can imagine it, teatime, BBC1: little usually happens around the customs post in the sleepy border village of Bally[insert wordplay here]. Mild amusement ensues when Proinsias

O'Shea cycles across the border with a pound of butter under his hat (he hadn't factored in the heat of the sun!); fleet-footed youngsters dash across nearby fields with bags of flour (they're good lads really); old Mrs Gallagher refuses to pay her five-shilling fine ('Customs officer! Didn't I take you to my own breast when you were a baba!'). It keeps coming, over the border, an onslaught of pre-Troubles tales, golden-lit, winking at you incessantly. One well-known tale captures the spirit of a thousand: every day a man cycled south, going by the customs post. Every evening he walked back home again into the north. The officials were infuriated by him, they knew he had to be smuggling something but they did not know what it was. They stopped him but his basket was always empty and he was never carrying a bag. They would check under the bicycle seat and get him to empty his pockets. He was carrying nothing. It was months before they worked it out; the man was smuggling bicycles.

A truth is captured in this tale: you were only smuggling if you were carrying more than you needed. One man, one bicycle, no hassle. But one man with two bicycles would get taxed. For this reason southern boys and girls buying new shoes in the north could simply walk across barefoot, buy the shoes, and return wearing them without problem.

However, newspaper reports from the time do turn up some real confrontations. In 1940 a gang of smugglers had a full battle with customs officials on the border. At the time a sack of flour was eight shillings cheaper in the north. The smuggling gang was in a convoy, over a hundred donkeys each carrying a hundred pounds of flour, driven by about ninety men armed with sticks. The gang must have looked like something out of the *Arabian Nights*, but with donkeys instead of camels and Cavan instead of the Sahara. They moved under darkness, the moon dimmed by cloud, crossing into the south on remote tracks. Fourteen officials lay in wait but had not been expecting so much opposition. It must have occurred to them to abandon the sting but they braved it, standing up and blocking the gang's route. There was swearing and shouting then fighting began, clouts on heads, punches, stones thrown, panicked donkeys rushing about and streaming flour. The smugglers' boss was on horseback, driving his men into battle and going in to take wallops at the customs men too. The fight did not break up until dawn; the customs officials got most of the donkeys and made many arrests. They claimed two tons of flour, less than half of what the convoy had been carrying. Not that the smugglers had gotten away with the rest of the haul; flour was strewn all about the battleground, coating several acres in a sticky glutinous web.

Even this story could be absorbed into the plot of our Sunday evening show. A clout from an aul stick generally heals in half an hour; just apply a comically large bandage. At the time the *Fermanagh Herald* put it mildly too, headlining the story 'Donkey Serenade' and discussing the 'exciting clash'. We are told that all of the Customs men took sick leave the following day as 'not one was left unscathed'. Now the distance of years has sepia-toned such events. We smile about that phase, the innocent border, the era of nudges and winks. It is easy to smile because of the contrast presented with the Troubles. Sacks of flour are transformed into crates of guns, or wraps of Semtex, or a young man with his wrists tied together. One way or another, few will be left unscathed.

Compared with the military hulks across the border,

the customs huts were like jokes, allotment sheds in the wrong place, each complete with a semi-retired man who enjoyed his own company. Customs huts continued to be staffed during the Troubles. My father and I would first have the tense experience of an army checkpoint then go on to the daft-looking hut. Customs never caused problems – as long as you didn't wave your contraband in their faces, as long as you had the decency to hide your gin under your child, then you were let on with a wave. The huts were staffed until 1993 when the European Single Market rendered them irrelevant, for a while at least. Some of the original huts still remain. Tiny, flimsy, yet still standing after the steel fortresses have gone. I encounter several on my border walk. One remote hut is actually for sale, ridiculous with a real estate sign tacked above the doors. I suppose it might make a holiday home for a singleton with a frontier spirit, or an eccentric with simple needs. It might make a primary home for more extreme versions of either. Anyone not already eccentric would soon be made so by the duality of the location. Not just dealing with the here/there, but the fact that the huts are in the middle of nowhere, yet only inches from the road. The border's low population is the vacuum that allowed these huts to survive, this is no development zone and vandals don't commute. So there they have stood, for decades, awaiting new orders.

*

I pass farm after farm. Evening shadows cast by corrugated sheds lie across the border. I make camp on a hillside and after dark I lie out on my tarpaulin, listening. There are no houses nearby but the still night air is a vector for sound. A dog's bark carries for miles, across from another country; a car door slams shut, tyres crunch on gravel, a distant acceleration. I think I hear cries from somewhere far off, maybe it's a football game. Then I hear something much closer, a heavy roll in the grass by my feet. I sit up and switch on my torch. A badger. A big badger, frozen by the sudden light, one paw held up. I can see the dirt under its claws. I am amazed the creature was passing so near without smelling something foreign and changing direction, what's that big nose for? The badger looks at me. I look at it. It looks at me. I look at it. In that long moment I sense the badger and myself coming to an arrangement. Slowly I reach over with one hand and switch off my torch. It's pitch dark again; I listen to the badger shuffle on without changing course or pace. We're both pretending it never happened.

*

The border hangs on a mile of hedgerow. I walk the fields or, if it is close enough, the nearest lane. At about 10 a.m. I call into a shop attached to a petrol station looking for something to eat. Like a farmer, I've taken to having two breakfasts. The owner is leaning heavily into his countertop, arms folded. I ask him if he is concerned about being taken out of the European Union.

'Be a terrible shame if I have to carry a passport on me all the time,' he says. 'We'll have to wait and see what they try to pull on us. In the meantime, I just keep an eye on the exchange rates. What are they thinking, wanting out?' I fail to give a good answer and he goes on to say, 'They aren't thinking about Ireland, that's for sure. The EU has been great for us, for the peace, for everything.'

I say that some in Northern Ireland want to leave.

'But not border people,' he replies. 'Not us.'

It is later in the day that I am struck by the term he used, 'border people'. He seemed to be giving name to an identity, a culture even. And he is proven right about the referendum. In June 2016 about 65 per cent of voters in the border counties choose to remain.

'Suppose tariffs are put on imports or exports?' I ask him.

'Then lads will start smuggling again, big time,' he says.

The shopkeeper enjoys a yarn about smuggling in the old days. He tells me the bicycle story, the fourth time I've heard it. He sees I'm not impressed so ups his game. 'There was a time,' he tells me, 'when you could make advantage from a dead cow. If you were taking it over the border to the knacker's yard someone might come around and do a quick bit of surgery. Crude surgery, mind.' He makes a gesture with his hands, a slicing action that looks experienced. He pulls himself up, wanting a better view of my reaction. 'You can get thirty bottles of spirit in a cow,' he says. 'Did you know that?' I did not know that, and I've since read one other source claiming this form of smuggling occurred. The shopkeeper also tells me that during the 2001 foot and mouth outbreak – when beef exports were banned – meat itself was smuggled, sides of beef hidden inside bales of hay.

'These days it's all diesel of course,' the shopkeeper says sadly. He is bored by the fuel's monopoly, not necessarily on business, but on stories.

Diesel smuggling is an industry and where I am walking today is its partitioned heart. Smuggling operations are uncovered by the police at a steady rate; it seems like once a fortnight another bust is reported on the news, but more operations replace them. Even within the Single Market, the duty levied on fuel is each country's own business. Diesel is cheaper in the south, a price difference to be exploited by entrepreneurs/criminals. The way they deal in fuel shows how large-scale and organised smuggling can be. At first I picture tankers of southern diesel driven across in the middle of the night, but that would actually be conspicuous, smugglers probably prefer 6 a.m. or the depths of a Sunday afternoon. The diesel they carry is licensed only for farm use – this is the sort with the biggest price differential. In the south it is stained with green dye, in the north it is stained red. Officials visit northern farms and 'dip' tanks, checking that the correct sort is being used, so to sell the diesel in Northern Ireland it has to be first cleared of the green dye. This is done with bleach and cat litter. The diesel laundries are hidden away in border garages; inside, rows of barrels stand on beaten clay floors saturated with spill. Other operations are larger, two or three massive tankers, separated from their truck beds and set on pallets inside warehouses that were built specifically for the purpose. A toxic fug hangs in the air.

The filtering process makes tons of waste that is trucked away and dumped. Five-foot plastic cubes are left in lay-bys, full of blackened cat litter or overflowing with poisonous fluid. Along isolated lanes you might find a few tons of waste spilled out on the ground, sticky with toxins. Near here an entire trailer, forty-five feet long, was left on a roadside just a few nights before I go by. In their haste the gang did not lower the trailer's jacks, so as soon as the cab pulled away the trailer slumped forward, crushing its nose into the lay-by and lifting its back wheels into the air, the swamp of waste pooling at one end. Next morning people found the trailer that way, tail in the air, the leavings of things that happen at night.

I hear about this and other events because my pocket radio, tuned to local stations, is strapped to my backpack. On some days I let it whisper to me for an hour or two. News stories begin to influence the way I see the landscape, I fully expect an encounter with criminality of some sort. I never seek landowners' permission, walking the border would take years if I did that, so everywhere I arrive unannounced. I pass close to isolated sheds and outhouses; any of them could be a diesel laundry. I pass through farms that straddle the border, a perfect base.

This morning the border leads me to a yard of abandoned cars and a half-dismantled lorry up on bricks. I must have been daydreaming – I did not notice the landscape get ugly so quickly. Sheds, warehouses and fencing

hem in most of the yard, there might be four or five different businesses operating from here. At the centre of this
one-acre enclosure is a grand modern mansion, still under
construction although nobody seems to be working today.
The project is in the last stages, doors and glass have gone
in. The living-room window will frame this view of
wreckage and locked sheds. There's a brutality about the
place, but also the hint of money. Guard dogs bark and
dash out of a garage towards me. Their chains are thirty
feet long, clattering over the rippled concrete surface. The
chains halt the dogs but they remain standing and barking, straining at the edge of their territory. Nobody
appears. Eventually the dogs tire and lie down. I make my
way towards a tall gate that leads out but discover it is pad-
locked. I rattle the lock pointlessly. When I turn around a
man is standing looking at me. He is wearing blue overalls
and a face mask that covers his mouth and nose. He is
coated head to toe in white dust.

'You're probably wondering what I'm doing here,' I say.
I point at my map and talk about passing through, about
following the border.

He pulls off his mask. The undusted patch exposed
around his nose and mouth gives him a canine look. 'The
border,' he says. He shakes his head in a way that is neither
negative nor positive. It is the headshake one makes in the
face of some impervious immensity; I might have said *the
Pacific Ocean*.

'It goes through here,' I say, showing my map, willing to
explain everything.

'Sure I know,' he says. 'Following it, are you?'

'I am.'

'The border,' he says again in the same tone and with the

same headshake. I am suddenly fond of him.

'What's the white stuff?' I ask.

'Plaster,' he says, indicating the door to his workshop. In the shadows I can see a few moulded ceiling roses leaning on their rims. 'Mouldings for houses and the like. Are you after any?'

'No thank you.'

'Call back if you ever are.'

He releases me and I go on my way.

*

I take a short hike into Northern Ireland to visit the Bonds Road. It is a single lane of bitumen with bungalows both sides; black wheelie bins await collection at their gates. The road has older names; dig under the Bonds Road and you'll find stones that were on the surface when this was the Old Coach Road and, presumably, the Coach Road too. Dig even deeper and you might expose traces of Bealach mor na Feadha, an Iron Age road used by traders, cattle raiders, warriors and wandering poets.

The road passes through an embankment, both steep sides covered in shrubs and bluebells. I might have taken it for an abandoned railway cutting had I not come here looking for it. Walking through the gap I experience a sense of antique transition. This embankment is called the Dorsey. It is a couple of miles long and one of Ireland's largest and most enigmatic ancient earthworks. It was a border defence with ditches, dykes and walls. However, the name sounds as if it might refer to something door-like, door-ish, and that would be correct. The Dorsey's defences funnelled travellers into an official entrance/exit point. The wall and the door are likely to have been built to control traffic, know who was coming and going and perhaps extract taxes. It was a doorway into the old kingdom of Ulster.

Stretches of the Dorsey look like they might have been cast up by a giant earthworm sliding below the surface. The embankments are up to twenty feet tall and the ditches below can be twenty feet deep. I am conscious that those figures may make the Dorsey sound more dramatic than it actually is; it has had two thousand years to blur with its hilly surroundings and blur it has. But most people probably don't think of any embankment as dramatic, no matter how tall. I am becoming calibrated to the borderland, its contained scales and slow unwindings. The Dorsey is sometimes hard to see among the land's natural dips and rises. Roads have been cut through it; trees have grown across it; farmers have bulldozed it; centuries of rain have needled it back into the earth.

Archaeological excavations have dug up palisade walls here, just off the Bonds Road. Layers were peeled back to reveal wooden posts set in long rows and reinforced with horizontal planks or flattish stones. The posts were thick oak branches or trunks, split and roughly squared. I have handled samples of these; they are in cardboard boxes in a basement of Queen's University, Belfast. They are thick discs with smooth faces, hard and heavy as stone. Tannins in the wood reacted with the bogwater and turned the wood black. Each growth ring is visible, black on greyblack. It is helpful that the Dorsey palisades were made of oak. Many trees skip a year of growth now and then but an oak grows with regularity, putting on a ring every year. This regularity makes them very useful for measuring time. In a year of good environmental conditions the ring will be thick, in a bad year the ring will be thin, creating a pattern of thicks and thins that can be plotted on a long sheet of paper, the results looking like a seismograph printout. By placing the printouts on top of each other, one tree's pattern can be compared with another's, running them back and forth until matches are found. An older tree will carry a certain environmental record in its outer layers whereas a younger tree will carry the same record close to its core. By matching up trees whose lives overlapped we can find out when ancient logs lived, and died. This is dendrochronology, and it tells us the oldest Dorsey palisades were made from oaks chopped down between 130 and 140 BC.

The existence of a first line of defence implies the existence of a core, the centre that projected the boundary. So where was the centre that the Dorsey defended? The ancient kingdom of Ulster was a much smaller place than Ulster is today and the capital was Emain Macha, about twenty miles north of where I am now. It was the royal seat and where Cúchulainn would have lived. Remains of a grand ceremonial structure were uncovered there and oak rings tell us it was built at the same time as the Dorsey. There seems to have been a phase of massive public projects for the kingdom, the Iron Age equivalent of a city about to host the Olympics.

Look at archaeologists' drawings of Emain Macha's central structure and you get the impression of concentricity, circles within circles. First a circular ditch was dug and then a huge timber structure was built over it. It was about 120 feet in diameter, a large round warehouse with a conical roof. The roof was supported by four concentric lines of posts radiating out around a central pole. We can't know how tall the building was but it was certainly imposing, judging by the depth of the postholes. It was probably the biggest building anyone here had ever seen. You would expect it to be some sort of royal residence, hosting feasts and rituals, but no, the building was itself the ritual and it was an extraordinary one. As soon as the wooden shell was complete, the people of Emain Macha began to fill it with stones, layer after layer, the work of many months. Limestone boulders were levered, towed and pushed to the site. Some rocks were the size of barrels, although not so conveniently shaped. The boulders were stacked inside the structure to a height of almost ten feet.

What were they thinking? We'll never know exactly, but just because you could not enter it doesn't mean it wasn't a capital building. It was still the axis point for the kingdom, all trails led to it, a centre point that society could look towards, experiencing social cohesion in the act. They didn't think of a capital building as a place for meetings and feasts, it was hardly a place at all but a kind of mystical task, half of this earth and half somewhere else.

The ritual was not yet finished. The wooden outer structure was set alight and burned away, leaving a mound of stones. The act of burning might have been an offering, sending the building to the other side, to be a house for the dead perhaps. The bonfire would have had a huge audience; there was mass entrancement as the mound of stones emerged from the smoke and drifting embers.

And still there is more. Soil was carted in from the surrounding country and the stone heap smothered in it. Archaeologists have found twenty-one distinct types of soil in the mound. This shows the builders ranged widely for the material and suggests another layer of meaning for the project; the mound was made of the land around it, was the embodiment of the territory, the part that represented the whole. Eventually, grass grew over the mound and, over the centuries, it settled into its surroundings. The people of Emain Macha had made a hill and it is still there today.

I'm struck by the primacy of the circle in all this. Beyond the rim of the mound a bank and ditch were dug too, enclosing the mound in another circumference. The posts supporting the circular building were arranged radially, showing an attention to geometric proportions unnecessary to simply hold up a roof and doubly unnecessary if, as seems likely, the building's only role was to be burnt as sacrifice. When the stones were brought in they were also laid with attention to radial lines. As we've seen, about three thousand years before, the tomb on Slieve Gullion was built with applied knowledge, made to align with the sun and seasons, but that tomb could have been built by an extended family whereas Emain Macha's mound needed a much larger workforce. In fact, it needed a whole society, one with a dominant priest class, able to whip the people up into the fervency such a project required. Mingling with its spirituality is something like politics, or at least ideas of society and homeland. Emain Macha radiates power and jurisdiction as far as the Dorsey, the gateway and defence being built around the same time. Take both projects together and a territorial sovereignty is being shaped, the centre and the rim, it would be difficult to have one without the other. It makes me think of an oak and its rings – the means by which we date both projects. A kingdom with a capital is sure to develop a frontier.

I step off the Bonds Road and onto a small field. To my left a section of the embankment stands over me, to my right is a farm's outhouse. A dog is barking somewhere nearby. I walk directly away from the embankment, counting my steps. Archaeologists stripped away the topsoil here some time ago. There is no sign of their work now, the grass is evenly thick again. But under my feet, a few steps inside the Dorsey, they found the foundations of a small shelter. It was built of sod walls overlooking the gateway. There was a fire pit next to it, lined with charcoal, burnt nutshells and animal bone. The shelter might have been the borderland's first checkpoint, first customs hut or a bit of both.

I imagine a couple of border guards sitting at the fire, roasting chunks of pork on blackened rods. Nothing happens for days at a time but the guards are constantly glancing along the trail. This was a dangerous posting if the amount of frontier violence in the *Táin Bó Cúailnge* is anything to go by. It is hard to know if guarding the gateway to Ulster was considered a lowly or honourable role, their shelter is tiny so I think lowly. Perhaps they are grumbling about the job, the cold, the exposure, they feel forgotten by Emain Macha. How do they conceive the land they are guarding, this kingdom that puts so much effort into building then sacrificing huge constructions? The policy may make perfect sense to them; they may take comfort in it. Perhaps it helps them to see their own role as part of the ritual, the guardians at the outer ring. We're important, they tell each other, even if nobody realises it.

Similar thoughts probably occur to anyone stationed on a European Union frontier. Such thoughts certainly occurred to the customs officers of Ireland's border. Sitting in the doors of their huts, waving on yet another car, it must have seemed to them that their true purpose there was to make the moment real, to officiate at the ritual when we pass from one state into another.

miles | 1 | 2 | 3
km | 1 | 2 | 3 | 4 | 5

N ↑

Au

39

St Patrick's Chair ⬡

Brackenridge's
Mausoleum
19th century

Slieve
Beagh

Tyrone

40 · 41

42

43

Em

Fermanagh

Columba McVeigh
Disappeared 1975;
burial site unknown

44

Monaghan

Scotstown

OB

Derryvullen
dancing deck

OB

Monag

Irish Arm
20th centu

Rosslea

OB

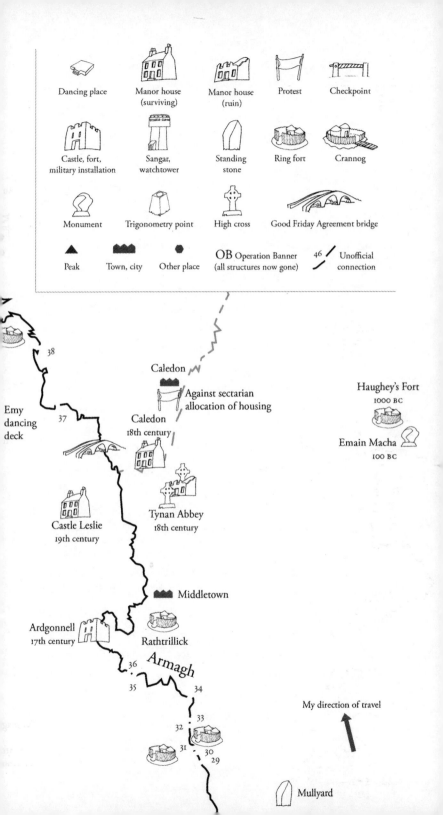

Legend

	Dancing place
	Manor house (surviving)
	Manor house (ruin)
	Protest
	Checkpoint
	Castle, fort, military installation
	Sangar, watchtower
	Standing stone
	Ring fort
	Crannog
	Monument
	Trigonometry point
	High cross
	Good Friday Agreement bridge
	Peak
	Town, city
	Other place
OB	Operation Banner (all structures now gone)
46 /	Unofficial connection

38

Caledon

Against sectarian
allocation of housing

Haughey's Fort
1000 BC

Emy
dancing
deck

37

Caledon
18th century

Emain Macha
100 BC

Castle Leslie
19th century

Tynan Abbey
18th century

Middletown

Ardgonnell
17th century

Rathtrillick

36   Armagh

35   34

33

32

31   30
              29

Mullyard

My direction of travel

Landlords, Tenants

The border swings around White Island then dives into the Blackwater River. Wider than a two-lane road, this is the most substantial border river I've yet encountered. There's no risk I'll lose track of the boundary here, it travels the Blackwater with complete fidelity for the next fifteen miles. Everything is scaling up along with the river, giving the border clarity not seen since Carlingford Lough. The fields on both banks are large and neat. The hills arch in a way that is smooth and regular.

There is a preserved order about this area, a new thing for me on this journey. I walk an hour without seeing a chicken-wire fence or litter in a ditch. There are no advertisements pinned to telegraph poles, there are no telegraph poles. The country is worked but not lived on, though I do pass grand stone pillars and walk alongside old walls with decorative crenellations on top, each block hand-cut. Some of these walls are miles long. All these things are clues that I am on the lands of country estates. There are three estates in this area, Caledon, Tynan and, in the south, Castle Leslie. Together, as one traveller put it, they make 'a kind of shamrock pattern out of the curious coincidence that here, in close juxtaposition, are the only three considerable mansions that stand virtually on top of the border'. These estates have curtailed modern influence in this part of the borderland. As evidence of this I have with me an eyewitness report from the summer of 1833. That was when Lieutenant C. Bailey surveyed these hills, the river and nearby villages and mansions for the Ordnance Survey.

Ireland's Ordnance Survey was more than the map-making project known elsewhere in these islands. Ireland's survey featured a side project, written 'memoirs' that were intended to form a portrait of the country. In the end only Ulster's counties were surveyed and those rather patchily. The manuscripts have been preserved and I have made a copy of Lieutenant Bailey's to get a picture of these grand estates from the time they mattered most: the nineteenth century. At the heart of each estate was the Big House, axis point of local social and political power. I am not alone in applying uppercase letters; they are earned because the Big House had a particular cultural position in Ireland, giving rise to a distinctly Irish literary genre, the Big House novel. The contrast between the Big House and the common cottage was ripe for dramatisation, stories revealing the tensions between landlord and tenant.

I am not sure Bailey was a fan of novels. His terse reports never exhibit flair or contain colourful detail. It's easier to imagine a man of military bearing, upright as he moved through the round hills. He counts cottages and jots down the names of the crops the tenants are growing. Bailey preferred measurable values and columns of numbers. He consults the ledgers in courthouses and schools, not engaging with folkways or ancient ruins. He does not speak much to the locals; unlike many other memoirists, Bailey never quotes local opinions. He does ask people if their properties are insured – the answer is always no – but he is pleased to report that here 'illicit distillation is not carried on'. Bailey is most interested in the land itself, and in the ways it might be more profitably managed. He approves highly of improving works. There is satisfaction when he notes that all the cottages have glass in their windows. Bailey also admires landlords' mansions and he makes a point of visiting them all, describing them not as Big Houses but Gentlemen's Seats.

I follow Bailey's footsteps to the Tynan Abbey estate. Bailey describes it as a 'remarkable handsome building'. It was never an actual abbey, the title was an affectation of the owners. There is a faux-medieval gatehouse overlooking the road. I have to clamber over the battlements to get onto the grounds. This is not as difficult as it might sound; it is a play-castle, a big toy, although of solid stone. Beyond the gatehouse is a long drive hemmed with spindly steel fences. Either side grow alders and oaks and a clump of bamboo has gone wild, shoots so tall they have collapsed under their own weight. Up ahead I should be seeing the house but there is only a backdrop of trees. Tynan Abbey is gone.

I must look to old prints to see the house. It was a hotch-potch of Gothic windows, turrets and Victorian gables, all bristling with top-heavy chimneys. Churchy windows and stained glass were installed to suit the fiction in the house's name. Tynan Abbey belonged to a family called Stronge and it seems the nineteenth-century Stronges were antiquarians, but of a grabby, indiscriminate sort, rifling through history for whatever took their fancy and sticking it all together. Bailey was taken in by the house's weight of authority but other members of the memoir scheme were not, one calling Tynan Abbey a 'fine specimen of a bastard'.

The Stronge family did a cheeky thing. They took some high crosses from the site of a medieval monastery up river and planted them around their estate. I find one among yew trees, the carved stone over ten feet tall, half-coated in

lichen, as if dipped headfirst in green paint. High crosses were medieval preaching stations, carved images on every side illustrating Bible stories to a non-reading population. These were God's imprints on the landscape. Their form, a freestanding bulky crucifix with an inset ring, has come to be identified with Ireland. Along with round towers, they were an emblem of Irish nationalism and are now one of Ireland's logos.

It was the cross's sense of history that the Stronges wanted perhaps. Continuity is vital to the families who own these estates. They keep detailed family trees. The Alexanders of Caledon began with James Alexander, who made a fortune in India, returned to Ireland and bought a substantial chunk of County Tyrone in 1775. The Stronges of Tynan trace their lineage as far back as 1363 in Scotland. The Leslies trace their ancestry back to Attila the Hun. The mixed design of Tynan Abbey might have been an attempt to ballast the house with history.

One night in January 1981 ten members of the IRA came across the border. They were dressed in combat gear, their faces blackened. They watched Tynan Abbey from the trees, eating sandwiches and drinking lemonade. After dark, they approached the solid oak door and used an explosive charge to blast it open. Sir Norman Stronge was at home with his son James. Both men had been Unionist MPs and examples of how the landed gentry, after the era of the landlord, had slid smoothly into a new kind of political power. The Stronges fired a distress flare up the chimney. The flare bursting above the slates looked like the house itself making a last gasp. Both father and son were shot and killed. The IRA gang set the house alight and it burned down around the dead men. James was the last of eight generations at Tynan. It is notable that the IRA erased the house: delaying to do so almost got them captured. Their statement referred to the action as an 'attack on the symbols of hated unionism'. Neither of the men they killed had played an active role in politics in ten years; perhaps the house itself was a stronger symbol than its inhabitants.

I sit at the edge of the house's footprint. A shape is implied in the air by the foundations and a couple of surviving sandstone arches. Tynan Abbey looked down between rows of squat yews to a lake. Someone is still coming here to trim them and mow the lawn. I imagine the groundkeeper at his or her task, keeping order in a garden that nobody sees. The ornamental rows are like spokes that have lost their axle, running from the garden's perimeter, leading to a void. Brambles are creeping in from the boundaries. Near the high cross a bed of bright red shoots, rhubarb perhaps, has burst from the untended kitchen garden and is marching towards the lawn.

Landlords, Tenants

*

I leave Tynan and walk into Caledon land. There are large well-tended fields and wooden gates where I usually see aluminium or steel. There are some quaint stone bridges, and a bridge of iron too. There are no washing lines, no B&Q garden furniture, no child's tricycle abandoned at the bottom of a driveway. Estates seem to be the only forces in Ireland powerful enough to keep bungalows at bay. The key difference between estate lands and the general country is that there aren't many small properties and the trappings they would bring. Much of the land is rented out, part of the reason it is so fully and intensely worked. But not so intensely that old gateways are modernised or hedgerows replaced with wire fencing. There is concern for preservation and, I think, an eye for the pretty. Clumps of trees have been allowed to stay, taking up good workable land. There are many mature oaks, leafy crowns so big they seem almost unnatural, freakish things. Everything has its place in what feels like a single composition. It takes me a while to figure this out: everything I'm seeing is the design of just a few people. These estates are intergenerational, ongoing projects but so dedicated to preservation that even the founders' tastes and leanings can still be read in the land. This is a rare experience; I'd say it amounts to a sensation. I think I am coming to understand something of the experience of a nineteenth-century tenant, living their whole life in an environment shaped and controlled by one person. The ubiquity of the landholder, Leslie, Alexander or Stronge: everything came from them or was allowed by them. Everything a tenant saw reflected the owner. I finally understand the word *landlord*. These were kingdoms.

Caledon is not just an estate, it is also a village with one main street running along the crest of a hill. According to Bailey, the inn was 'excellent'. It looks like it probably still is. Bailey noted that the solidity of the buildings, arranged in terraces, made Caledon appear to be a street in a large town rather than the entirety of a village. Much of it was built in a short phase by the second and third Earls of Caledon; homes, flourmill, courthouse, barracks, all placed along this arrow-straight street. I walk the generous pavement. It still looks like the street of a large town; it still looks the way the Alexanders of Caledon wanted it. From the town clock to the carvings above the doors, everything still reflects them.

I walk alongside the wall of the Caledon demesne, the biggest beech trees on the border towering over my head, crows' nests clumped in the branches. The gates are black steel hung between whitewashed gatehouses, decorated with establishment detailing: crowns, plaster sphinxes and coats of arms. I have to look past all this to see the firm security, CCTV and electronic mechanisms that pull the gates open or, like now, hold them shut. The Earl of Caledon, seventh of the line, still lives behind these gates. His house cannot be seen from the road and cannot be approached.

Bailey says Caledon House is 'magnificent . . . a fine building with a handsome front supported on pillars of the Ionic order'. Watercolours from the same era show a cold grandeur. This house was a far bigger statement than Tynan, it looks like the parliament building of a medium-size nation. In fact, there are constituted nations smaller than Caledon estate. A more recent image, a photograph, shows the same house but closely surrounded by a high fence. With concrete posts and barbed wire, like the perim-

eter of a Second World War prison camp, but with the top angled outwards instead of in, surely erected because of what happened at Tynan. Despite tensions between landlords and tenants in the nineteenth century, this estate would have been more open then. Bailey was probably able to walk right in. Now, with an institutional firmness, the gatehouse keeps me out.

I peer between the bars and am surprised to see a young man sitting on the doorstep of one of the gatehouses. He is smoking an electronic cigarette and enjoying the evening sun. I ask him if he lives here.

'I rent it,' he says. 'I've been here three years. This is my main house, that's the spare room.' He indicates the other gatehouse, across the drive.

'So you're a tenant of Lord Caledon, how's that?'

'It's grand,' he says blowing out vapour. 'I've only met him once. It's a mile from here to the house and I don't have much call to go up there.'

We look along the curving drive to where it disappears between hills. Giant oaks are silhouetted against the sky. A herd of deer are rounding the hill, each head down, cropping the pea-green grass.

'Do deer make good neighbours?' I ask.

'They'll be down here in a while,' he says. 'They come down here every night.'

*

The common image hanging over from the nineteenth century is of a few Protestant landowners lording over thousands of Catholic tenants, but with a large population descended from the Plantation, the north of Ireland was different. Although all the landlords were Protestant, not all tenants were Catholic. Lieutenant Bailey visited six schools, noting student numbers and their religions. This information indicates that Caledon's population contained equal numbers of Protestants and Catholics.

I feel I've been getting to know Lieutenant Bailey. I think he is shy, which leads him to be overly officious. He is too impressed by mansions, but that's forgivable. It is while reading his school reports that I'm frustrated with him. All those young, nameless lives, lined up in his columns – he makes no effort to enliven them, to let us hear their voices. But even through the statistics one school stands out as unusual; it was inside the Caledon demesne. Bailey gives only the most basic information about it; I look at the report's fifteen words for a long time, feeling like Pip at the beginning of *Great Expectations*, calling up a picture of his parents by gazing hard at their tombstones. The whole entry reads: 'Caledon Demesne, 20 Protestants, 20 Catholics, 40 females;

supported entirely by Lady Caledon, established 1829.'

While her husband built Caledon village, Catherine Alexander also had a project, the improvement of local girls and the improvement of society. Picture forty girls trooping across the fields to the gates every morning, twenty Catholic, twenty Protestant, all going to be educated together in the heart of the estate. Forty was a small number compared to other schools nearby; I sense a selection process. Did Lady Caledon ask the village schools to send the smartest girls, or the most needy? We don't know; all we have are Bailey's clipped phrases, but they are enough for things to gleam in the distance; a woman unwilling to lead a life of needle-point, a zeal for the improvement of the lower orders, an idealism. Due to the lack of other clues, the numbers themselves have to take on meaning. Twenty and twenty, equal of course, they have the air of an experiment, of controlled conditions. Twenty and twenty: firm and square.

Think of a new girl on her first day, terrified, passing between the Caledon gatehouses. Her parents have told her to behave herself. There's nothing unusual in that, but this morning their tone had a strange solemnity. She knows her responsibilities have widened. Even this young girl understands that she represents the family name here. The Big House emerges as she rounds the hills, astounding, beautiful, monstrous. White pillars, stone urns and dozens of chimney pots. Gravel crunches under her feet all the way up the long, long drive.

*

Each of the three Big Houses in this area can be taken as an example of how all of Ireland's Big Houses fared after

Irish independence and partition. They were destroyed, like Tynan; they hunched down and built defences, like Caledon; or they adapted, like Castle Leslie.

I leave Lieutenant Bailey behind, he did not survey County Monaghan, and, in addition, the Leslies will lead me into the twentieth century. I follow a wall across the border, into the south, and to a gateway. This is a back way into the Leslies' lands, rarely used. The three arches and decorative spires hint at Asia. Under each arch is a drooping gate. The ironwork features rather preposterous curves and spearheads, points coated in a silver paint that has not entirely worn away. The whole thing is like something from a Gothic novel or old horror film. I can already see the Leslie line were more bohemian than their neighbours, and prone to posing. A few bars have snapped away so I climb through the gate and follow a muddy lane to the Big House.

The Leslie estate dates back to the 1600s and the baronetage was created in 1876 for John Leslie, MP for Monaghan. He passed the land and title to his son, whom he had named John. When this second baronet had a son, in 1885, he called him John in turn. Names, like lands, were to be preserved and passed on. This John was sure to be another establishment man: first cousin to Winston Churchill, he grew up in a secure network of wealth and influence, in line to inherit the estate and title of third baronet. A lot of his youth was spent in Ireland but, as he later put it, 'behind our demesne walls, behind our gates, we are brought up as Englishmen.' Despite this, John found himself attracted to land beyond the walls. The estate gamekeeper made an impact on his childhood, inculcating him with the ways of Ireland's woods and wildlife. Later John Leslie remembered him as a 'magnificent red-bearded Celt'.

In England John received the correct education, Eton then Cambridge. It might have been here that he was first referred to as Irish and, up against strong contrasts, a sense of Irish identity developed in him. He became an activist for Irish independence and stood for election, although failed to gain a seat. He became a Catholic, which meant he could not inherit the Leslie land and title, throwing his family into a protracted crisis. He changed his name to Shane.

The dual nature of Shane Leslie's conversion, to the cause of Irish independence and to Catholicism, shows us the cultural landscape at the time. Many of Ireland's first nationalists were Protestant but by the beginning of the twentieth century Irish nationalism and Catholicism were completely intertwined. Nationalist and Catholic, Unionist and Protestant: it was unusual to be one and not the other. Political stances had become fused to religious traditions, making compromise even less likely. This, and the fact that there was a Protestant population concentrated in the island's north-east, was a recipe for a border. As soon as Ireland gained independence, it was partitioned.

In his memoirs Shane Leslie recorded his irritation at the border. It ran right by the estate, cutting him off from his titled neighbours and leaving a bedevilling no-man's land; 'a maze twisting between bogs and rivers giving a tolerable living to customs-officers and smugglers'. He offers this telling snapshot of life on a border estate: one day Shane and his father saw a group of men carrying sacks and walking towards one of the outhouses. 'My father, believing the march of men bearing mysterious bags meant that his house would be burnt, faced the visitors.' The men, laughing, opened the sacks to reveal struggling cockerels. It turned out that the Leslie estate was being used for cockfighting bouts, the birds representing the north and south. Now that they had been found out, the men asked Shane's father to preside over the cockfight.

A landlord asked to provide impartiality; this is a feature of tenant life that often appears in recollections of the time. A landlord might be called upon when neutrality was required. It was a kind of honour, I suppose. It indicates trust, but also highlights a landlord's remoteness from the tenants. Tenants could trust their landlord's adjudications because their lives did not overlap. Shane Leslie wanted to close the gap between landlord and tenant, his conversion was part of that mission. He expressed a wish to find a third way, not just for him but the entire landlord class, setting out his beliefs in essays and a pamphlet called *The Landlords of Ireland at the Cross-Roads*. He expounded on a few semi-legendary landlords who, years before, had taken on the religion of their tenants: 'They exemplified how pleasant Irish life could be when the Big Houses and the cabins went to Mass together.' Shane Leslie believed the landlords of Ireland should make similar switches, be useful to an independent Ireland by becoming curators of its history, turning their estates into preserves of woodland and wildlife. He believed it was the landlords' last chance to retain a meaningful role.

But, south of the border at least, the era of the landlord was ending. Government acts took their lands and redistributed them. Unsympathetic tax laws forced estates to shrink until they were just farms with massively out-of-proportion houses, crumbling away. To survive, Castle Leslie became a hotel and equestrian centre. It is still a hotel and equestrian centre, run by a board of family members.

Having slipped in by a back gate I come at the hotel from

the wrong direction, the wrong side of the concealment shrubbery. I see the staff car park, smell the wheelie bins and hear the hum from the kitchen's extractor fans. Through a window I see a staff room with lockers against the wall and plastic chairs around a large table. A waiter, from the Indian subcontinent perhaps, is sitting with his head in his hands.

I go around to the main entrance. 'Have you booked, sir?' asks the receptionist. Yes, I have, but I feel awkward standing there with a backpack and hiking boots. I expect some chap to prod me out the door with his horsewhip. I have returned home to Belfast a couple of times since my border walk began but have been camped out for the last three nights. I look and feel out of place in this luxury hotel, with its tinkling piano music and carefully tossed cushions, but nothing in the receptionist's demeanour suggests she has noticed this. A pro, she's unfazed. She leads me to my room, pointing things out to me along the way, the bar, the restaurant, the boot room. Opposite my bedroom door is a display of reins and riding crops, for decoration I assume. I try to adopt the tone of the confident upper crust: smile, be polite, grateful, interested in what you're being shown while making it clear you've seen it all before. I add a dash of *I don't want to be any trouble* – an easy position to take when everything is so clearly perfect. Before leaving me, the receptionist opens the door to my bathroom, revealing a freestanding tub on clawed feet. I almost weep.

Later, over roast lamb, mint sauce and a pint of Guinness, I decide that landlordism has contributed a lot to modern Ireland's definition of luxury. Shane Leslie said landlords should go beyond their gates and be among the tenants, but meanwhile it seems the tenants were trying to get in the gates and be among the landlords. Now we too have the landlord experience for a few days, or even just a night. The prim grounds and mannerly staff, all lined up to meet us, all beckoning us to the Big House like it is our house, like we were supposed to be here all along. If you're like me, you hang back, unsure about passing through the portal, but a visit does one thing consistently, you are always made to feel like you deserve to be here. That you should be accustomed to this treatment. Just when you're starting to believe it, it's time to go home.

Shane Leslie died in 1971. Whether or not he achieved the fusion with Ireland that he so desired is hard to say, his later writings on the topic are evasive, but he did admit that his dual conversion had isolated him, an attempt to change sides that left him without a team. 'The convert is impeded and discouraged on every side unless his social position or mental indifference makes him independent enough to laugh at both sides.' Shane Leslie was gifted with some mental indifference, and he certainly had social position. He was born into a stratum from which it was hard to fall completely; that he hung on there despite himself can be seen as evidence of this. His life was a blend of writing, long travels, politics – radical and then diplomatic – and unfinished projects, such as a translation of the *Táin Bó Cúailnge*. He never stayed still. He was interested in forestry, the paranormal, fairy tales and mental health. Income from the estate paid for these pursuits. Despite his Catholicism, Shane's line has continued to hold the estate, and he took the title of third baronet. He had found it easier to make the journey from Protestant to Catholic, and from Unionist to Nationalist, than to go from the Big House to the cabin. When Shane Leslie had a son, he named him John.

I sleep very well, thank you. Walking north I leave the big estates. Soon every hill has a bungalow, with B&Q garden furniture and kids' trampolines out the back. Above my head power lines span the fields. On a tarmac drive I see a girl on a tricycle, head to one side, trying to figure out what I am doing. I wave but her expression does not change. I think I am done with landlords when another grand structure comes into view. With the names Leslie, Alexander and Stronge, I want to mention the name Brackenridge. I had not heard of him until I walked this way, his estate has now dissipated, but in the nineteenth century he owned much of the soon-to-be-borderland along here.

The structure is a tower. It stands about two miles inside Northern Ireland and perplexes me at first. It has a telescoped design, three cubes of decreasing size stacked on top of each other to a height of about sixty feet. It isn't a defensive structure: the lowest cube has wide arched windows. It can't be a bell tower, because the top storey is solid masonry. I decide it is probably a folly, but most follies in Ireland are whimsical things, open, airy structures with pillars and domes, and located for the convenience of strollers. This tower is a brutal upright, sharp-cornered, wilfully ugly, tall and weighty and isolated on top of a hill, visible for many miles in every direction. The builder wanted it to be seen by everyone but did not care if they liked it. I get the beginnings of an explanation when a middle-aged woman comes walking along the lane from her bungalow. Arms folded across her chest, stoic expression; I suspect she was already thinking about getting home again the minute she left. She has no dog, she is out walking herself. I detect external compulsion to her gait, doctor's orders. 'Brackenridge's Mausoleum you call it,' she says when I ask about the tower. 'A right sore thumb, isn't it?'

'Someone's buried in it?'

'Aye, yeah. Brackenridge was his name.' She thinks about it for a few moments. 'His bones were pulled out of it, way years ago. Schoolboys used his skull as a football.'

I am straining my eyes for details of the tower. 'Is that an Irish flag flying from it?'

'Aye, probably,' she says, not bothering to look. 'Brackenridge won't have liked that! But they'd stick a flag on anything around here. If we stood here long enough they'd stick a flag on us.'

She isn't able to tell me much about Brackenridge, only that he was a landlord and 'a right conniving bastard'. She says this as if he was her own landlord rather than one who, it turns out, died in 1879.

Everything I read or hear about Brackenridge begins with 'It is said . . .' or 'The story goes . . .' It seems his tenants disliked him; he was vengeful and inappropriate with the women. What is clear is that he was a barrister who through some smart purchases ended up with a huge amount of land and wealth. What he could not buy, however, was a place among the gentry. He changed his name from Trimble to Brackenridge, he became a layman in the Church of Ireland and built his own Big House, all in an attempt to gain respectability, but the Leslies, Alexanders and Stronges would have nothing to do with him; his money was too new, his manners too coarse.

I want to know why he built the tower, so for some sense of Brackenridge I read a novel by William Carleton, a writer from this area who wrote about peasant life during

the nineteenth century. The author knew Brackenridge and based a character on him for a tale of stolen inheritance called *The Black Baronet*. As with Trimble's name change to Brackenridge, the semi-fictional landowner in the novel wants to change his name to something with gravitas, something that sounds like it might have lineage. That he chooses Crackenfudge is our first hint that he is out of his depth with the gentry. 'A' had a right to change my name,' he says, 'when a' got into property. A' was ashamed of my friends, because there's a great many of them poor.'

Crackenfudge, like the real man that inspired him, wants to hang around with earls and baronets, sip tea with them at their lawn parties. To raise his status he wants to be made a magistrate and for this he needs the approval and recommendation of the baronet, Sir Thomas Gourlay, who resides at Red Hall (based on Caledon). The baronet insults Crackenfudge and sends him away but he comes back for more. This time Crackenfudge is physically whipped by Sir Thomas, but again he comes back.

We are given insight into Sir Thomas's thoughts on Crackenfudge and what kind of magistrate he would make if given the role: 'This fellow, now, who is both slave and tyrant, will play all sorts of oppressive pranks upon the poor, by whom he knows that he is despised; and for that very reason, along with others, will he punish them.' Despite this, he does make Crackenfudge a magistrate, partly because Crackenfudge's sycophancy eventually wears him down, but mainly because Sir Thomas Gourlay is an even more dastardly character, and flippant with it. 'Crackenfudge must get to the bench,' thinks Sir Thomas, 'if it were only for the novelty of the thing.'

I think this insight that Crackenfudge is 'both slave and tyrant' cuts close to the real Brackenridge. I think so because of this mausoleum. The tower is such a contorted statement; simultaneously scornful and needy; simultaneously enraged with everyone, but desperate for their recognition. It looks like a big finger stuck up at everyone for miles around, but perhaps most especially at the Leslies, Alexanders and Stronges. Brackenridge is said to have wanted to be buried under this tower so the gentry who had looked down on him during his life would have to look up to him after his death. He had the tower built decades before he died, presumably not trusting anyone to build it afterwards, but this means that Brackenridge himself spent much of his life looking up at his own grave, awaiting him on a hilltop, a monument to his own vanity and dislocation.

Highs, Lows

The border has many moods, but not as many as me. I walk by the river, between encroaching hills. I am always heading into a fold that, when I get there, I find leads to another that is just the same. The same dead-eyed cows stand in their fields, chewing grass, the same bright yellow tags in their ears. When it is time to make camp, I march straight up a round hill that is unpopulated and divided into about five fields. These hills are called drumlins and there are thousands of them in a thick band stretching across Ireland, much of it corresponding with the borderland. Although this particular round hill form is found in many parts of the world, the name was shaped here, in the Irish language, from *droimnín*, by way of *drym* and *druim*. It means little ridge. At the top of the drumlin, the relief of far horizons strikes me in a way that is almost bodily. I feel I've pushed through some sort of clingfilm ceiling. Up here I'm bathed in new oxygen, the sky is huge and in every direction I can see miles of cresting hills. I whoop out loud, using my voice-box for the first time in hours. The sudden openness boosts my mood. I feel lucky to be here, to have the freedom to pursue this quest. It is summer, I am healthy, I am free, I can go and camp on a hilltop any time I like. I walked a lot of miles today and I have earned this high kingdom. I kick my boots off and drop into the crisp grass.

Later I pitch my tent, then lay out my tarp as a picnic

blanket. Roast lamb is a memory, I'm back to sardines and noodles. My tent and tarp could be seen by anybody but I feel an open hillside gives its own kind of protection. If you are going to sleep in thinly populated country, under the sky, it is safer to be exposed, to be boldly present. Skulking away only puts you in the path of other skulkers, and makes you attractive to them.

The sky is grey-pink. I watch the curved evening shadow inch up the drumlin towards me. I've read descriptions of drumlins that compare them to ripples left on sand after the tide has gone out. They can be a mile or three long, cigar-shaped, indeed like ridges in sand, but Ireland's border drumlins have a much closer length-to-height ratio and the description does not fit. A border drumlin is more like an egg half-buried on its side. You might also say a drumlin is like a church's copper dome, coloured with exposure; or a desert dune on a planet with green sand.

Border drumlins are often symmetrical on one axis, so simple geometric descriptions come to mind. Looked at head on, some are the top fifths of perfect circles, or emerald suns rising from a plain. One aspect of their arrangement reinforces this sense of geometric order: many drumlins don't merge with their neighbours, rather each rises and falls from the same flat plain. They may rub their outer circumferences against others but are mainly independent.

Look at a lot of drumlins together and other metaphors occur. One writer describes driving by drumlins as like passing by an endless rollercoaster. A walker's interpretation, mine, is of a landscape slowly filling then exhaling. There is also something oceanic here. Drumlins look like full sea swells, bulging more to one end, but still a long way from breaking. From my campsite I can see miles of drumlins. Between any two I can see another and the caps of others beyond, until I'm looking across crests of a wavy sea.

Waves, swells, ripples. Watery imagery gets into lots of descriptions of drumlins; perhaps when seeking metaphors, writers have consciously or unconsciously drawn on the process that made this landscape. During the last ice age glaciers passed this way, a few hundred feet above my campsite. Down here was the uneven bed of a concealed sea. Although pressurised and sluggish under the glaciers, the water did flow, slowly dragging rocks together in drifts across the seabed and pressing them into hills. A drumlin's orientation tells us the direction the ice age flow was travelling when it was shaped, the tapered end pointing the way. If you pick up some loose soil and press it between your two palms, then work it with a circular motion, you'll create a rounded form. You'll have made a model of a border drumlin in a way very like how the real ones were made.

Drumlins define many stretches of the borderland. More, they helped create the borderland in the first place; it is a landform well suited to ambushes, harrying and conspiring. There were always hills to hide behind and high ground to claim. Local knowledge was an enormous advantage, the outsider was hampered, denied a view forward and easily got lost. The drumlin belt was a barrier. It is hard to imagine a centre forming anywhere in the drumlin belt. This landscape tended towards the peripheral, helping distinct cultures to evolve north and south.

A geographer called Estyn Evans wrote many books about Ulster and often considered drumlins. He was fascinated by rural traditions and handmade objects, loving the way the design of spades, baskets or boats changed from county to county, showing the slow currents of influence that moved under folk craft. Evans wished for Ulster to develop a regional consciousness that could jostle along confidently with others in the rest of Ireland and beyond.

Evans described Ireland's drumlin belt as a necklace of beads and also gave us a collective term for them, a swarm, but he was less interested in the metaphors that could be applied to drumlins than in what drumlins could do. He suggested that living among drumlins created certain psychological types. 'One might think of the moulded drumlins as moulding, in turn, the outlook of the farmers who lived among them,' he said in a public lecture in the early 1970s, suggesting that living in small valleys had given some people an outlook concerned mainly with the immediate, whereas life on the uplands, plateaus and naked bogs found further west along the border produced people of far sight, imagination and poetry. There is certainly contrast; I know I find a day down among the hills oppressive, although sheltered, while hiking highlands often feels airy and expansive. It's too bad Evans had to fall for stereotypes and apply this pair of mindsets to Ireland's two main religious groups. He felt the uplands were Catholic, the valleys Protestant. It is hard to know who is worse served by this ethnic labelling. It's not true either, I should mention. Compare two maps of Ireland, one of religious distribution and one of drumlins, and you will see that people of all sorts are found in all sorts of landscapes. We are a little more complicated than Evans could credit. But I think I see what he was trying to get at with drumlins and it's well-intentioned, he wished to show us two primary landforms in Ireland, open and closed, hilltop and valley, and use them as a metaphor for diversity among the people. He believed that embracing this diversity would lead to a 'culturally productive borderland'.

There are troughs, there are crests, the land undulates with these and other rhythms. Evans believed we should try to enjoy our different values and learn to live with pluralism, in a social landscape as varied as the one under our feet.

*

The border travels up a tiny tributary, ascending to higher country, across rising heath to Slieve Beagh. For the first time on the border I camp in a forest, under leafy maples, among ferns, on a bed of clover. I sit in the flap of my tent. When the light fades the darkness is complete. Denied the use of my eyes I strain to hear a distant engine, the flutter of a bat, anything, but the forest's soft furnishing renders the night soundless. There is, however, plenty to smell: flora, moisture, oozing sap. This is the most enclosed campsite I've made but with branches low overhead and the air muggy with smells I feel exposed and self-conscious.

In the morning I find a border-crossing footbridge among younger trees. There is a latched gate across the midpoint, perhaps just there to mark the crossing's internationality. It's hardly a secret, this bridge, but it's not on the Ordnance Survey so I record it, number thirty-nine on my map. It has a nameplate: Millennium Bridge. It seems a comically grand name for these few planks until I realise I'm standing in a Millennium Forest, part of a project in which a tree was planted for every household in the Republic of Ireland. Each of these trees has somebody's name on it.

All day the border creeps higher. Hedgerows give way to wire fences. The grass becomes coarse and yellow. I follow a track with staked saplings growing on both sides. Up ahead a man stops whatever he is doing, puts his foot up on a tree stump and waits for me to approach. Moustache, body warmer, work boots: a solid countryman with a solid countryman's authority. I know the situation before he speaks: this is his land and he wants an explanation for my presence.

'I'm making a map,' I say.

'A map of what?'

'Things I find along the way.'

He prefers to look elsewhere when talking to me, like a warden issuing a fine. He has not forgiven me for being here but he talks about the land. He tells me there's a lake up ahead, the border going through it. His phrasing is more scientific than a farmer's, he offers no judgement on a thing's beauty or value, only stating that it is there. 'I'm a forester,' he says, indicating the saplings. 'I'm planting all this.'

We hear a cuckoo, the distinct call that gives the bird its name, soft but with something mechanical about it; it could be produced by a delicate steam-puffing gadget. 'There he is,' says the forester, pointing. I see the small grey head poking out of the grass.

'Do they nest on the ground?' I ask, before correcting myself. 'Of course not. They don't nest, famously.'

'If you find a cuckoo's nest,' says the forester, 'you should put it on your map.'

At the end of the track I find the promised lake. Grey water a quarter of a mile wide but too high to be seen from any road or public path. Bog meadows run down to the shore, flecked with bright yellow and white dots, thousands of buttercups and daisies. Trees have been planted in rows but are still only one foot tall. Some day the lake will be surrounded by tall trees and thoroughly hidden. Perhaps the forester dreams of this, a secret oasis where he can be alone.

I continue up to higher ground, past scrappy firs and lean-ing hollies. My footfalls squish as the bogland gets boggier. Beyond the last tree I make camp. After a cold dinner I sit in the flap of my tent, lonely and doubtful. I could be at home, throwing another log on the fire, drinking a glass of wine. Instead, I am looking out across cold empty heath. There will still be light for a couple of hours but I can't think of any reason to stay awake. I unfold a printout of a newspaper report that I have carried with me and reread the words of an investigator whose search for a missing body brought him to this area in 2013. 'Imagine your final steps taken up here . . . Your last view. It's a dark, grim place.'

He and his team were searching for the body of an IRA victim called Columba McVeigh. He was aged seventeen when he vanished in 1975. Every newspaper article about his killing uses the same photograph; perhaps it is the only one that exists, something a twenty-first-century seventeen-year-old will find hard to fathom. The photo comes from a performance in amateur dramatics. Dapper, Columba is wearing a bow tie and a white top hat. 'He was a big child,' said a relative in an interview, 'a very bubbly character but gullible and naive, very close to his mammy.' Someone in the IRA accused Columba of spying for the British army; he was taken away, killed and buried near the border in this remote bog. He was not the only one; Columba is part of a group called the Disappeared. Disappearing was not a thing they did, but a thing done to them. They were disappeared. Some bodies have been found in recent years, some have not. I walked right by fields where two victims were finally located in 1999, twenty-one years after they were shot and buried. Even after the area was identified it still took a month-long search to uncover them. I did not know the history of the place when I passed; I saw only ferns and mud. Anonymous tip-offs about the location of Columba McVeigh's body were received in the 1990s also but they were too vague and four searches were abandoned without finding him. Then, in 2012 more precise information made its way to the investigating team.

It is frustrating that everything is unattributed – *made its way* – but there is no other way to describe these histories. The information arrived, the teenager was killed. This facelessness stops us doing something that might soothe: containing the killing in one place, attaching it to one or two names. Instead it spreads, the whole landscape is touched and we are supposed to accept that Columba McVeigh was not killed by people at all, but by a three-letter acronym.

Columba's sister Dympna was aged twenty when Columba was taken. When the fifth search began she was approaching sixty. She wanted his body so she could bury him with the rest of his family; his name was already carved on the family plot's tombstone. She did not want to know any details about his death and any idea of justice was given up long ago as unobtainable. 'We know how he died,' she said in a television interview; 'they are walked to the spot, sometimes they dig the grave, sometimes there is a hole dug for them. They are shot in the back of the head and they fall in. That's execution, I don't need to know any more.'

The search reopened near here. The team used ground-penetrating radar to identify the spots most likely to hold him. A fir plantation was bulldozed and three orange diggers scraped at the black peat, working on blanket-sized steel plates to avoid sinking into mire. Workers in hi-vis gear examined the turned earth but did not find the body. Columba McVeigh has still not been found. He is somewhere in this bog but has been denied a marker, a small upright to say he was real, he existed.

Dympna says that she cannot visit the bogland that holds her brother. It is too sad a place for her. 'I refused to go because I have an image in my head of Columba standing there crying, looking into a hole.'

*

With the remaining light, I decide to follow the border to the top of Slieve Beagh. This boggy plateau is the most remote corner of three counties. Tyrone, Fermanagh and Monaghan all meet in a damp hollow here. Everything dims gradually as the day fades, losing definition. Tufts of grass make tough going, this is more like kicking than walking. Having my progress slowed creates a simmering frustration that soon boils over. Clear thoughts do not formulate, instead I feel a general aggravation, something blunt and stupid that can neither be released nor understood. Everything that made me angry in the last year is remembered and makes me angry again.

I pass depressions holding pools of brown water: Lough Naheery, Lough Eshbrick, Lough Navarad, Lough Sallagh. They are thin on nutrients, supporting little but spiky quill-wort. I navigate by the pools as it is hard to know where the peak is. Slieve Beagh's highest point turns out to be a water-saturated bulge. I feel it sink when I stand on it. In a week it may have drained and squeezed up elsewhere, or been shifted by the wind.

Slieve Beagh got its name from the legendary Bith, one of the first people of Ireland. In a fusion of Christian and indigenous story-telling, we are told that he came to Ireland to get away from the biblical Flood, stepping ashore in Ireland with his daughter, Cessair, her male consorts and fifty maidens. Conscientious monks recorded the names of all the maidens: Tamall, Rodarg, Luam, Baichne, Femar, Foroll, Cipir, Torrian, Rinne, Irrand, Espa, Sine, Samoll; a list that may be of interest to anyone seeking an unusual name for a baby girl. Bith died on Slieve Beagh. His tomb was a great stone-heap that could be seen a hundred years ago but has now vanished, gradually eroded by human hands, the rocks used to build walls. Where were the folk of far sight and vision that Estyn Evans told us about? I am 1,300 feet above sea level, the sky is wide open and the horizons far, but Bith's tomb was destroyed for a haul of stones. I wonder why this ancient landmark was so devalued. Was it insufficiently mythologised, or was there a particularly aggressive stone shortage up here? I picture a farmer standing on his poor land. He finds no poetry in the distant horizon, only adversary. Slieve Beagh is an upturned bowl and clinging to it is a punishing existence. Winds roll over it, ripping at his crops and wearing him down too. He needs a wall to protect his harvest. He scoops one load of stones from Bith's tomb and carts it to his field. That is all he wants, just one load; maybe he did not realise that this would be enough to shatter the spell. Suddenly an ancient tomb is just a heap of rocks. Neighbours who had previously held back now rush in. They pick it apart.

The border sits in a brackish brown ditch. I step over it, into the south, and follow a beaten path. I have never seen evening light like this. Instead of getting darker it is getting greyer, like sheets of tracing paper are being dropped over the scene. A figure takes shape in the grey; he is on my path and running in my direction. I stop as his definition increases. Then I see his white earphones and the flash of fluorescent running shoes. I step off the path to let the jogger by. Ahead, other figures materialise, half a dozen of them all slicing into the ground with spades. The land is divided into family turf plots and they're harvesting their winter fuel. Cars take form, sitting up on banks. I realise that on the southern side of the border, unlike the northern, roads go near to the top of Slieve Beagh. The turf cutters see me approach and they lean on their spades, preparing to give me some time. They know I have walked a long way across rough country to get here. It's fanciful but I feel like an ambassador from the north and, emerging from the haze, I might look like one as well.

I stand among a group of men. Bricks of turf lie about our feet, stacked in little pyramids so the breeze will dry them out. The older men look at me silently. One has cataract eyes that stream tears when the air gusts; he opens his mouth and makes a guttural sound that might be a greeting. Another lifts a flask from the heather and unscrews the top. Hot tea would help now; I say thank you about three times. But I'm out of luck, only a thimbleful dribbles into the cup. 'Fuckit,' he says. A younger man raises his arm and points south across the valley under Slieve Beagh. Each steeple means a village and he names them all for me. Distant tungsten streetlights are coming on, glimmering orange dots, guiding people to their homes and firesides. Between the villages are dark lines, each about as thick as a horse hair: roads. My guide names them too, not by their allotted codes but by their destinations. He tells me lots of things but after a while I realise that everything he is saying adds up to one thing. Behold our civilisation, he is saying, behold the land of the south.

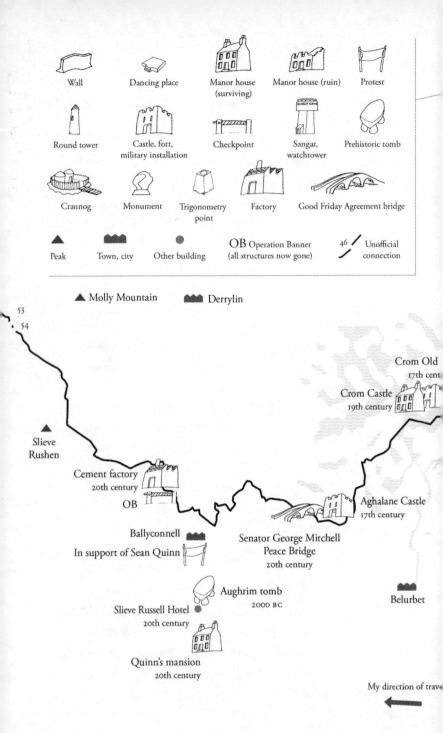

Wall · Dancing place · Manor house (surviving) · Manor house (ruin) · Protest

Round tower · Castle, fort, military installation · Checkpoint · Sangar, watchtower · Prehistoric tomb

Crannog · Monument · Trigonometry point · Factory · Good Friday Agreement bridge

Peak · Town, city · Other building · OB Operation Banner (all structures now gone) · 46 Unofficial connection

▲ Molly Mountain   ▰▰ Derrylin

53
· 54

Crom Old
17th cent

Crom Castle
19th century

▲ Slieve Rushen

Cement factory
20th century

OB

Aghalane Castle
17th century

Ballyconnell

In support of Sean Quinn

Senator George Mitchell
Peace Bridge
20th century

Aughrim tomb
2000 BC

▰▰ Belurbet

Slieve Russell Hotel ●
20th century

Quinn's mansion
20th century

My direction of trave

Cuilcagh

Carnmore
1952

Carrigatuke

OB

Derryvullen
dancing deck

OB

Rosslea

OB

45

Aghafin Lough

Fermanagh

Tirnahinch

OB

Clones

The Borderland
Ballroom

Barry McGuigan's
route to first club

Newtownbutler

Hilton Park
18th century

OB

46

OB

48

47

Saunderson
th century

51

49

50

Drumaveale Lough

Black Pig's Dyke

Monaghan

Cavan

miles   1   2   3

km   1   2   3   4   5

N

A Boy Racer, a Buster, a Boxer

The border runs with barbed-wire fences down off Slieve Beagh. The colours brighten and swallows zigzag by. The border falls in with a hedgerow and I walk in its shade. It is producing berries in abundance. Blackthorns are the bricks and mortar of border hedgerows, and now their dusty-purple fruit is plentiful. These berries are used for sloe gin but they are not suited to immediate needs. For my second breakfast are blackberries, growing from thorny shoots that arc downward as if for my convenience. I throw the berries in my mouth as I go. Try to forget the familiarity of a tangled hedgerow and look at it as if for the first time and an Ulster bramble might suggest as much generosity as a coconut palm or an orange tree.

Other things can be foraged from a border hedgerow. Wild strawberries are tiny and melt on the tongue. I stop to suck the sweetness from a honeysuckle flower, as my mother taught me to do. The leaves of wild garlic can be eaten and then, to cleanse the palate, the leaves of wild mint. I feel the landscape is being kind again, I feel like its guest. Things are looking up. The sun is shining and I've got a ticket for a festival that starts in a couple of days.

The track joins a narrow lane. I hear a car coming and step up against the hedgerow to give it space and preserve my own life. The woman driving the saloon gives me a full palm greeting, backed up with a smile. By 'full palm' I mean she unwraps all four fingers of one hand from the steering wheel, leaving only the thumb hooked around it. This is an enthusiastic greeting compared to the more common 'single finger'. Here just the index finger is raised from the wheel and can mean as little as *I acknowledge your presence*. Other drivers use a dip of the head, or mouth a hello through their windscreen. As the border often travels close to lanes, I often walk along them. I see a lot of drivers and a lot of drivers see me. I've developed observation-based theories about their greetings. Whatever style of greeting a driver uses, I will probably see it again from the next driver who passes. And the next too. This morning it happens as well: a few minutes after the woman in the saloon, a man in a four-wheel drive goes by and also employs the full palm. It seems to me that I am hiking in and out of areas where single tra-ditions hold sway, micro-traditions, only a few townlands wide. A process of unconscious imitation creates these hyperlocal customs. They will be waving to each other too, not just to strangers like me. When the same few dozen people drive back and forth on the same few lanes for about twenty years, an agreed form of greeting is sure to develop. They all wave in the same accent.

The raised index finger is the most common. The gesture is neutral, so the expression on the driver's face tempers its meaning a great deal. The single finger is often delivered with an impassive gaze, the driver unwilling to commit to friendliness. Often they are not even looking at me as the finger goes up. I could be anyone, and the border has long fostered suspicions. In the meantime, they don't want to be hostile either, so they're letting me know that my existence has been registered.

There are 'horn-tooters', rare but can appear anywhere.

They lightly tap the horn, just enough to produce a half beep as they go by, using the car to say hello. Horn-tooters seem never to be part of a local trend. Individuals, jocular, a little overbearing perhaps, they weave in and out of other gesturing traditions. The 'empty handshake' is the rarest of all, I have only seen it four times. Here the driver raises one hand completely from the wheel and holds it towards me, loosely open, shaped as if about to shake hands. So far I have only seen this from older men. Gender has a big role in the culture of driver greetings. The 'salute' entails taking one hand off the steering wheel to make a quick go of the traditional nautical gesture. It is, so far, exclusively male. It is almost entirely men who use the 'sideways head tick'. This greeting is a hard thing to explain. It is not a nod, it is a diagonal dip of the head leading with the chin and is much sharper and quicker than a nod. You could blink and miss it. The sideways head tick projects a similar character to a wink and can be accompanied by a wink but by itself is not as presumptuous. It is by far the most common greeting you'll see from a farmer, nine times out of ten it's what you get from a tractor cab. Rather like a wink, the sideways head tick carries a sense of conspiracy, of mutual understanding, of thin warmth. It says, 'I understand that you walk a hard road, a three-hundred-mile task, pack on your back,' while at the same time saying, 'I too have a hard road, all this silage to pull, arthritis in my knuckles.' A sideways head tick from an old man handling a tractor can somehow acknowledge all your trouble, all his trouble, all the trouble in the world.

This morning I encounter a new wave, one that I will go on to see a few times on the Fermanagh/Monaghan boundary. I see it while walking a lane where I can touch one hedgerow then touch the opposite hedgerow in only three strides. Many lanes in Fermanagh are so narrow and have hedges so tall that they feel like channels or chutes. They are pretty, but worrisome for pedestrians as there are no pavements. I notice that school uniforms in this area have reflective strips sewn into their design. Lanes like these are the reason.

From around a curve up ahead I hear a tiger's purr. It turns into a roar. Sunlight flashes off the bonnet as the car comes into view. The low-slung fender makes it look crouched even as it rips along. It is a hatchback and tangerine orange – a non-standard colour that the young driver must have paid to get done. The car blares along, exhaust rigged to snort in a bassy, too-full way. The side mirrors are only inches from the hedges; the car occupies the lane like a pea occupies a peashooter. I step off the hard surface and wedge myself in among berries. The car's pilot is slouched low in his bucket seat, his nose behind the top of his steering wheel. If he hit a tree he would shoot straight under his seatbelt and get compressed in the foot well. He spots me ahead and makes his greeting, his hand out flat and at a right angle to his outstretched arm, his palm back towards his face and his knuckles almost touching the windscreen. He does not wave it, he holds it static. I might call it 'street'. It is an urban, hip-hop kind of gesture, out of place here among the fields and whiff of silage. It is a youthful greeting, friendly but ultimately very little to do with me. Unlike the equalising and unifying salute or sideways head tick, this greeting is all about the young man making it, him and his unprocessed influences. I can imagine him making the same gesture when passing livestock. The car goes by emitting a loud drone and a sense of heavy gravity. I watch him disappear. That was a boy racer.

[123]

*

Boy racers are chasing the border day and night. The motor-car is their art, something to spend their money on. There isn't much else to spend it on around here. In bungalows every evening boys are poring over car magazines. They are saving for alloy wheels, new trims, a spray job. The border boy racer does not go for the same level of flamboyant modification seen in cities. They may add fenders, spoilers and flame transfers but a link to the normal is maintained – they are still going to their jobs in these vehicles, they are still dropping their grandmothers to the shops. I can imagine one of the grandmothers, disapproving of the excessive horsepower, the show-offy stripes and the fiddly stereo. 'And this visor!' she says every time she squeezes into the bucket seat, reaching up to pick at the vinyl band across the top of the windscreen. 'Sure, you can hardly see out at all!' Her grandson will bring her to the shop and then do three circuits of the village rather than park and wait.

You can see boy racers out after dinner, motoring from one borderland car park to another. They park their hatchbacks in parallel but facing opposite directions, so they can roll down their windows and talk without getting out of their seats. Again, if this was Bristol or Birmingham, their faces would be revealed by the stereo's blue neon lights, or the smartphones glowing in their hands. In Fermanagh/Monaghan the car interiors are black but for the burning tips of cigarettes.

Boy racers feel too big for this landscape. They are certainly too big for these donkey-cart laneways. Their hearts thunder with feelings they can only express with a foot on the accelerator, a rapper's greeting, but ultimately all they are doing is cruising to the chip shop to see who's about. They will race back and forth into their twenties and eventually trade the car in for something more sensible. I don't mean to suggest they'll decline into bitterness, weighted down by the sense of having missed out. Not at all. They understand that life is about choosing a small place somewhere or another, about keeping your expectations in check. Their grandmothers taught them that.

The boy shooting by me in the tangerine car is on a borderland of his own. He has recently done his last day in school, sat his last exam. He has only recently gotten a driver's licence and just started earning money. There are girls around who appreciate him, perhaps one special girl. It's an intoxicating time, crossing the line to manhood. There are new freedoms but he is not stupid, he knows there are pressures too, far greater than any found in a school day. Across the border stretches a wide plain, a thousand possible routes, a thousand ways to mess up. He will park here a while, engine ticking over, on the line.

*

A pack of boy racers have occupied the car park in the centre of Clones. The town's name is not pronounced as the plural of clone, rather as *cloh-ness*. I arrive just as the boy racers receive some bit of news on their mobiles. They throw down their cigarettes and start their engines. The cars snort then streak out of town, leaving me standing in exhaust fumes and drizzle. They seem to have sucked the town's colour away with them. Clones is mainly dense terraces of grey houses, slate roofs covered in moss. There is a net curtain across every window and plaster Virgin Marys in a lot of them too. There is no one left on the street but me and some boys in school uniform. They are cupping their hands around their mouths and bellowing to each other up and down the width of the town. One has a fully-grown moustache.

In a Clones graveyard is the border's best surviving example of a monastic round tower, dating back to the tenth century. I go to look at it. The cap roof is gone but it is otherwise complete, each block black with wet today. Crows are picking around the base. The door slot is above the ground but any Viking could have got in there with a boost from one of his mates.

Clones is in County Monaghan, in the south, but was always closely linked to County Fermanagh. In the 1830s, the Ordnance Survey's memoirists visited Clones during their Fermanagh survey and included it with their Fermanagh reports. Locals will tell you that the town's northern orientation is because of the hills; drumlins crowd it from the south and east, whereas to the border and across is gentle pasture. A Northern Ireland exit from the EU would shake the economy here, just as partitioning Ireland in the first place hit Clones hard. The town went from being an axis point to a cul de sac. Four roads out of Clones immediately hit the border.

The canal was the first thing to go after partition. From the mid-nineteenth century the Ulster Canal had connected north and south but it was finally drained in the 1930s. The borderline follows the canal's route for a while and so, leaving Clones, I walk on it for a mile, a wide grassy track. The light is fading but such an easy route encourages me to walk on through dusk. I pass a warehouse of solid stone blocks. Its upper-storey doors are still in place and there is a winch and crane waiting for the next barge. Then the railway closed in 1950. This was a profound shock for the people of Clones, upsetting their sense of their place in the world. There was no hope that trains might one day return, the rails were lifted and sold for scrap. The land they ran on was sold as well.

Clones is at the beginning of the border's twistiest stretch, where it folds back on itself multiple times, meaning even a short journey can cross into Northern Ireland, out again, in again and out again. It also means I have walked an hour and am still near Clones. I can see its lights from my campsite. I am on a peninsula of the south inside the north, a landlocked headland called the Drummully Polyp, the Wee Republic, the Salient or Coleman's Island. It has a lot of names. Its neck is only about four hundred feet wide but from there the south balloons out again to an area of five or six square miles.

Dealing with this bewildering border brought about, in the 1950s, the 'concession road'. Concession roads crossed the border but could only be used if your ultimate destination was back in your own country. These roads did not have checkpoints or customs huts but drivers were obliged to keep their wheels turning until back in their own jurisdiction. If you had friends along the way, you could only wave as you went by. The concession of the concession road was not enough to save the Clones economy, and traffic fell to a trickle as trade went elsewhere. Emigration was a common Irish story but Clones suffered large-scale abandonment. Boarded-up shops, vacant houses, the damp rising.

After the canal and the railway, the roads. During the Troubles people were nostalgic for the eccentric concession roads, now these same routes were 'unapproved'. The British army spiked them, blew craters in them or blocked them with oil drums full of concrete. Wanting to get about their locality, people would group together and fill in the holes again. When the army collapsed a bridge, another means of crossing would be crowbarred into place by the locals, rough fords of rubble and scrap metal. A challenge for the ford-builders was making sure they didn't dam the river in the process. Concrete pipes were too expensive, so the builders dropped wrecked cars into the water and built across them. The cars were set upside down with their windows open so the river could flow through.

A couple of days further along the border, I spot a JCB digger parked just inside the south. It is too clean, an impossibly bright yellow. Approaching, I see that it is on a raised plinth and there's a fence around it. The digger has been retired from service and transformed into a monument, its mechanical arm permanently outstretched and bucket resting on gravel. The plaque says it is a tribute to the Borderbuster.

Borderbusters were the diggers used to reopen border routes, filling in cratered roads and shoving aside concrete bollards. The wording on the plaque makes me suspect this particular JCB did not see action, it represents the machines that actually worked around Clones. The digger's plinth is made from steel cubes that I recognise. They are the black and yellow containers that, filled with concrete, were used by the army to block roads. If this monument is making a claim on victory, then the plinth is actually the most effective part, more effective than the stand-in digger. The people who created the monument have been able to appropriate their opponents' tools, using them to honour themselves and their own history.

Crossings near Clones were opened and closed uncount-able times, one fought over so fiercely that it was nicknamed the Khyber Pass. It sounds like a game but relations between the local population and the British army were toxic. Soldiers deployed in this area were often accused of harassment and assault. In 1972 two men were killed on a farm north of the border, knifed to death with such ferocity that the murder weapon was at first taken to be a pitchfork. It was ten years before two soldiers were convicted of the double killing.

Bursts of violence; vacancy; poverty; border defenders and borderbusters, growling at each other across the line; this was the atmosphere that a boy called Barry McGuigan grew up in. He and his friends would pass the afternoons exploring abandoned houses around Clones. In a decaying front room he found a boxing glove. He slipped it on and it felt right, appropriate, the logical extension of his arm. He was able to give his pals a solid thumping, even the bigger ones. He went home and told his parents that he wanted to join a boxing club.

The boxing club was in the south but the most direct route for McGuigan to travel cut straight along the zigzagging frontier. He got there and back on his Triumph bicycle, crossing the border eight times in an evening. There is something affecting about his descriptions of these journeys, a tough nut of a boy ignoring any potential danger, all for a couple of hours at the punching bag. If the way was blocked he would hoist the bicycle over his shoulder and carry it. When he got to the club, he'd get straight into a workout, 'not that I knew what a workout was at that time; I'd just belt away at the bag until I was knackered.' Apart from his left hook, something else was getting exercised on those evenings; I think the cycle there and back was shaping McGuigan's identity as a border crosser. Featherweight McGuigan started winning fights. He took the Mid-Ulster title at fourteen and won the Golden Shamrock, an Ireland-wide contest, at fifteen. At sixteen he became the youngest ever Ulster Senior Champion. The location of Clones enabled McGuigan to operate under a certain borderland blur. It is in an Ulster county but not a Northern Irish one, a southern town that looked north. To some, this was a confused identity and yet another reason to abandon it, but McGuigan carried on as if its border position was an advantage. Double the country, double the opportunity. McGuigan fought for Northern Ireland in the 1978 Commonwealth Games and for Ireland in the 1980 Olympics. He was an example of a third identity forming between Ireland's north and south. A new citizenship, there for those willing to take it: the borderlander.

In the ring, McGuigan did not accept any national branding. No harps or bulldogs, and he avoided national flags. I imagine he was too busy training to spend much time on politics, or maybe he simply did not want to be associated with a single nation because he was a likeable man who liked being liked and liked having friends everywhere. He was certainly up for anything – boxing, singing, having a go at rally driving – all with a springy and relentless positivity. He never stopped. When it was advantageous to his boxing career McGuigan took British citizenship, although some around Clones considered this treachery. For McGuigan, it meant he could compete for the British featherweight championship, a stepping stone to the European title, which would give him a shot at the ultimate prize, the world title.

In 1985 he got that chance. The fight took place in London and was a contest that everybody in Ireland watched. Neighbours crowded around televisions. Every pub was packed. People who had never watched a boxing match in their life and never would again made sure to see this one. The roads cleared and stayed clear, not a single tractor engine was heard along the border. McGuigan's father, a professional singer, stood in the ring and sang 'Danny Boy' before the opening bell. The fight ran to the full fifteen rounds, advantage rocking back and forth between McGuigan and his opponent, Panama's Eusebio Pedroza. It was going to be decided on points. Towards the end McGuigan lost all sense of time, he did not know what round it was until his trainer leaned over and said, 'Go out and give it everything this round. You've got to have a big last round.' At the final bell McGuigan threw his arms around Pedroza. In a low voice Pedroza said, 'You'll be a good champion.' McGuigan was hustled away by his crew and never saw Pedroza again. He had done it, he was World Champion.

Of all the reactions to McGuigan's victory, there is one

small example I like best. The local dairy products plant, Monaghan Milk, changed its name to Champion Milk. It has stayed that way ever since, you see its branded tankers going from farm to farm.

Barry McGuigan was born before the term was thought up, but I can see the boy racer in him. His first car was a Volkswagen Golf with go-faster stripes. As reward for winning the world championship, McGuigan bought himself a new car. It was waiting for him in the car park when he flew back into Belfast, a red Lotus Excel, with cream seats and one of the first in-car CD players. The registration plate read: BOX 1T.

Belfast's mayor was there with a limousine to bring McGuigan to a public event, but McGuigan wanted to try his Lotus straight away so he followed the limo into the city centre instead. Afterwards, he drove it to Clones where thousands more people awaited him. McGuigan wanted to see his parents before giving himself over to the throng, so a few miles from the town he turned the Lotus right down a lane, his police guard of honour trailing after him. I think I can imagine it, a streak of Italian-crafted racing car somehow at home and confident on the tight bends and narrow routes of the border's backways.

*

I go to the Flatlake Festival. It is in the grounds of a Big House called Hilton Park. Setting up my tent in a field with hundreds of other people is strange. I find myself pitching in the most distant corner, up against a hedgerow. The campsite is the crown of a wide drumlin. The grass is dry and soft, it makes you want to lie in it. I do lie in it, listening to the banter of other campers. One woman is exclaiming with pleasure as her tent pegs slide smoothly into the ground. 'What was Kavanagh going on about, *stony grey soil of Monaghan?* This soil is great!' Flatlake, by the way, is a literary festival.

The days and nights are a jolly cocktail of performance, readings and music. There's a karaoke tent and a knitting circle. Food is being served out of a London Routemaster bus. Musicians play on pallet stages. I become a fan of Jinx Lennon, 'Stop Giving Out about Nigerians'. In a tent on Sunday morning there is a combined Catholic and Protestant service, giving all but five or six festivalgoers the opportunity to attend neither more efficiently. Displayed in a fish tank in its own enclosure is the biggest slug I have ever seen in my life. There are pop-up sculptures made of books. In one tent ten-minute lectures run all day – Mars, mathematics, the Annals of Ulster. There are many children, chasing each other between caravans and far into the night. Alexei Sayle is reading from his books on the trailer of a truck. A woman wails from the audience, 'I've never in my life understood any joke.' It is not a heckle, it is a genuine cry for help. Sayle tells a joke. She gets it. Everyone cheers.

There are lots of other writers here. Look, there's Anne Enright, releasing a Chinese lantern into the sky, as excited as a schoolgirl. There's Patrick McCabe playing records in a caravan, a large man in a bright shirt, looking like a gangster on a budget holiday. Long after dark I am returning to my tent when I am drawn towards a powerful voice belting out soul classics. It's a big band; drums, bass, a couple of guitars, backing singers and wind section, filling a trailer stage from end to end. The lead singer is giving lungfuls. It might be 'Mustang Sally', I can't remember now. What I'll never forget is realising who the singer is. The small, sprightly man in a white shirt, one large hand wrapped around the microphone. It takes me a few seconds to believe my eyes. It's Barry McGuigan. He never stops.

Bridges, Dead Ends

Wattle Bridge has three stone arches. Its name refers to an earlier wickerwork version, daubed with mud to help pre- serve the material's springiness. I would like to have seen that bridge, the organic extension of the trees and rushes along both banks. A woven bridge, without a nail or screw, knotted supports, plaited horizontals. I imagine it creaking, tensing in the wind, rising when the river did.

Close by I find where the Clones canal joined the Erne river system. All that is left is a short inlet – the length of two barge poles. There has been much discussion about reflooding this canal, to let it bring boats across the border and into a network that extends over much of the island. Until then, this is just a swampy dead end, a gathering place for lost footballs. Primordial goo covers the water.

The borderline slides into the Erne. Moving against the flow, it disappears between green islands. Here ground and water mingle until it is hard to say which is in charge. Is this land flooded by a wide river, or a wide river interrupted by land? Here is what happens when you take a chunk of the drumlin belt and pour lots of water through it. The drum- lins are now islands. Some are round but others are formed by two or three drumlins and look like the half shells of monkey nuts. The border twists between them, sticking with the water. It is the thread that will lead Paddy and me through the maze.

I find Paddy parked up on a roadside. He steps away from his station wagon and gives me a big wave, his whole upper body rising into it. 'Howya!' We lift the canoe from his car's roof rack and lower it onto the water and there is a satisfying sense of immediate buoyancy, the surface hardly rippling against the canoe's underside. I ruin the effect when I clamber aboard. Paddy hands me a paddle and I love the change from legwork to armwork. Up ahead all we can see is land; we have to trust the Ordnance Survey map and move towards the impasse, a passage will open as we get closer. When I raise my paddle, water droplets run from the tip, flashing like crystals in the sunlight. The Erne itself is dark though, leaden and yellow with earthy particles, the flat of the paddle indistinct only inches under the surface. The air is warm and drifting while the water has density, smacking against the paddle and the peeling bow. Up ahead I see a row of flapping white shapes along the shore. I take them to be turf sacks caught on a fence but, paddling closer, it turns out they are six swans drifting on the current, taking it in turns to shake out their wings.

Partition and the Troubles preserved this area, it would surely be peppered with hotels and holiday homes were it not for the border winding through. Decades of pervasive threat have protected it better than UNESCO could have. The only house we see is a mobile home set on bricks, surrounded by trees, at the tip of a crooked finger of land. A tin chimney means a stove and hints at quiet evenings with the smell of wood smoke. I am suddenly attracted to the idea of dropping out, nestling away in a cabin here between woods and water. Everywhere I look pools, rivers, forests and laneways compose themselves into soothing views.

We paddle a stretch of water called the Bloody Pass. It is

only a few dozen feet across at its narrowest point. Reeds stand swaying over our heads. The Ordnance Survey shows it is open but fenceposts come into view, irregular jagged things with rusted barbed wire, going right across the waterway. Closer, we see that they are planted in a causeway. Truckloads of stone and concrete have been laid, fording the border. Paddy and I have to carry the canoe over the crossing. From there the Bloody Pass widens, the border slides up the middle. The pass is silent but for the slosh of our paddles. Forests – maple, alder, beech – stand on each bank. Sometimes – a strange sight among trees – we see cows watching us go by.

The Bloody Pass got its name by swallowing up about five hundred men in 1689, during the Williamite War, a conflict arising when the English throne was taken from the Catholic King James by the Protestant King William. In England this was a reasonably swift and bloodless changeover; it was in Ireland that the rending was felt. James's reign had promised some freedom of religion and losing him was traumatic for Ireland's Catholics. A force of his supporters were bombarding a castle nearby when an army of Williamites arrived and overwhelmed them, shouting, 'No Popery!' as they drove them back, stabbing and shooting. This war would load Ireland with some resilient invective, phrases that would be repeated for centuries to come – 'No Popery', 'No Surrender' – terms that disallow compromise or even discussion. The Jacobites were forced to the shore where they were shot, hacked to death or drowned. There was no ford then, although one description claims the slaughter itself created one, the weight of the dead filling the watery pass. Only one Jacobite soldier made it across, clambering over the bodies of his comrades perhaps, or a good swimmer, and nimble enough to shed his equipment before leaping in. He escaped the future north and came ashore in the future south.

*

'You're wasting your time . . . we've been killing each other for centuries, and we're going to go on killing each other forever.'

This was what the United States Senator George Mitchell was told again and again in Northern Ireland during the 1990s. He heard it from strangers on the street, in restaurants, in the arrivals hall of Belfast airport. He believed the statements were the self-protective reflexes of a people who had been disappointed many times and that, in fact, behind them lay hope. Mitchell had to believe this; he was the independent chairman of the Northern Ireland peace talks. In interviews he was measured, professorial, distant yet generous. He wore sensible glasses.

The talks went on for two years, and much of the time were not directly about peace at all. They were talks about talks, about ground rules, about who should be at the table and who should not. Political violence in Northern Ireland was ultimately about the border, to keep it or not, so you were either one side or the other and it was difficult to find space for compromise. As Mitchell entered the first cross-party meeting, a Unionist leader got to his feet and said, 'No. No. No. No. No. No,' repeating it over and over again until Mitchell was in his seat. Then the no-sayer and several others walked out. Mitchell later wrote, 'I had the fleeting urge to get up and go home and leave these contentious people to their feud.'

Mitchell makes a strong and accurate choice of word. *Feud* describes the nature of the politics while also capturing the slow strangulation of hope. Choosing the right word was one of Mitchell's skills. When the talks finally began, he and his team opened up new possibilities daily with deft linguistic arrangements, words picked and put together in ways that led to solutions. The peace process was built on this skill. 'Decommissioning' was a clever term, free from associations 'disarming' would have brought. Disarming might be forced on you, whereas decommissioning is something you'd have to decide for yourself. It was a word that allowed the paramilitaries to maintain face, which was important to them, but they were still unwilling to decommission completely before the talks. Hence 'parallel decommissioning'. This allowed them to gradually disarm alongside the talks process. The new language emerging used many pairings like this, two-word phrases where each word modified the other. The overarching title, 'peace process', itself follows this model. Taking two things and making them one: language as bridge. 'Weighted majority', 'sufficient consensus', 'north–south bodies', 'power-sharing'. Mitchell and his team brought the delegates a long way from just shouting 'No'.

Paddy and I discuss George Mitchell as we paddle from the Bloody Pass onto a meandering river. Paddy remembers those days well; it was difficult to be apathetic, everyone read the newspapers. There was a sense of last chance, of all or nothing.

'The vocabulary of the peace process got to everybody,' he says. 'You'd hear words like "decommissioning" used in everyday conversation.'

'Can you give me an example?' I ask.

He thinks for a few seconds before saying, 'Is there a toilet around here? I've got something I need to decommission.'

The new language could also be called duplicitous. 'Decommissioning' might just be admin-speak for surrendering. 'Power-sharing' was compromise with terrorists. There was an overly clean, corporate tone that was easy to undermine. I wonder if the tone came directly from Mitchell himself; the other negotiators were politicians whereas Mitchell was also a man of commerce, director of several companies. The name of Northern Ireland's new leadership structure, created in the talks, is 'the Executive'. And it's true, 'power-sharing' was a carefully spun way to avoid saying 'compromise'. 'Sufficient consensus' meant leaving people out, including victims. It is disconcerting to realise that the peace process was held aloft on a spindly framework of linguistic construction, pinned together with hyphens. Yet it did hold. Tongues were held, mainly. The ceasefires held, mainly. The talks toured to London and Dublin as reinventing Northern Ireland meant the British and Irish governments would have to rewrite their relationships with it and each other. One contention was the Republic of Ireland's historic claim on Northern Ireland, an aspiration to a borderless island in the Republic's constitution: 'The national territory consists of the whole island of Ireland, its islands and the territorial seas.'

Mitchell was eager to move the talks into endgame, leaving less time for sporadic violence on the streets to intensify and cause the negotiations to fail. In March 1998 he set a deadline and it was close, the eve of Good Friday, just a couple of weeks away. Mitchell's skill with words was now important again, but in a different way. On the first day of the negotiations he told all the delegates that every word of any agreement would be theirs. He and his team then set about drafting an agreement using only words spoken by delegates. Of course, Mitchell made judgements all along the way, leaving things out, mixing things up, splicing ideas. Millions of words had been spoken and written by the delegates; the final agreement was constructed from that lump of raw material, building sentences, and from them paragraphs, and from them feasible aspirations. Mitchell was the editor of the peace process. 'I made certain that every single word in it had either been spoken or written by one of them,' he says. 'And when I distributed it to them, I put in the cover sheet: Remember what I said two years ago, it would be your agreement? Here's your agreement. Everything in it is yours.' And it was. By then the politicians had gained a whole new vocabulary.

The Thursday deadline was missed by a few hours and the document gained a resonant title, the Good Friday Agreement. It was not the end of political violence in Northern Ireland but it was the beginning of peace. The accord led to the destruction of weapons stockpiles, the reform of the police, increased cross-border co-operation and the recognition of both Irish and British identities in Northern Irish institutions. The Irish Republic's constitution was amended to define Ireland in terms of people rather than territory, offering aspirations of harmony and diversity. There was a provision in the agreement for a vote on Irish unity, a border poll, so when enough people in Northern Ireland want a referendum on that big question the mechanism is there to allow it. Hours after the 2016 Brexit referendum result nationalist politicians were calling for this poll to be run as soon as possible. There are probably more people in Northern Ireland who would now vote for Irish unity than would have previously, but not enough for the poll to be run, at least not yet. In the meantime the Good Friday Agreement is transforming the border. New bridges have been appearing ever since. I saw three on the Blackwater so fresh they aren't yet on maps, and there's a new bridge on this river too.

Paddy and I see it up ahead, a perfectly dull concrete span with steel railings. Rough stone cladding has been cemented on, nostalgic for the traditional trades that the steel and concrete replaced. The bridge that used to be here was destroyed in the Troubles and the crossing broken for twenty-five years. This new bridge was built shortly after the Good Friday Agreement and is called the Senator George Mitchell Peace Bridge.

Paddy and I keep moving, dusk is on us and we need to find a camping spot. As we approach the bridge, a white

cruiser appears around the next bend. Yellow fenders hang symmetrically from each side. The cruiser is just ticking along, creating little wake. Our dipping paddles probably disturb the fish more than this boat's tidy prop. Two men by the wheel look at us through their windscreen as they slip by. The pilot is wearing mirror shades and drinking from a can of Coca-Cola. His friend has his jumper draped over his back, the arms tied loosely over his chest, like something from a Marks and Spencer advertisement. Paddy and I, on the other hand, look as if we might smell. We're in patched-up trousers and need haircuts. We all gaze at each other. Their expressions are flat, they don't wave but neither do we. I think we all feel the same incomprehension and for a moment are united by it.

A Tomb, a House, a Hotel

Slieve Rushen is either a small mountain or a big hill, with a thin coating of peat, heather and little else. There are no animal tracks, birds pass over it without landing. The border goes over it too but does not bother visiting the peak. Slieve Rushen was formed under a tropical sea full of life. Layer after layer of animal shell, bone and coral was compressed into a mass of carboniferous limestone. Inch by inch the mass shifted north across the planet towards this destiny. Carpets of sediment fell on it, solidifying into shale and sandstone, giving Slieve Rushen a hard cap that would protect it from the erosion eating away much else around here. The sea level around Rushen rose and fell. Ice ages went by, glaciers grinding down the land while letting Slieve Rushen stand in relief. Melting ice dropped valley loads of sand and gravel around its base. I imagine a pause then, the way diagrams charting geological phases seem to invite us to, implying everything stopped for a while on the clean line between the Pleistocene and the Holocene. Picture a fresh, stony land. Trees fill the valleys and delicate flowers poke from cliffs. It is silent but for pebbles clattering together as they are pulled along riverbeds. It stays like this for a few thousand years.

Humans showed up. This was no land of plenty but there were many crystal-clear lakes and rivers with thrashing, thick-bodied fish. These first Irelanders left almost nothing behind, just a few flakes of stone worked into points. The next wave made bigger statements. They saw the possibilities of Slieve Rushen's limestone. This rock is highly soluble and often, after millennia of rainfall, fractures into slabs. The people stood some of these chunks on their ends to create a tomb on Slieve Rushen's side. It looks like a corridor, with a chamber at one end and a slab across the top. It is about four feet tall and ten paces long. Pottery and human bones were interred beneath it. Later it was called the Aughrim tomb, named after the townland that developed beside it. As a substantial landmark, the tomb was used to mark the edge of a district and later the Cavan–Fermanagh county boundary. Nineteenth-century farmers could draw little wealth from this land. The soil was heavy clay, prone to flooding. It was an area of small fields and high emigration, doomed to complete stagnation when the border was laid through it. Aughrim tomb had come to mark the international frontier.

In 1960, one mile north of the border, a boy jacked in school and began working with his father on the family farm. The boy was no better suited to farming than studying, but when he was only twenty-one his father died, leaving him to work the damp slopes alone. His name was Sean Quinn. Under his land were tons of pebbles, dropped by the last glacier to exit the valley. Quinn's attention would make these pebbles into something else: gravel; aggregate, a construction material. The flow of meltwater had even sorted the gravel by size. He dug it out and sold it to builders, first in wheelbarrow loads, then in lorry loads. Confident, he bought a brand new Bedford truck, then several more. Soon he was operating a substantial quarry.

In time Sean Quinn's story would attract the attention of

writers – I can't go through this area without joining the tradition. Travel writer Dervla Murphy was one of the first to notice the Quinn effect, although she did not take note of his name. She was at the customs hut here in 1978 talking with a policeman when three lorries came thundering past, laden with gravel for construction sites in the south. 'Dozens come across every day,' said the border guard. 'At this rate we'll soon have one of the Six Counties back.'

Colm Tóibín came this way about ten years later and interviewed Sean Quinn. By then Quinn was a millionaire and producing all sorts of building materials, bricks, flooring, roofing. 'Strength Through Diversity' was his company's motto. He revealed to Tóibín that he was beginning to trade in stocks and shares. Every day one of his employees brought him the *Financial Times* from the nearest big town and Quinn would study it, buying stocks in gold and oil over the phone to his broker in London. He also told Tóibín about the cement factory he was planning to build. Quinn was well positioned to produce cement because he had an abundance of limestone close by: Slieve Rushen. Later he would begin digging sand out of Slieve Rushen too, using his next factory to make a billion glass bottles a year.

Rich business people often move abroad for tax reasons or shift operations in pursuit of cheaper labour. Quinn did neither; he still lived on the border and based most of his businesses here, vitalising a place that had been deprived for decades. Quinn industries created hundreds of jobs. Without him, it would have been just another patch of peripheral Ireland, empty houses and old people with American grandchildren they saw once a year. Instead, there was life and activity, and for this he gained fierce local loyalty. The entire Quinn business group was his, no shareholders to report to. If he wanted to expand into something, invest somewhere, buy anything, he just did it. Although he got his children and other relatives involved, everyone knew that Sean Quinn was the business, the business was Sean Quinn. Centring an empire on one person can lead to problems. Sometimes, as one insider put it, things would go 'a bit Quinny'. Unminuted meetings and verbal arrangements led to uncertainties, but the staff could only fall in behind their leader. There was something of the chieftain about him, he was known as the Mighty Quinn. Up close Sean Quinn was hard to distinguish from any of his generation of country businessmen – he loved Gaelic Football and a round of golf, he settled deals with a spit handshake.

In 1991 author Carlo Gébler travelled in a Quinn truck. From his conversation with the driver, I get the sense that taking a job with Quinn was like joining a family, or an army perhaps. They worked in a steady and focused way. Drivers were not paid by the hour but by how many loads they transported. The driver and Gébler approached the border. At that time the crossing was known as Bomb Alley and the army checkpoint was fortified. Gébler's lorry was let through with a wave. The drivers were sure to maintain a cordial relationship with the soldiers; they crossed the border many times a day and delays would cost them. Gébler's driver was hauling a load of stone from Quinn's quarry to the site of a hotel Quinn was building south of the border. The hotel was called the Slieve Russell, the anglicised Slieve Rushen.

The landscape had made Sean Quinn, giving him the gravel that was his first break, then the limestone, then the sand. Now he was remaking the landscape. By 2007 vast sheds both sides of the border housed Quinn Glass, Quinn

Radiators, Quinn Packaging, Quinn Plastics, Quinn Insurance, twenty separate facilities. Acres of borderland had been polished up into a golf course. Wind turbines stood across the cap of Slieve Rushen, the turning blades visible from five counties. Above the fields power lines crackled with Quinn Energy. His factory pumped out Quinn Cement.

*

For at least four nights I've been seeing the blinking red light at the top of Quinn's cement factory chimney. It is right beside the border, so was my inevitable destination, all my journeying has seemed dedicated to reaching it. Every night I've checked the beacon to see it get closer. I was beginning to feel I had been heading to Quinn's cement factory all my life. It is up ahead, up ahead, up ahead until suddenly I am in its orbit. I meet a woman at the bottom of her driveway, deadheading flowers. 'It's still keeping everybody

in work,' she says, referring to the factory, 'it's still keeping the trees covered in dust.'

The factory overlooks the north–south road. The Troubles-era fortifications are gone, Bomb Alley is gone, now this dust-spouting giant dominates. It is more raw machine than building – all conveyor belts, chutes, exposed vents and pipes. Around it are tall silos and a huge round warehouse with a domed top, like a grey drumlin.

On the border is a petrol station with a shop. I go in and walk about the aisles. A customer has settled against the counter, he and the owner having a quiet conversation, leaving long gaps between statements in which they discover they agree about things. My hand hovers over the apples but settles on a chocolate bar. I also buy a newspaper. As I step back out one of Quinn's fleet, a dumper truck displaying his Q logo, goes across the border. Roadside sycamores swish about in its wake. Quinn's trucks are a distinct green, a green that I can imagine on an Amazonian frog but not found in nature around here. By now, though, Quinn's branding is so ubiquitous on the border that you could call it a part of the environment. The trucks are in movement, but in such numbers that they create the impression of a stable feature, going somewhere but always there. Five minutes later another truck goes by.

The border is marked by a lane up Slieve Rushen. The factory is always audible and the tallest stacks always visible over my left shoulder. The lane turns and so to stay with the border I push my way through ferns. I find a ruined cottage, a single-room cabin built of irregular stones, perhaps one hundred years old. Such ruins are common in Ireland but strange now within earshot of the cement factory. Pushing on I begin to hear something else, a regular *beep-beep* from somewhere ahead. It is the alert produced by a truck when reversing but where is it coming from? I shove through gorse and suddenly a great hole in the world opens up beneath me. I throw myself back a few steps, then approach the edge again, more carefully. It's Quinn's quarry, bigger than a football stadium. The bottom is flat from the weight of daily traffic. Quinn's trucks are rolling around like toys down there, the same acid-drop green that I saw on the road. This is where they were coming from, this is what they are doing, hollowing out Slieve Rushen. The sheer walls are lined horizontally with layers of strata and vertically with long white scrape marks, boreholes and mineral stains.

The immensity of the void stays with me as I draw away. I had taken Slieve Rushen as another regular round hill but I was wrong, the quarry has profoundly altered its contours. The future Ordnance Survey might call the hole Quinn Valley.

*

I walk to another of Sean Quinn's landmarks. It is not as profound as the quarry but much more public. Quinn's mansion was built in 2004 – he was a billionaire by then. It stands just a few miles from where he grew up, on a junction as if to maximise exposure. Looking at the house makes you think of first lessons in geometry. There are lots of forty-five-degree angles and triangles. It is four storeys tall and about ten times bigger than any other house in the area. I'm told there's a cinema inside, a golf simulator and a swimming pool in the basement. Out front is a long curving drive, guaranteed to give you that sweeping feeling as you pull in. Rows of immature trees stand either side. I see no cars, although there could be one in the garage. In fact, there could be nine cars in the garage. It's that kind of garage. Modern, brash, loud, the house reminds me of the mansions in 1980s American soap operas. I think there might be a real connection between those houses and this one. Quinn had no peer group, nothing nearby to aspire to when designing his house. To find a local parallel to his own wealth and all-encompassing presence, he would have needed to look back in time. He might have considered the model of a nineteenth-century landlord. Not since then had a single person shaped an environment and community the way Quinn had with this stretch of the border. It would have been fitting: a grand Victorian pile with stables, plaster urns and a fountain, set back from the road, perhaps behind a wall. But no, a house like that would have sent the wrong message to the neighbourhood. His was a modern wealth, levered from the stony ground with canniness. Quinn had no desire to pretend he was old money. It was better to think of the United States, the unashamed attitude to wealth, where a rich man did not always have some dubious smog about him. I suspect there is a generation of rural men and women in Ireland who got their ideas of how modern wealth should look by watching *Dallas* and *Dynasty*.

When this house was built Sean Quinn was investing heavily in shares but 'Strength Through Diversity' had been forgotten; he was fixated on one particular business, the Anglo Irish Bank. It absorbed much of his time and money, a fixation some describe as blindly illogical, or even pathological, like the actions of a gambling addict. Things were very Quinny. He had bought so many shares in the bank that he now owned a quarter of it. The bank was slow to discover how much was held in one pair of hands; Quinn bought shares through an arrangement that concealed his identity. The bank's fate and Quinn's fate were now linked, both of them riding the crest of a property boom. And that boom was ending. The world banking crisis, beginning in the United States in 2008, soon swept across the Atlantic, sinking Iceland, Portugal and the Republic of Ireland. When the housing market collapsed, Anglo Irish Bank's share price dropped sharply. The bank loaned Quinn money to cover his investment debts, debts he'd built up investing in them. Quinn and the bank propped each other up for a while, but the pressures were too great. They both fell into a tangled mess.

All these border businesses still bear the Quinn name but none of them actually belongs to Sean Quinn any more. Not the cement factory, nor the quarry, nor the hotel. Three more Quinn trucks pass while I am outside the mansion but they are now directed by a boardroom of professional executives, parachuted in to run all the businesses. When Anglo Irish Bank collapsed it was nationalised and its debts became the taxpayers'. Quinn owed the state 2.8 billion euro. His empire was taken away from him and carved up.

'How can I pay it back?' said Sean Quinn in an interview. 'They've taken my businesses off me.' It was startling to see him on television; he rarely spoke publicly before his bankruptcy. I saw a plain countryman, leaning forward in his chair, defensive in an offensive kind of way. Using no contemporary management-speak at all, he had preserved his original self perfectly despite the money. He could have been any rural businessman, he might have owned an undertaker's and a corner shop. He delivered an impenetrable set of evasions and half answers. I could detect no hard centre to what he was saying. Colloquialisms added another layer of obscurity; he talked constantly in terms of pennies. 'They never loaned a penny.' 'We don't owe them a penny.' 'Our children never borrowed a penny.' 'We never saw a penny.' I had to remind myself that Quinn was talking about billions of euros.

Assets vanished as the state came to collect its 2.8 billion. A court found that money was being slipped abroad. Properties changed hands in a flurry, keeping just ahead of court injunctions. Secret new companies were formed off shore, assets signed over to associates. It was claimed that 455 million euros' worth of assets had been spirited away, a judge calling the actions 'blatant, dishonest and deceitful'. So, in the end, a dubious smog gathered around Quinn very quickly. The court found both Quinn and his son guilty of contempt and sent them to prison. Quinn's nephew, who was also found guilty, escaped across the border to avoid serving jail time.

There is confusion on this stretch of the border now. The king has fallen, there is no successor. After his release, and mainly to make peace, Sean Quinn was brought in as a consultant by the new owners of his former businesses. That arrangement quickly turned sour. Now it seems that Quinn is alone and resentful. Nothing moves around the mansion, curtains drawn, every window reflecting the grey sky. It is still Quinn's, protected from repossession as the law allows bankrupts to keep their primary home. After prison he came straight home and could well be in there right now. I imagine him at the back, in the kitchen, at the table, his big farmer's hand around a mug of Nescafé Gold, looking out across the lake and the golf course that he used to own.

*

The Slieve Russell hotel is still open for business. A red carpet has been rolled out, not for me. I hang back on the lawn, take a photo of the facade. The design of the mansion came from elsewhere, but the hotel got the full Big House effect: pillars, pediments, lots of sash windows, a fountain, Victorian-style lamps and lashings of ivy. Add to this plenty of bling and multiply with sheer scale. It is an enormous edifice, known as 'the Jesus Christ hotel' because as people drive over from Northern Ireland they come around a bend and the hotel's front, like a cliff face with windows, is suddenly before them. 'Jesus Christ!' is the common reaction.

'Are you here for the wedding reception?' a man on the lawn asks me. He is not part of the wedding either but is waiting so he can watch the bride and groom's arrival. I suppose he likes to see such things, perhaps it's the sense of continuity he enjoys.

'No,' I say, 'I'm just having a look around.'

He takes me for a pilgrim to Quinn's great temple. We stand side by side, looking at the hotel.

'He was a great man,' he says.

I note the use of the past tense. 'I hear he still comes around here quite often,' I say. 'He walks over from his house.'

'He does surely,' he says. 'You know, he did a lot for this area. And then they put him in jail. It's a terrible thing.'

'But, let's face it,' I say, 'asset stripping is a crime.'

He shifts on his feet. 'Well, things can be complicated,' he says. I have ruined our friendship before it began.

Inside the hotel are a few early wedding guests; silver waistcoats strain around beer bellies, heels clatter on Quinn slate. In contrast, the concierge skims around, smooth-talking young and old alike. Everything about the decor is big and shiny and expensive.

'Can you tell me where the Aughrim tomb is?' I ask the receptionist.

'It's only a small thing you know,' she says, concerned I'll be disappointed.

Prehistoric Irelanders built the Aughrim tomb on the side of Slieve Rushen but that put it in the way of Quinn's quarry. So, with government permission, Quinn had it shifted three miles, not to a different part of Slieve Rushen but here, to his hotel garden. I go to find it. The reconstructed tomb has a hedge around it and is overlooked by the hotel. Ivy has been allowed to grow over the limestone slabs. Someone has carved their initials into one. It is hard to appreciate the monument in this neat garden, the noise of a lawnmower coming from a fairway. This tomb was originally built for someone with high status, a spiritual leader or chief; they became orientation points in death. The tomb was supposed to be on raised land, supposed to command an area, but has been made subservient to a new chief. A four-thousand-year-old monument is now a garden ornament.

*

I join a road that follows the border over Slieve Rushen. It is a private road, built by Sean Quinn to connect the quarry to another on the other side. A truck thunders by, heading north. Five minutes later another comes along, heading south. The drivers give me full waves and overhead salutes.

When I say a truck goes by every five minutes I don't mean on average, they are very regular. The trucks are essentially parts in a mountain-wide mechanism, going up Slieve Rushen, down the other side and back around again, like evenly spaced buckets on a giant excavator.

Just as I have been seeing the cement factory for four nights, I have been seeing Quinn's wind farm for four days, up ahead, the turbines calling me on with their arms. At last I am under them. Each four or five storeys tall, they are spread over Rushen's cap, both sides of the border. They are revolving at top speed as I go by, producing a textured wall of noise. Inside the swish of the rotation is another rhythm, a respiratory in and out.

To the north is another rise called Molly Mountain. Definitely not a mountain, it's a bump, overlaid with a dozen fields and, from the west, getting eaten away by the quarry. It is named after a group of agitators called the Molly Maguires, only gaining 'Mountain' due to a fondness for alliteration. The Molly Maguires operated in this area in the 1840s and the hill was said to be their hideout. They were just the latest manifestation of agrarian revolt in the border counties, unrest born in tensions between land-owners and tenants. In general, the Molly Maguires didn't fight existing land systems, but they sought to stop anyone who broke from established understandings and put fur-ther pressure on tenants. Their enemies were modernising landlords, their agents and any tenant who moved in on land from which someone else had been evicted. Various folktales claim to know who the original Molly was: an old widow evicted from her home; the owner of an illicit tavern where the gang met; or a fierce young woman, pistols strapped to her thighs, leading the men on their night-time attacks. The gang referred to themselves as Molly's Child-ren. The Molly Maguires were convinced their own laws were fairer than anything the courts would apply, present-ing themselves as guardians of community values. Their methods were vandalism, cattle maiming and death threats, soon moving on to actual executions. Theirs was a localised, targeted violence. In disguise, they would walk out of their homes, assault someone or something, then slip home or to their hideaway on Molly Mountain.

There is still something of the Molly Maguires in the air on Slieve Rushen now, some twenty-first-century vandalism in the same tradition. I knew I was going to see it; the story is covered in the newspaper. Back in the petrol station the owner and his friend were discussing the attack, going quiet when I approached the counter. There is an electricity substation by the road, a cabin on a brick foundation, for managing the power the turbines create. The whole thing has been buckled and blackened by arson. Its doors hang open. The rain has washed ash into puddles that have dried out, leaving black stains on the ground. The substation was set alight by someone demonstrating loyalty to Sean Quinn, attacking the things that were taken from him and now belong to banks. This substation was not the only target. A company director, newly inserted into a Quinn business, had his car burnt out on his driveway; Quinn vans and a bus were torched; two dozen electricity poles were chainsawed. One afternoon someone drove a lorry into the Quinn Group business headquarters, leaving a lorry-shaped hole in it. These new vandals might like to be considered Quinn's Children but, from his cell, Sean Quinn disowned them.

Not all complaints are delivered clandestinely. There are rallies; thousands gather from both sides of the border to show their loyalty to Quinn. A general mistrust of banks has helped to portray him as a victim, overthrown by the enemies of any honest-to-goodness worker: bankers and boardroomers. 'Free Sean Quinn' is daubed on walls. A local country singer has recorded a song in his honour. 'The Mighty Quinn from Derrylin / They closed him down, it is a sin'. It gets a lot of plays on local radio.

Most of Ireland, north and south, mocks this surge of support for Quinn. I hear them scoffing on national radio stations, I read their irritation in newspaper columns. Quinn's supporters are gombeens, they are plain eejits. Journalists ask what on earth these people think they are doing, Sean Quinn has stolen from you, don't you get it? They did not predict Quinn's ongoing popularity and cannot compute it. 'There is, however, a historical meaning to it all,' goes a letter to the editor. 'This is the Irish people marching for their chieftain. It is a form of feudalism that Irish people seem to love. They love to be ruled . . .' For me, I take it as evidence that there are other values on the borderland, rattling in the gravel, rushing down the rivers. One journalist in the *Irish Times* captures some sense of what's going on when he writes that those loyal to Quinn are 'good Cavan people, good Fermanagh people – those are the "imagined communities" that command respect and allegiance.' Most city folk just don't get it; Quinn's supporters aren't dumb, aren't in denial, they're members of another state. It is small, inward-looking and centred – if such a thing can be said – on the border. I spot them every day, in garages and waving from trucks, working border fields and resting on doorsteps. In their wallets are both pounds and euros, they skim back and forth across the line, paying no heed to the distant city parliaments. To outsiders their orientation points can seem obscure but they themselves don't suffer much angst about this. The larger states didn't show much interest in them, they were left on the side, so they have elevated other figureheads and other values. They are the borderlanders, this is their two-chambered heartland.

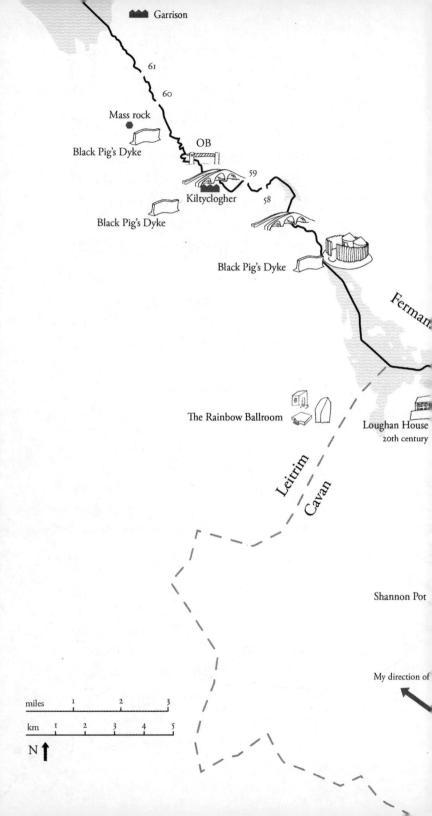

Garrison

61

60

Mass rock

Black Pig's Dyke

OB

59

Kiltyclogher

58

Black Pig's Dyke

Black Pig's Dyke

Ferman

The Rainbow Ballroom

Loughan House
20th century

Leitrim

Cavan

Shannon Pot

My direction of

miles   1   2   3

km   1   2   3   4   5

N

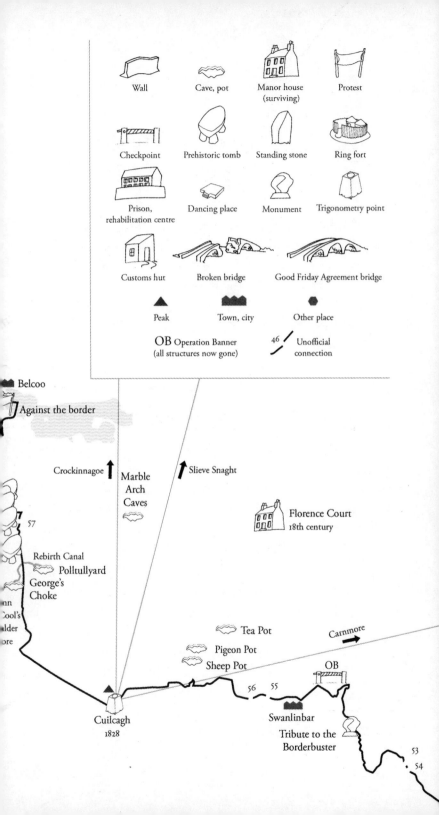

Wall

Cave, pot

Manor house (surviving)

Protest

Checkpoint

Prehistoric tomb

Standing stone

Ring fort

Prison, rehabilitation centre

Dancing place

Monument

Trigonometry point

Customs hut

Broken bridge

Good Friday Agreement bridge

Peak

Town, city

Other place

OB Operation Banner (all structures now gone)

46 Unofficial connection

Belcoo

Against the border

Crockinnagoe

Marble Arch Caves

Slieve Snaght

Florence Court
18th century

57

Rebirth Canal
Polltullyard
George's Choke

nn
ool's
lder
ore

Tea Pot

Pigeon Pot

Sheep Pot

Carnmore

OB

56   55

Swanlinbar
Tribute to the
Borderbuster

53
54

Cuilcagh
1828

A Peak, a Pot, a Tunnel

I've heard it in Belfast, been told it in Dublin: there are smugglers' tunnels under the border. Nobody can say exactly where. They haven't seen them personally – they don't live near the border. But they believe in them.

They are wrong. The tunnels are border mythology. The border is potent as an idea but rarely visited; this is a recipe for myths, cooked up between the imagination and a few half-remembered news reports. Tunnels were dug under the Berlin Wall, maybe the idea comes from there, but tunnelling made sense for Berliners in a way it never did for borderlanders. To get from one side of the Wall to the other, you had to beat a narrow strip, saturated with guards, where getting caught could mean getting shot. The stakes were very high and the West was very close. Tunnelling was the obvious answer. Ireland's border was different. Guarding and patrolling took place over a wide band; a tunnel would have to be miles long to be of use. Moreover, even during the Troubles there were remote stretches without checkpoints. It was much easier to make your crossing there than dig a tunnel. You could simply hack your way through a border hedgerow or lay planks across a border stream.

However, there are natural tunnels under the borderland I'm walking today, it's an area shot through with subterranean voids and fractures. Rain running down the slopes of Cuilcagh Mountain has bored holes in the soft stone below, creating a hidden network of caves. I'm walking over them, towards the mountain. Cuilcagh rises from miles of heath. North or south of here I could appreciate its length – Cuilcagh is a ridge that looks like a capsized ship – but following the border from the east I am presented only with the bow, its smallest face.

Cropped green grass turns into yellow-grey tufts as I move away from the road. The fields become threadbare then give up and turn to bog. Songbirds fade away; here there are only crows. A rusty yellow digger has been parked halfway into a ditch. The engine lid is ajar and parts have been swiped. A squall of rain passes over and I shelter in the cab, reading the five-year-old magazine I find under the seat.

I set off again. The border moves against the flow of a narrowing stream. I see black fissures in the streambed. The water has run off the mountaintop, which is impermeable sandstone, and here flows across limestone, a soluble rock that gives way to it. Water is sapped through the cracks, down and away. The stream is just a brief horizontal detour on the water's journey from cloud to water table.

My Ordnance Survey map shows lots of boreholes just over the line in Fermanagh. I succeed in finding one, tugging the heather back from its craggy lip. Its rim is a foot-deep layer of turf and exposed roots, dropping to a void. The floor is a shelf of rock, wet with running water. I would need ropes or a ladder to get down there. Cavers with the correct gear have done it. If you squeeze around the shelf, I'm told, you find yourself in a chamber the size of a house.

Boreholes like these have several different names – dolines, swallow holes or sinkholes – but around here they are called pots. Many Cuilcagh pots have their own given names: Goat Pot, Long Pot, Black Pot, Pigeon Pot and, yes, Tea Pot. Even on dry days they drip with moisture, fed by tiny rivulets from the mountainside. Animals sometimes claim a pot as a den. One caver found this out the hard way, writing in a report: 'Exploration was terminated by a combined badger and wasp onslaught.' That pot is called Buzzish.

I watch my step as I return to the borderline; to me the claustrophobic depths are more frightening than any animal. I picture throats lined with calcium and smooth as marble. Fall into one, you'll slide along it as if greased, water sloshing around you, your fingers finding nothing to grip. Even a narrow point in the tube might not save you. Momentum and the suction of the deep earth will tug you through and down, down.

I continue towards Cuilcagh. Just below its cap I can see stripes of sandstone and shale. Below that the mountain is coated in scree, some patches held in place with vegetation, the rest exposed and loose. From a distance the contrast makes what look like huge letters, green on grey, from an unknown alphabet.

The border follows a nameless stream for another hour. At one point I stop and turn a slow 360 degrees. I am in the centre of a bogland swell, a sodden bulge measuring miles across. The horizon is soft and receding. Not a road, sheep, tree or house, as far as the eye can see. I feel as lonely as a Mars rover. The tiny stream is fed by slow weepings from the peat each side, contributions that could be measured in cups per day. I walk further to where the border suddenly disassociates itself from the stream and makes a straight line towards the inverted bow of Cuilcagh. It's as if the pull of the stream was finally too weak to compete with the mountain's call.

Mist is collecting along the ridge when I reach Cuilcagh and begin to climb. Ascending is the work of hands as well as feet. I search the frost-shattered scree for boot- and hand-holds. The stones are unfriendly to fingertips, freshly snapped, with cold sharp edges. Several times they shift under my weight and there is the sound of rock scraping rock as everything I'm clinging to shifts. There's nothing I can do but lock my body and hope the avalanche is small and stops soon. I am sent back five or six feet but luckily the stones stay together in one loose conglomeration. It's a two steps forward one step back kind of ascent.

I pass up into fog. Dew makes my hair stand on end. The mountain curves over and I no longer need my hands. There will be no views from the top today, I am in a close mist. I almost go by the cairn that tells me I am at 2,185 feet, Cuilcagh's peak and the highest point of Ireland's border. For most of the walk along the three-mile length of Cuilcagh's cap I can see only a few yards ahead, but by keeping my feet to the upper ground I stay on the borderline. Giant mudstone boulders materialise. They are black with wet, fog becoming liquid on contact. The mist is so dense that rivulets pour from only a few square feet of stone face.

The name Cuilcagh means Chalky Peak, but you should not think of soft crumbly chalk. Cuilcagh's calcareous deposits are smooth and rock-hard. There are lots of drip-feed formations to be seen north of here, in a cave system called Marble Arch. As I walk along the mountain's toothy edge I see streams, fed only by mist but heavy enough to gush away. Cuilcagh is a water catcher, pulling down rain and moisture, making it milky with calcium and funnelling it away underground. The peak feeds the pots.

Some pots are fed from below too; rainwater washing

down meets other water rising up. The best-known pot is one of this sort. It is at the mountain's western end, two and a half miles inside the south, the size of a swimming pool, much bigger than most pots, and permanently brimming with water. It is the source of the River Shannon. The Shannon Pot appears to be spring-fed, the river rising from the deep earth. A 'mighty fountain' one nineteenth-century traveller called it. On still days a strong upwelling can be seen pushing up at the surface. The Shannon is already a reasonable size as it leaves its pot and flows south-west, picking up tributaries along the way, soon becoming the King and Queen of Ireland's rivers, bigger than any other in these islands.

Legend puts the Shannon Pot at hundreds of feet deep but I've met a man who worked for fisheries and had access to sonar equipment and so decided to measure it. It was thirty feet deep. After this investigation cavers in scuba gear went to the bottom of the pot. Their torches were useless in the heavily stained water, but they felt around with their hands and confirmed the sonar reading. They also found a narrow slit through which the pot was being fed. A caver called Artur Kozlowski was first to go in. I have watched a few online interviews with Kozlowski; he seems like someone to whom caving had become a spiritual pursuit, an attitude I recognise from surfers. Working handhold by handhold, he dragged himself down the narrow tunnel against a stiff rising flow. The floor of the tunnel was unstable, rocks shifting at the slightest contact. For me, this is a nightmare: utter blackness, rock above you, breathing through a tube, and going deeper. After about thirty feet Kozlowski was in another chamber. The floor was littered with loose stones, a strong current pushing up through the gaps. Kozlowski took hold of one rock and lifted it. There was an instant reaction, a flushing effect, sand and stones sinking rapidly from all sides, tumbling towards the new opening. Kozlowski plugged the hole and got out, quick.

The following week it rained a lot. When the cavers returned, they found that everything at the bottom of the pot had been jumbled about. The slit into the narrow tunnel had shifted and was even more unstable. 'Obviously,' they comment in a report, 'a high water flow creates a very violent environment inside the chamber with rocks and gravel being tumbled around like inside a washing machine.'

If the amount of water feeding the Shannon Pot increases with rainfall, then it is clearly not just fed from underground, but perhaps by runoff from Cuilcagh. The pot is close to Cuilcagh's western tip, a narrow wedge with a small catchment area, surely not gathering enough water to feed the mighty Shannon. Cavers started to wonder where else the water could be coming from. They wondered if the limestone erosion under Cuilcagh was more complex than was previously thought – the boreholes not just tending downwards but winding sideways under the mountain. Such a system would catch water from the entire nine square miles of mountain face and deliver it to the Shannon. Perhaps Cuilcagh is like a cap on a termite mound, sitting over a whole maze of hidden passages and caves, all funnelling water to the Shannon Pot. This would mean the pot is not the source of the Shannon at all – it could be traced further back.

There is something iconoclastic about this idea. The river has often been a kind of spiritual resource to Ireland, the focus of songs and poetry for centuries. 'Bend ye hills, on either side / In solemn, deep devotion,' Gerald Griffin wrote of the Shannon in the early nineteenth century, using the same lyrics to hail the river as an economic resource: 'On his heaving surface sails / Half the wealth of Erin's vales.' In the first years of Ireland's independence the Shannon was dammed, creating electricity to power the new nation. The Irish Republic's identity mingles with the Shannon just as a large fraction of its land gathers to it. The Shannon is special and questioning its source is a thing of significance. A team of cavers got together and did it anyway.

*

Back in Belfast I meet with a gang of cavers who are exploring beneath Cuilcagh. They are Stephen, Jock and Rocky. Two of those names are nicknames. Nicknames develop among cavers as they can help avoid confusion in the dark confines of the tunnels, especially in the Cuilcagh group as they have lots of Connors and Stephens. Kozlowski had something of the guru about him but these three cavers are different, explorers in the more traditional style. They are practical, self-effacing, not given to romanticising their adventures, no matter how much I try to encourage them. They are just looking for undiscovered places in a fully mapped world and have realised that this means they have to get under the planet's skin. Their rewards are the camaraderie, the satisfaction of opening new caves and the thrill of being first. 'People have been walking around Ireland for ten thousand years,' Jock says, 'but nobody has ever seen these caves and chambers before.'

As a boy Jock loved reading about mountain climbers, adventures that were all a long way from Blacklion, the border town where he grew up. He had to make do with joining the Scouts. One day a potholer came and spoke to his troop. He told them that they could have Himalayan adventures right here, minutes from their own village. For Jock, that was when it started. Exploring a cave is in many ways similar to climbing a high mountain. It's all teamwork, nobody does anything alone and there is a comparable fixation on equipment. The adventure is rooted in taking care, planning and preparation. Making twenty feet of progress might be considered an achievement. If someone is injured deep in a cave, it may take days to get them out. Similar perils, therefore, to mountain climbing. Both a mountain and a cave can trap you, although in different ways.

How does it happen, I ask, that a person can squeeze through a passage but is then unable to get out again? Stephen demonstrates, sitting up straight and pressing his hands down on his ribs. When sliding through a narrow gap the human ribcage will compress and allow you through. Once through, your ribs pop out again: you experience the kind of shove and click that sometimes comes with putting together tubular furniture, except you're in the tube and it's your ribs that have clicked. It is a system that does not work backwards. Your ribs only compress when going headfirst. If, as is often the case, the space you have entered is not big enough for you to wiggle yourself back around, then you are trapped. You are plugged.

Stephen, Jock and Rocky will clear rocks if that's what they must do in order to make progress. Sometimes they bring lengths of scaffolding down to shore up loose sections. Their ultimate mission is to 'open up' routes, traverse them, map them and make it safe for others to follow. It is often plain hard work and the thrills are slow ones. 'A sedate extreme sport,' says Jock, referring to the pace. 'It can be nerdish too,' remarks Rocky. 'There's the caving itself, but most of us are also into related aspects of it, the science, conservation or the mapping.'

I ask about the Shannon. These cavers were among the group who, with careful timing, poured dyes into various pots around Cuilcagh then travelled to the Shannon Pot to see if any of them emerged there. I had imagined the cavers in muddy overalls, squinting and uncomfortable in the light, sitting at the Shannon Pot's rim and waiting for the water to turn pink or green. In fact, tracing experiments do not work like that. The dyes are quickly diluted to invisibility as they travel the waterlogged tunnels, too thin to be seen by the human eye. Charcoal detectors were used. When unopened, these look like tobacco tins and are about the same size. They were placed under the rim of the Shannon Pot for a time, then sent to a specialist lab for analysis.

In this way the source of the Shannon has been pushed back under Cuilcagh Mountain, back its entire length, all the way to its eastern slopes. While I was walking today, the last five or six hours, the Shannon was running beneath me. Back when I thought of a Mars rover, it was there. The Shannon's source was a mile to my north while I sheltered from the rain in the abandoned digger. The Shannon has been traced to Pigeon Pot in Fermanagh, meaning it has not just been pushed back miles, it has been pushed back under the border, into the north.

Borders do not mean much to people who spend all their free time underground. Stephen, Jock and Rocky are unfazed by having demonstrated that the Shannon is a cross-border river. To them, this was just a starting point. The experiments were timed: the dye travelled from Pigeon Pot to the Shannon Pot at more than one hundred metres per hour, a speed that showed the water was in free flow under the mountain. They had proved there was a tunnel. The next challenge was locating it and then, maybe, opening it up. The cavers' ultimate goal is to join the dots, traverse the whole system between Pigeon Pot and the Shannon Pot. This is a distance of six miles. Consider the implications of this ambition and it becomes hard to grasp. A mountain must have a peak but a continuous traversable route under Cuilcagh may not even exist. The dyes showed there is a link but that does not mean a human being can travel it. Years could be spent exploring winding, rib-crushing caves without finding a connection but never, for sure, proving its non-existence either. It is extraordinarily tantalising. After the next bend – a bend taking a day to get around – you may meet a wall of shale, the water sloshing around your boots and disappearing through bores only the diameter of your wrist, no further progress possible. Or around the next bend you may find yourself in a massive chamber, able to walk upright through an echoing cathedral, pillars of limestone and calamite towering around you, a place no one has ever seen before.

Dropping into the middle of a connecting tunnel would be a good way to get started. Stephen scanned the maps and reports looking for other pots that might join a trans-Cuilcagh system. His attention was caught by a site called George's Choke, which had been abandoned for years. Stephen was interested in it because it is about a mile and a half from the Shannon Pot, just a few steps south of the border. In 1980 the Reverend George Pitt descended into the cave and was trapped when large boulders fell across his exit. In an example of cross-border co-operation police officers from north and south worked together to pull him out.

Stephen formed a team, they called themselves the Shannon Group, and investigated George's Choke. It would not relent but nearby, over the border, they found another promising pot, Polltullyard.

Descending Cuilcagh, I hike over heather to go and look at this pot. It is hard to miss Polltullyard, as it is the centre point of a large rocky sump. I clamber down to the bottom. A jagged hawthorn stands over the hole, as if on guard, its roots wrapped around the pot's mouth. I wonder how many fairy stories have been set here. The cave, I'm told, ends at a hundred-foot drop. Stephen's team abseiled down to the bedrock and found a water-bored tube going west, surely leading to the Shannon.

All Stephen's spare time went into this cave, years of weekends and holidays. Dangerous sections had to be shored up, rocks shifted to clear the way, tight squeezes negotiated. Eventually, the Shannon Group arrived at the site of George Pitt's calamity. So somewhere in the zigzagging depths they had crossed the border. It seems my original informants were not entirely wrong; people are digging their way under the border. Not for profit, but for exploration and sport.

It took fifteen weekends for the Shannon Group to reopen and shore up George's Choke, working under the ground for up to eleven hours. Now they have a base camp set up almost a mile further. It takes four hours just to reach it. They go under on a Saturday morning, work all day opening up the system, sleep in tents in their underground campsite, then dig more the following day. They do not see light until Sunday evening. Linking with Artur Kozlowski's descent into the Shannon Pot will eventually mean donning scuba gear, but so far they have pushed more than two miles into the south without needing to, although they are occasionally up to their waists in water. And so they slowly make their way – this mission is still ongoing. I'm sorry to report that Artur Kozlowski died in 2011, while diving another of Ireland's cave systems. His work is admired by all the Shannon Group, the mutual appreciation of explorers who see their adventures as, ultimately, teamwork. 'He was a force of nature,' says Jock.

Advancing into new country, Stephen and his team get to do what explorers love to do, name things. Finn McCool is a giant in Irish legend and so Finn McCool's Boulder Store is a fine name for a wide chamber littered with large rocks they found just beyond George's Choke. Other names are based on the tunnel formation: a chamber encrusted with gypsum crystals is called Starlight Evening. Some names recall the experience of passing through. The Rebirth Canal, a breakthrough made by Stephen, is a choke where you must go slack and allow yourself to slip down through it, dropping onto the floor beneath. Names might indicate misadventure or wasted time – Mistake Passage, Pointless Cave. Duck's Arse, I assume, is a particularly tight squeeze. Not for a hundred years have individuals got to add so many names to the map – though admittedly cavers' maps are rather specialist documents. Other sections are named for the day on which they were found. Paddy's Parade, for example, was opened up on St Patrick's Day. There are quite a few like this, a reminder that a lot of potholing happens on days off work. In reaction to Ireland's sectarian traditions, tunnels are sometimes given grotesque, satirical names; Fenian Terror, Prod's Pot, Papist Passage. I like this subversion of the way religion has been used to make claims on areas or routes above ground. These names mock such attempts, they giggle at sonorous claims.

It has taken extraordinary effort and commitment but the Shannon Group has still only opened a fraction of the Pigeon Pot–Shannon Pot system. 'How long might it take to open up the whole route?' I ask Stephen.

He laughs and shakes his head. 'It would take twenty people three lifetimes,' he says.

For big achievements you must think across generations. The tunnels only relent in tiny increments. The pace of exploration is best measured in feet per year, like erosion or the movement of the earth's plates. Tunnels can also sit still for years between pushes, untouched, until the right set of people come together and decide to give it a go. Of course, these short breaks are nothing compared to the millennia these voids have sat undisturbed and untitled before the likes of Artur, Stephen, Jock and Rocky crawl in, let torch-light bounce off the walls and think up a new name.

Relics

The border passes through a bowl-shaped dip, dividing a small lake. It's a hidden place, no road comes near. Few of us would ever have reason to follow the narrowing trails that link this lake to the outer world. Even people who live nearby probably never visit. To find places like this, you must set yourself peculiar projects, shake yourself out of the well-worn routes, follow a border for example. Sunshine, lush pasture, the blue of the lake and the natural quiet; an atmosphere of freshness and clarity. It is early in the day but I am tempted to set camp and enjoy it. Frolicking in the grass, like they know they're on to a good thing here, are four European hares. These creatures are a shock to someone used to the much smaller Irish hare. They are large and look like they might thump you. Robust brown packages of meat and muscle when they are close to the ground, they suddenly reconfigure into something svelte but no less powerful when extended into a leap. European hares are not widespread, I had never seen any until today. Charts of their distribution across Ireland do not place them in this area but there they are, looking very much at home.

I feel the border will bring me to strange places today. I ascend with it onto a plateau.

*

Adventure writers have come up with various lost lands where their characters can find trouble, creating almost plausible settings where ancient mammals and reptiles have survived or unique species have evolved. In *Journey to the Centre of the Earth*, Jules Verne tells us about a vast underground chamber where prehistoric creatures live around a subterranean sea. Edgar Rice Burroughs used an island for *The Land that Time Forgot*. Arthur Conan Doyle came up with another way to isolate an ecosystem – the Lost World is removed from the familiar by being raised, it is a plateau.

The plateau the border crosses is not a large formation, just a couple of square miles of limestone, coated in thin soil and trees. The acidic bite of rain has carved channels and runnels into the rock, giving it a buckled appearance. The whole thing is slowly dissolving from the inside. Locally, the plateau is called the Cavan Burren. It is a landscape of relics – although without Conan Doyle's dinosaurs or bubbling tar pits. Time has not stopped, but has slowed to something better measured in geological terms. The plateau has preserved wonders. Left by the last ice age, there are many hundreds of sandstone boulders, known as erratics, scattered around erratically. A few have cracked down the middle and fallen open like hatched eggs, others have been absorbed into field walls. It is unlikely that the massive boulders were shifted to the course of the wall, rather the location of the erratic dictated where the wall was put. The big stones were probably boundary markers for a long time before the wall reinforced the boundary. Many of the field patterns here are prehistoric, laid out in a style that is completely different from today's squares and rectangles. To create regular fields, irregular features must be moved or smashed up but these walls developed organically from a central area, outwards in a spiral, a bit-by-bit style that was able to absorb the plateau's features – like the erratics – and actually helped protect them.

I find a boulder resting on a much narrower stone pedestal, an arrangement that came about because the boulder is sandstone, almost completely insoluble, and has protected a small column of limestone while the rest was washed away. The rough sandstone is pleasing against my palm; the push it takes to open a door is enough to make the whole boulder sway. Such features attract stories and this plateau is a deeply storied place. If a site is not associated with giants – the Giant's Grave, the Giant's Leap, the Giant's Table – then it is associated with an ancient priest class, with their prayers and curses: the Druid's Chair, the Druid's Lightning Stone and the Druid's Rocking Stone, the thing I am touching right now. Historian Séamus Ó hUltacháin suggests that natural, but striking, formations like the Rocking Stone may have fired the imaginations of earlier Irelanders, helping turn them into monument builders. Nearby is another erratic, a rectangular block the size of a small car. It was dropped here by a glacier to later infatuate humans; it was raised and other stones wedged underneath, making the cap high and flat. A burial chamber was carved out of the space below. This is very special, remarks Ó hUltacháin, a link between natural geology, the erratics and the entirely assembled megalithic tombs that were on the way.

Near the plateau's highest point is a tomb called the Giant's Grave. Slabs were stood on end and five big lintels laid across them, forming a wedge-shaped passage over twenty feet long. It is constructed of sandstone erratics that would have settled naturally hereabouts but, as each weighs over a ton, it would still have required an enormous collective will to set up this truck-sized monster. I stop a while to examine the tomb and eat wild strawberries growing between the stones. There are round hollows in one of the capstones, prehistoric cupholders of ritualistic purpose. I run my fingers inside them and feel a tingle, not a shock making me withdraw my hand, rather a magnetic pull keeping it there. Now my fingers are where, four thousand years ago, the creator of this hollow had theirs. Time is suddenly compressed, everything foregrounded all at once.

The original builders could have lived in this state perpetually. They had no written histories, and surely little sense of societal progression. The arrangements of rocks were simply there, meaning as much twenty generations after construction as two generations afterwards. At a nearby site called Legalough, ten steps from the border, a trio of tombs stand together. Their stones mingle but the span of their creation covers at least a thousand years.

It is not just the plateau's elevation that preserves these and other relics, it is the border. Economic fragility, an atmosphere of threat, the way the border always seemed to be challenging one's identity. Few could be persuaded to make any place on the border a destination. The Cavan Burren has more treasures than some of the more celebrated sites in Ireland, but they sit unvisited mostly. If the border did not run over this plateau there would be tour buses parked in its shadow, a shop and a busy visitors' centre. You could stroll around the features on gravel paths then retire to the cafe for a scone, maybe purchase some expensive knitwear. Instead, there are just a few paths and handmade signs. You have to pick your way from stone to stone, get a little sweaty, get a little muddy, get transported back in time if you're tired and susceptible to that kind of thing.

I move on, following the border to the plateau's edge and finding a path down. A red squirrel dashes along the up path. I stop and it does too when it sees me. The squirrel is smaller and more delicate than the common grey squirrel. Trembling, it leans into its front paws. It's my move, but I don't move. I'm remembering someone whose name I never knew, a frail red-haired girl in my primary school, she always looked underfed and stood alone in the playground too scared to speak to anyone. The squirrel looks just like her. Red squirrels are becoming rare, getting beaten back by the greys. When grey squirrels arrive in an area, the red population is usually gone in fifteen years. It seems red squirrels have held out on the plateau. Suddenly it flashes into action, dashing off the path, up a scattering of lime-stone rocks, leaping from slab to slab and vanishing among the relics.

*

Soon after seeing the squirrel I meet another walker, called Michael, and together we hike down from the plateau. He is retired and lives near here. It was Michael who dropped the sonar device into the Shannon Pot and found it not as deep as people liked to suppose. He has views on plenty of other things, his hiking pole is used more for pointing than leaning on, it's his teaching aid. He delivers his various wisdoms dryly. 'Of course, those tombs were only for people with high status,' he says, pointing back in the direction of the Giant's Grave. 'The poor man had to go into the woods and bury himself.'

We leave the path to take the direct route down through

fields, the border woven through a dry-stone wall to our right. Michael hits the wall top with his stick – *a clatter of his stick* is how they might word it around here. 'These walls are thousands of years old,' he says but I think he is mistaken. We are off the plateau now, away from its prehistoric boundaries. This wall is straight, from the era of formal land division, of plans, maps and rent books. We are back down among the ordinary. If we see a squirrel it will be a grey one.

When Michael pauses it is not to catch his breath, it is to light another cigarette. His face's yellow tint comes from a lifetime of lighting another cigarette.

'Where do you get your breath from?' I ask.

He looks at me carefully, as if I'm implying something distasteful. 'I'm only sixty-nine,' he says.

Below we can see neighbouring villages, Belcoo and Blacklion, and two connected lakes, MacNean Upper and MacNean Lower. The border passes through the middle of the cross they form. There are islands on both lakes, the border swimming among them. If I squint I can project the black line, making angles, south of one island, north of the other. The lakes are part of one of Ireland's major freshwater systems, the Erne belongs to it too. It brushes up against the Shannon system, they flow to within only a mile or two of each other, but they do not mingle. This is because of another border, a thin barrier of dolerite rock running through the land and keeping the two subterranean flows apart.

The surface is stark, hungry ground. Fingers of limestone poke through the fields, reminding us of the erosion below. Michael points out a hollow known as Lost Valley. It is a deep cleft in the land. You could hide a double-decker

bus in it, although you'd never get it out again. It marks the place where one day a mass of perforated limestone just gave up. It would have been a disturbing thing to see: a rock-chewing crunch and the land suddenly slumped, air pockets collapsing and spouting dust.

'It's like Swiss cheese under these fields,' says Michael, tapping the thin soil. 'And to think that they want to frack here!'

Along with the dolerite and limestone, there are bands of shale below us, rock that holds reserves of gas. Conventional gas is held in linked reservoirs through porous rock, so a single bore can tap large amounts. Shale gas is locked in small voids, bubbles in the stone. The rock must be shattered side-on to release it. That is what hydraulic fracturing does. Boreholes are made in the rock and then water and chemicals are pumped into the bores, opening up cracks and allowing gas to be extracted. Both sides of the border, gas companies have requested licences to frack and from both sides of the border a protest movement opposes them. Twenty years ago a cross-border protest movement could not have happened, if only because of the difficulties of travel, but there is one here now, and it's strong. Placards are nailed to telegraph poles hereabouts, homemade signs saying, 'Our lakes Are Not For Shale', 'No Gasholes', 'Farming, Not Fracking' and simply, 'Frack No'. Anxieties surround fracking; the protestors say chemical cocktails will seep into groundwater; the level of the lakes will fall; there will be tremors. Michael is concerned too. 'See if they do that fracking here,' he says, 'you would not know in what way the land could be affected. The Erne could break into the Shannon. The Shannon could start to flow the other way.'

We reach the main road. I say goodbye to Michael and walk into Blacklion. The border tiptoes along flowerbeds before sliding into the lake and passing under a north–south bridge. A protest is taking place on the bridge. I hope it's an anti-fracking demonstration; I'd like to see one of those. They are big, noisy get-togethers; kids running around, hooters and homemade banners. Farmers bring their tractors out in large numbers, forming protest convoys that twist back and forth across the border. As I get closer I see there are only two dozen people on the bridge, few compared to an anti-fracking demonstration. They stand in a line along the road's central division, down the middle of the bridge. They seem stiff, they've taken position but now don't know what to do. They've made a show of themselves yet still seem furtive. This is because many of their faces are covered.

They are members of the 32 County Sovereignty Movement – a group dedicated to the removal of the border, getting all Ireland's counties back together rather than the current 26/6 arrangement. They reject the Good Friday Agreement, which they see as propping up Northern Ireland's illegitimate existence. Their position on the European Union is unclear although a fixation on sovereignty suggests Irexit would please them. Everyone on the bridge today is male; one has a long beard and a wheelchair, a veteran of something, while the rest are young. They are unrehearsed; some face into traffic from the north, others face south. They are chatting, texting and eating bags of crisps.

'What's this about?' I ask a twenty-year-old returning to his comrades with a bottle of Lucozade.

'National sovereignty!' he says. He scuttles on, he doesn't want to be a spokesman, but then spins around to add, 'Up the thirty-two!' He raises his bottle of Lucozade, indicating his energy for the task.

I wonder if the protest's real energy comes from frustration, frustration at having missed the Troubles. If these lads had been born a decade or two earlier they could have been fighters, they could have had rank, instead they look awkward. Passing drivers slow down a tad but otherwise ignore them. The protestors' placards are printed on corrugated plastic boards, there are no kitchen-table art projects here. The placards are all printed with same image of Ireland, the island a seamless mono-green. Every day I refer to my Ordnance Survey maps constantly to make sure I don't wander off the border. I think the line is scored into my retinas by now, so I find this map disorientating. I suppose they find the borderline disconcerting, although it was there long before they were born. They consider the border a relic. For others it is they who are the relics.

Romance, Break-ups

At the beginning of this journey birds were an anxiety to me. I had no names for them. Beyond the big hitters, the crows, swallows, blackbirds, birds most of us know, I was unsure what I was seeing. The calls I heard in forests were mysteries too – the throaty clucks and lovelorn cries I could hear from my tent at dawn. It wasn't just that being able to identify them is a desirable connoisseurship, a romantic skill; I felt my lack of knowledge was shameful. As if a thing isn't actually witnessed unless you can label it.

So I put a guidebook in my handiest pocket and learned a few things. At Carlingford Lough I saw black guillemots and razorbills; I imagine a birdwatcher would be pleased to see both species in the same few minutes but I am more pleased that I can tell them apart. It's the beak, the razorbill's is thick and stumpy. The cat-like mewing of a raptor means it is a buzzard, its hunter's silhouette hanging on an updraught.

'I saw a buzzard try to take a rat today,' a farmer told me. 'Kept dropping it and snatching it up again. The rat was too fat for it to lift.' He paused to insert a sideways head tick into his story, using it to mark the rat's luck, to ensure luck's role was given due regard. 'It was fat on my barley,' he said.

Crows are plentiful, noisy as helicopters. After harvest it is common to see a dozen picking their way across a cropped barley field, black dots marching across a yellow background. Wood pigeons are common too, heard more often than seen. If, as I am starting to feel, the border did not divide Ireland in two but in three – the north, the south and the borderland – then the wood pigeon should be official bird of this third state.

In the summer swallows are everywhere along the country, their wings making rapid, hard thumps against the air. Overlooking a border lake, I find a one-hundred-year-old barn claimed as a nesting site. Through the loading hatch, I can see the shadowy interior under the roof, made extra dark by the day's brightness. I can see nests, clumps of denser shadow pressed inside the rafters. Dozens of swallows are darting in and out of the hatch. When outside the swallows are zippy and seem fickle, changing direction every second. I have the notion that this barn is source of all border swallows, this is their maternity ward and HQ. Not close-packed enough to be called a flock, they are more like loose smoke trailing from the hatch. I stand watching for fifteen minutes.

*

I'm at another of the border's watery stretches, so I've arranged to meet Paddy Bloomer. We lift the canoe from his car's roof rack and slide it onto the river we will follow to meet the border on Lough MacNean. 'A fine day for it,' he says, tightening the straps on his life vest. We set off. Trees line the banks, branches mingling above our heads and keeping the air shady and still. The water oozes more than flows, brown and thick. Junk has been dumped by the riverbank; coated in mud, the broken machinery is hard to distinguish from exposed roots but for rusty red lines running from them through the water. The stains take a full minute to diffuse and disappear. The river has been in flood lately, a tree has fallen across it and we must lift the canoe over its trunk. A calf drowned in the swell and the high water has left it hanging over a branch.

'Or the calf died and someone didn't want to deal with the carcass,' says Paddy. 'There's a load of regulations about disposing of dead stock, so a farmer might have just thrown it in, let the river take it.'

Paddy knows country ways and is never shocked. I think he has a grid in his mind, its vertical edge defined by human nature and its horizontal by the limits of physics. He quickly assigns any eventuality to a position on the grid. Nothing is surprising, everything has a place.

The first bird we see is a duck caught in rushes by the bank. It is not real, it is a rubber duck. Its bright body stands out in the murky light, a chemical yellow that mud does not stick to. Paddy tells me that village festivals often include a rubber duck race. People scratch their names into the ducks' undersides then gather on bridges to release scores of them. Nets are put up at the finish line and a winner is declared. Inevitably, a few ducks slip by the net and escape into the wild. That's probably what happened to this one.

An electric-blue flash cuts across the gloom. I have never seen this bird before but need no guidebook. Kingfishers are the most striking creature you'll see on the border. The paddle hangs still in my hands, my rhythm broken by the sight. The kingfisher glides ahead of us, going only a little faster than we are, before our bow for half a minute or so. Its blue is amazing, it is like a little tear in the material of this world, a hole into a different, brighter place. One heavy downbeat of its wings and it cruises right, into the trees, and disappears. I hope for another sighting but it never comes. From stern Paddy says, 'I've seen more rubber ducks in the wild than I've seen kingfishers.'

The river opens out onto Lough MacNean. There are several islands on the lake, all farmed but for one covered in trees, a drumlin cap packed with alder and sycamore. We paddle towards it and when we step onto the island the ground crunches under our feet, years of bird droppings layered up into a yellow crust. Paddy and I push into the interior. It is a tiny island but so dense with flora that we can't see the lake. The treetops are full of birdlife. Hidden in the upper branches are crows, wood pigeons and many songbirds, all squawking their objection to our visit. Held in by the canopy, the smell of droppings is cloying and full-bodied. The air pressure seems to rise. The birds get louder, alarm calls and shrill protests.

Free of mammals, this island has become a haven. Geese nest with impunity on the open ground. Some of their nests are made entirely of feathers. In the centre of the island we find a soft grey ring the size of a cafe table-top. In it are four big eggs, well loved and entitled-looking. Lives are condensing inside but the sight feels more deathly than anything. Having stepped into their realm, I am struck by the strange, unknowable ways of birds, the weirdness of their straw-light bones, hair-trigger instincts and sideways eyes. Overhead the crows have launched and are circling, the ducks have hunched down along the shore. The gamey smell is so thick I can feel it lining my throat. Every leaf on every tree is streaked with white and yellow droppings. Wordlessly, Paddy and I return to the canoe. It is a relief to get back onto the water, to escape the kingdom of birds.

*

The lake narrows to a stream, funnelling the border along with it. We paddle under the bridge where the 32 County Sovereignty Movement held their protest. Stones scrape the hull. To lighten the load I have to take off my boots and walk alongside the canoe. Sharp stones pressing into my feet make me yell out. 'Stop complaining,' laughs Paddy. I recommend wellington boots if you're canoeing this way.

There is a railway bridge a four-minute paddle beyond the road bridge. The trains ceased in 1956, the rails were unbolted and trucked away but the bridge itself remained, handy for smugglers and cattle herders. In time the planking rotted, leaving just the girder structure. If your balance was good you could still toe your way over the girders and across the border.

When a bomb killed three policemen in Belcoo in 1976, some thought the explosives had been brought into the north via the skeletal bridge. The army were called in to destroy it. Locals doubted the bridge was to blame, it was a difficult crossing even unladen. They complained that destroying the bridge would just be posturing, rooted in the army's frustration at another IRA attack left unpunished. The *Fermanagh Herald* called for the bridge's protection, saying it was a landmark in the district, 'adding to rather than distracting from the beauty of the surrounding countryside . . . a monument to the skill and ingenuity of the builders'. But one morning charges were taped to the supports and whether just posturing or not the spectacle found a willing audience. Hundreds of people sat on hills both sides of the border to experience the boom. The bridge was enveloped in brown smoke, a mushroom that rose nine hundred feet above the water and bristled with red flame. Seconds later the ground shook. Windows shattered in Belcoo and Blacklion and light fittings fell from ceilings. The smoke cleared and everyone could see the bridge now broken in two. The *Fermanagh Herald* remarked that it was still a landmark, but with a different message. 'The break occurred exactly on the border, in the middle of the bridge,' ran the editorial. 'Its broken back protrudes above the water into the bank on the Cavan and Fermanagh sides, a monument to man's inhumanity to man.'

The bridge's two halves are still here, bowing to each other across the river, chins in the water. From the canoe Paddy and I examine the blast points, inch-thick steel peeled back like banana skins. I put my fingertips to the steel's exposed innards, pitted and rough against my skin. There is a certain charge to this, touching the epicentre of a blast, an event that radiated shockwaves for three miles.

'Good luck through there,' says Paddy, shielding his eyes with his hand and surveying the fenland. He is leaving me at the lake's far end, where sluggish water is invaded by rushes. I say goodbye then squelch my way inland, arms raised to keep myself balanced. Tall grasses block the view. I sink to my ankles, the land grabbing hold. The flies too have taken a liking to me, divebombing my forehead. I am stung by nettles, white hives rising instantly. I am ridiculous and cursing myself when I see a man standing only twenty-five feet away. He is using a clamp to twist ends of barbed-wire fencing together. I laugh; it is funny after all, to have been caught looking so undignified. He is about sixty years of age, black suit jacket, dirty work jeans, wellingtons, out-sized woolly hat. He is thrown by my sudden presence, almost frightened, even though I look more stupid than anything. I think it's just that he had not expected to see anyone this morning – this can be an isolating landscape, not just because of the border. Among these hills are hard-scraped livelihoods, emigration taking away your children and your neighbours, it is easy for an individual to drift from sight. It feels appropriate to speak slowly. 'I'm follow-ing the border,' I say.

'Grand, grand,' he says. He turns away, as if to attend to something else but leaving the wire split at the site of our encounter.

*

A landscape shaped for loneliness: the writer William Trevor went after this idea and, I think, captured it best. His tales of rural isolation highlight the people that every-one else has forgotten. In Trevor's vision the drumlins divide us, not because they helped create the border but because each small hill is a world upon itself, with only one farm, one family. Homesteads are dotted on the other hills around but each is kept apart and tends to look inwards. In Trevor's stories the hills produce people who are self-reliant but do not easily mix. There are untended aches, wishes unfulfilled, people who hesitate so long at the periphery of things that hesitation becomes their lives. 'The Hill Bachelors' is an example. After his father's death a man named Paulie returns to his family's hilltop farm to care for his widowed mother. He slips back into the slow rhythms and long silences. His first meeting in years with their only neighbour is respectful and brief, only a few sentences are exchanged. Trevor's narrative voice tells us, 'It wasn't a time for conversation, and that was observed.'

Paulie realises living here will make it hard to find a wife. His few acres of hilltop, complete with an arthritic matriarch, has no appeal when compared to London or Dublin. All the unattached women are clearing out and he is in danger of being left stranded and alone. He fights this fate, stepping out with women from the nearest village, including one who works as a cashier in the supermarket. But she never cares to visit his farm and the relationship cools. 'Paulie took to steering the trolley to one of the other pay-outs even when the queue at hers was shorter. His mother didn't ask why.'

The local girls soon know that he is after marriage, they make excuses and back away. Up on his farm, Paulie begins to fold into himself, get acquainted with his own company. When his mother eventually dies it is too late for him. He is another silent countryman. 'Enduring, unchanging, the hills had waited for him, claiming one of their own.'

There are such people around still. I meet them on the border, on lanes or fields, looking towards the horizon from the edge of their land. When they see me an anxiety that is almost childlike hovers about their eyes. They are shy as deer. Their mouths open but they don't know what to say. Others may feel the same way but express it more briskly. 'That'll do,' a man said to me once after we'd exchanged three sentences, folding his arms solidly and looking away. Others are smiling, a gentle look about them, but they evade your eye. They may give you a few words but their style of conversation is to shut it down quickly, their tone is always closing. 'I'll let you go,' they say, looking ahead up the path, withdrawing from the conversation. These are the people who never get into travel memoirs, they are unquotable, they leave no trace. These borderlanders say hello in a way that makes you aware it is also a goodbye. Anything else they say, right from the beginning, is an attempt to sum up all that is to be said and get me moving on, leaving them in peace. 'That's it then so.'

'The Ballroom of Romance' is probably the story for which William Trevor is best known in Ireland. It follows a heartbreaking course similar to 'The Hill Bachelors'. Again there is the lonesome hill dweller, Bridie, on a few 'scant acres' caring for an aged parent. On Saturday Bridie does something for herself, cycling seven miles to the Ballroom of Romance for an evening of socialising and dancing. The dancehall is a plain place, 'miles from anywhere, a lone building by the roadside with treeless boglands all around,' but for Bridie it is both weekly release and glimmer of hope. Bridie wants to fall in love. She is not the only one, many converge on the ballroom each Saturday night. 'People came on bicycles or in old motor-cars, country people like

Bridie from remote hill farms and villages. People who did not often see other people met there, girls and boys, men and women.' The dancehall was just a shed with coloured lights but Trevor understands that the building's real meaning is what people assign to it, the possibility it represents. This is the possibility of love.

The dancehall was not Trevor's invention. It was a real place close to the border. Trevor saw it while passing on a motorcycle in the 1960s, and a story was suggested by the building's sheer size, brashly optimistic given its lonely location, and the hopeful words painted across the front: The Ballroom of Romance. The ballroom is still there now and still has the same name, although this is actually its subtitle. The Rainbow is the hall's proper name. I have arranged to meet Jerry and Michael there, a different Michael from the one I met on the plateau of relics. Unlike some borderlanders these are talkative men, and both are light on their feet, great adverts for ballroom dancing. Both have been regulars here much of their lives. Jerry looks like a cheerful Samuel Beckett. Michael is eighty years of age and fairly skims across the floor as he tells me about the nights there in the 1950s and sixties, when the ballroom was busiest. He has his own grammar around the word dance, he says things like 'I would dance a girl' and 'I was dancing a girl'. They bring me inside. The dance floor is about the size of a tennis court, decked in bright maple. There is a stage at one end. 'All along here was packed with girls,' says Michael, his voice echoing as he glides along the left wall. He points along the opposite wall. 'And over there were the boys. It was all live music, the band would start up a foxtrot, quickstep or waltz.'

'There might be a certain girl that a few fellas had their eye on,' says Jerry, 'but nobody would move!'

'We'd wait, watch,' says Michael.

'But once one fella moved everyone was away—' says Jerry.

'That's it!' says Michael. 'One boy led the way and all would be straight across. And jeez you could be half killed. You could be rammed up against the wall with the gang coming behind you.'

'But this hall wasn't so bad for that,' says Jerry.

'People here were civil,' says Michael. 'But Drumshanbo! There was a dancehall in Drumshanbo with a fierce rough crowd.'

Jerry shakes his head and says, 'I was afraid to go to Drumshanbo.'

'Coalminers went there,' says Michael. 'Big strong boys, they'd burst in and take over.'

'Here we'd a thing called an Excuse Me dance,' says Jerry. 'Michael could be dancing with a girl and I might come along and tap him on the shoulder. He'd have to let the girl go, that's the way it was. But I'd only have gone a few steps with her when—'

'Another lad would tap you,' says Michael. 'You'd keep hearing it on the dance floor, excuse me, excuse me.'

'Did women ever do the tapping?' I ask. 'Cutting in on another woman?'

Michael and Jerry look at each other, thrown by this radical suggestion. 'Maybe if she'd enough drink in her,' says Jerry.

'But there was no alcohol here,' says Michael.

The Rainbow was a wholesome place. The refreshments were fizzy drinks, still called minerals in this area, and biscuits. For one shilling and sixpence you'd get a cup of tea and a sandwich. Here, dancing was the thing. Dancing sober, for pleasure of pairing, for the touch, for the arm around you and, perhaps, as compatibility test. It was dancing with intent. Michael met his wife here, they have been married fifty years and still dance in the Rainbow. There were other dancehalls in the 1950s and sixties, all with equally whimsical names – the Silver Slipper, the Cloudland, the Wonderland and the Drumshanbo's infamous Mayflower – but this one has outlived them all. Why is this, I wonder?

'I'd say it was the personality of John McGivern,' says Jerry.

This was John McGivern's ballroom. It was the only business he ran, it was all he wanted to do. A photograph shows a trim gent with his hair oiled back. He worked for a time in New Jersey and had come home in 1934 with a new sense of showmanship and a business idea. He bought this site, a boggy field full of rushes, and built the first manifestation of the dancehall. With few houses nearby, it might have seemed a foolish location for a business that depended on people gathering, but crossroads are traditional meeting places in Ireland. Middle ground to the rural people they serve, they are close to few but not too far from many. Before McGivern's ballroom there was a custom of dancing at crossroads, people meeting where the neighbourhood roads did and dancing to music provided by a fiddler. Sometimes a dance floor would be put down on the grass, twenty square feet of planks nailed across a framework, boosted here and there where the ground was uneven. I've been able to chart the locations of a couple of these dancing decks. They reveal just how basic architecture can be and still be architecture. The floor was the only essential; the rest was done without. A bare wooden square laid flat marked off a small space and

gave it a special role, creating a destination.

It was surely no coincidence that McGivern built the Rainbow on a crossroads. What he built was not quite so basic, not quite. The first version of the ballroom was made of corrugated steel bolted together, like a military Nissen hut. The floor was the essential element, the superstructure was just there to protect it and allow dancing throughout the year. McGivern knew people would come and he was right, they came from miles around, down off the hills, from across the border. There was no electricity in the hall, men and women danced by the light of oil lamps.

'I don't remember those days,' says Michael, in case I've mistaken him for an old person. 'I didn't start dancing until 1953.'

By then McGivern had bought a little more land and expanded the ballroom. Understanding the importance of appearances, he put up a brickwork facade facing the junction, but behind it remained essentially a hayshed with a deck. For the ballroom's first decades there was a train sta-tion two fields away, the first stop after the Belcoo–Blacklion bridge that Paddy and I examined from the canoe. Some people came by train to dance but the closure of the railway did not stop them. 'At that time you weren't allowed to take a car across the border from eight at night until eight in the morning,' says Michael. 'So they came in specially arranged buses, or walked, or cycled.' Half the clientele came from across the border and kept on coming during the Troubles. They would hoist their bicycles onto their shoulders to walk around the craters. During a dance, scores of bicycles would be stacked against the front of the ballroom. 'It was a world of bicycles out there,' says Michael.

When the railway closed, John McGivern bought up the corrugated sheeting from railway sheds and used them to patch up the ballroom. He also bought a truckload of rails. These were lengths of milled steel, over twenty-five feet long, and he used them to support a new dance floor, laying the deck across them. The rails gave the floor a notable bounce, a feature much commented on and appreciated by the dancers. I like this idea. The railway connection was broken but some sort of fundamental purpose in the rails could not be thwarted. Perhaps that purpose was to connect people. With no more trains to carry, the rails lost their first role as connectors but went straight into another, support-ing this dance floor, supporting the ritualised steps we make in the hunt for love.

McGivern had a sharp business mind but also seemed genuinely dedicated to bringing people together. He might have sprung from the mould of an old Irish character, the matchmaker – men and women who set up meetings between boys and girls, with a view to marriage. Perhaps it was in the United States that McGivern discovered upscaling; the dancehall rolled out a matchmaking service on an industrial scale. During dances McGivern would take to the stage to announce any recent engagements or marriages that his ballroom could claim credit for, over two hundred in the years he ran it. He would also sing a few slow numbers, a part of the night called the Romantic Interlude. Many relationships moved up a notch during the Romantic Interlude. The effect of dimmed lights was achieved by switching off every second bulb.

'John would direct us all to shake hands with our partners before starting,' says Michael, 'that was a kind of first step you could move from. The girl you were dancing might be a stranger but afterwards you might ask her for a mineral.'

'John always sang "Have You Ever Been Lonely?" during the Romantic Interlude,' says Jerry. 'He was a reasonably good singer but with that song he'd go more for drama. He wouldn't sing the words, he'd speak them slowly, giving it force.'

'He'd kinda throw the words down to the people,' says Michael.

'Have . . . You . . . Ever . . . Been . . . Lonely?' says Jerry.

Walls, Ways

The border passes between small lumpy hills. Banks of ferns have dried out and fallen over, turning bronze. Stunted trees poke through blankets of yellow moss. There's a metallic yellow tint to the grass as well, like there's something nasty in the soil. The lawn of an abandoned cottage stands out as it is a vibrant green, a plot where years of laying down manure has continued to pay off after the owners have gone and the house fallen in. A mass rock overlooks the lane, and I climb up to examine it. It is a boulder, probably an erratic, used as an altar in the seventeenth century for Catholic rituals outlawed at the time. Hollies and prickly sowthistles stand around it. I see why this site was chosen for a mass; you could see someone coming from a mile away. I make camp close by and go looking for another landmark, the Black Pig's Dyke.

This is the name attached to about a dozen earthworks dating back to the Iron Age, two thousand and some years ago, several corresponding closely with today's border. They were linear defences, dykes and ditches. The Dorsey is sometimes included among the set. Gathering so many earthworks under one name makes them seem related – this is almost certainly a false impression – but some people like the idea that the builders aspired to a continuous barrier dividing the island in two. They claim the Black Pig's Dyke as a proto-border, evidence that the island's twentieth-century partition has deep foundations.

As with the Dorsey, the dyke's wooden palisades are long gone, we are left with trenches and raised earth. As with the Dorsey, the dyke has had two thousand years to soften, erode or get shovelled apart. At its best the Black Pig's Dyke looks like an overgrown railway embankment. The remnants never offer the thrill of discovery, the moment when the ivy is pulled back or the lid lifted. You don't discover the Black Pig's Dyke, you notice it. Travelling for the Ordnance Survey memoir scheme in 1835, the scholar John O'Donovan was among the first to notice the earthworks, have some inkling of their antiquity and start asking about them. He was first to wonder if they were the remains of some sort of Great Wall of Ireland. But it was a butterfly expert called William Francis de Vismes Kane who actually tried to make the case. In 1909 he attached the label Black Pig's Dyke to every linear earthwork in a wide belt from the Dorsey to the west coast and claimed everything north of it was the ancient kingdom of Ulster, making it bigger than anyone had imagined. Kane was joining the dots, linking up old walls and saying they were one project. A weakness of Kane's theory is illustrated by a map of the earthworks; there are lots of big gaps. It is far more likely that the walls were built by completely different peoples, but Kane ignored this and told the story he wished, and found an audience willing to listen; his theories were published in the years leading up to partition. Kane attempted to fill the distance between earthworks by explaining that the wall-builders had lakes and bogs to use in defence as well, they needed to build only where the natural barriers weren't strong. This is a good point, and the best example is where I am walking this evening. From Lough MacNean it is four miles to the next large lake, Melvin. I will camp by it tomorrow night. Just plugging the gap between the lakes gets you a defended frontier ten miles long.

People living near the earthworks had their own names and their own stories explaining how they got there. In 1957 R. S. Rogers walked the dykes and ditches, looking out for old people and asking them for stories about the earthworks' origins. They were calling them various names, like the Dane's Cast and the Worm Ditch, as well as the Black Pig's Dyke. Rogers heard dozens of versions of the Black Pig story, each beginning in a different way but with the same ending: a black pig thundering across Ireland, making a furrow with its snout. In the townland where I have pitched my tent this evening, he met a seventy-six-year-old man who recounted what Rogers reckoned was the original foundation story, the base the others sprang from. In the story a man notices his son's health is declining. His son says it is because of the daily cruelty of his schoolmaster and his magic book.

The young lad says, 'The master puts us into different shapes, and he makes me a hare and the others hounds and they run after me. And I run at the same fret as a hare every day. And then through the power of this book, he turns us back every evening to our usual selves.' Then the father says to him, 'I'll go to the school tomorrow.' So the father goes to the school and he says to the teacher: 'Is it true that you can do these things?' And he said he could, so he says, 'Change yourself now into a pig.' So the master turned himself into a pig, and the man took the book, and the master was in the form of a pig and he couldn't take it from him and he burned it in the fire. So the pig lost his senses altogether

[201]

when he saw this and he ran through the country tearing up the land as he went. And somewhere in the neighbourhood of Tullaghan he ran into the sea and was drowned.

The 'tearing up' is the creation of the dyke; Tullaghan is where the most western of the works runs up against the Atlantic. Judging by the length and width of the dykes, the father did not just challenge the schoolmaster to become a pig, but a giant pig. It must have been the size of a shipping container to plough up so much soil, but no version of the tale refers to the creature's size. This illustrates something: in these stories scale is incidental, the mark on the land is more like a text than a remnant. The Black Pig's Dyke isn't a prop in the story, it is the story. The storyteller reads the landscape like a book.

*

I walk the yellow hills. According to the Ordnance Survey, there's a section of the Black Pig's Dyke here, between two bungalows, but I can't see anything. A dog leaps from a doorstep to bark at me and a man emerges from around the back. He is tall, beer-bellied and has craggy stained teeth. Both sleeves have been torn from his leather jacket.

'Is there a bit of the Black Pig's Dyke around here?' I ask.

'There's not much to the thing,' he says, and he points into the trees across the road, telling me where I'll find it. The dog keeps barking.

'Sorry about setting your dog off,' I say.

'Her bark's worse than her bite,' he says, 'but you need a dog, what with the times that're in it.'

I plunge into a forest. Mud clings to my boots. I stomp

around a while in the gloom, trying to find ways around bracken and bog pools. Mushrooms grow from trees, looking like small flying saucers that have become wedged in the trunks. I finally identify the dyke where it runs over the brow of a hill. It's a let-down, two ridges that are only a few feet high and a slight depression down the middle. I would have missed it without the man's advice. It continues fifty feet into the undergrowth. Hawthorns grow densely on both sides and it looks as if the dyke, in more recent years, was used as a path – perhaps by deer, farmers driving sheep or the people who lived in a ruined cottage nearby. Raised sides and a trough down the middle: it makes sense that the eroded Black Pig's Dyke fell into this role. Sometime in the last two thousand years the barrier's personality flipped, a wall became a way. In this area the dyke was known as the Little White Lane and the Great Man's Track. The name Black Pig's Dyke too tells the story of a journey, a rampage, not an impediment.

I follow the dyke's route until hawthorns crowd the ground and its impression slips away. I am left standing in a meadow, unsure exactly when I lost the dyke, or when it left me. Swallows flit overhead, I hear the distant thrumming of a hydraulic hammer. This is always the way with the Black Pig's Dyke, no sooner have you found its trail than it vanishes under bracken, not rising again until somewhere beyond the horizon. I feel like a whale-spotter out on the waves, glimpsing an arching back slipping under again. This ought to be enough, but there's the niggling sense of having not quite grasped the thing, of having failed to properly witness it. Similarly, the original purpose of the dykes eludes us. We don't know what scale of feud built them, a single valley or something much wider. The dykes might have been a fashion, built to satisfy a local chieftain's desire for fortifications like his neighbour had. Some archaeologists reckon the construction would have required resources out of all proportion to anything the earthworks could have done to hold sway over a landscape. Perhaps showing you had the power to build a rampart was more important than any tactical use. A dyke showed who was boss. The names of kings who had them built must have stayed in local memory for generations but were eventually forgotten and replaced with the story of a grumpy pig.

*

The next morning the border joins a river. The landscape reverts to green and I walk by several Good Friday Agreement bridges: steel railings, stone cladding, like mini versions of the George Mitchell. But I don't see a car on any of them; it takes time for daily patterns to rediscover old routes. Meanwhile, crows perch on the railings and squawk. The original bridges were dismantled or knocked down in reaction to IRA incursions. Around the time R. S. Rogers was seeking stories of the Black Pig, the IRA began a border campaign, swooping across the line to dynamite or fire upon their targets. The campaign was called Operation Harvest, evoking ideas of acreage and crops, wealth drawn from land. They wanted something like a conventional war, aiming to invade, overrun and claim territory in the traditional manner. Operation Harvest opened with a big statement. One hundred and fifty volunteers hit ten different targets along the border; customs huts, transmitters, police stations and army bases. In an attempt to stop further attacks, road cratering and the systematic destruction of border bridges began, breaking two hundred connections, leaving only sixteen official links between north and south. However, the craters were shallow and farmers filled them in easily. 'They were like ponds really,' recalls a man who grew up here. Even left unfilled, the holes only impeded cars and there were few of them anyway, the borderland was a world of bicycles.

Operation Harvest petered out and the border went quiet again, returned to the fields and farmers, until the Troubles. The IRA had dropped any desire to fight in column formation. Ambushes, hijackings and home invasions were the new methods. Here in 1972, a few hundred feet inside the north, Tommy Fletcher was stopped at his gate by four men wearing stocking masks. Fletcher and his wife were held at gunpoint while his house was searched. They found his rifle: Fletcher was an army reservist. The masked men then took him away, telling his wife they would not harm him, that they were using him to cover their escape back over the border. They did take him to the border but there they shot him more than a dozen times. Tommy's wife saw them then strolling away into the south.

I stop for a few minutes at the bridge the killers used. No cars go by. Sheep are eating grass both sides of the single-lane road, I can hear the cropping action of their stumpy teeth. Low cloud. Dark green fields. Sycamores.

The week Fletcher was killed, the army blocked this bridge and every other border link between Lough MacNean and Lough Melvin. This time they did it properly; you couldn't even get across on a bicycle. The craters were the entire road's width and, when filled with rainwater, deep enough to drown a person. One night a well-known local storyteller fell in a crater, failed to claw his way out and was found dead in the morning.

People shunned the border and communities either side soon lost knowledge of each other, the closest Ireland ever came to a complete north–south divide. But there were always ways across the fields. The killings continued and few perpetrators were ever caught. As with Tommy Fletcher, convenience to the border was a factor in selecting victims. Fermanagh is a roughly rectangular county with the border on three sides, so was dangerous. Many Protestants left the borderland, abandoning businesses and farms, their homes becoming the vacant wrecks I see as I walk the border. I stop to examine them sometimes, pulling aside ivy to peer through windows. At first I did not know why some houses seemed abandoned in a hurry, furniture left behind, wellington boots standing by the fireplace. 'The bark of a dog in the night sets you reaching for your shot-gun,' a Protestant farmer told a journalist in 1980. In one border village a few family dogs died from poisoning; it was immediately feared to have been an IRA move, clearing the dogs away before further killing. The poisoning was later shown to be accidental but not before several families had left. The IRA seemed to come and go as they pleased. There was a sense of getting picked off, of being exposed. To protect Fermanagh's Protestants some politicians called for the county's border with the south to be fenced. The leader of the Unionist Party thought even bigger, calling on Prime Minister Margaret Thatcher to seal the entire border. Whatever it took: walls, mines, razor wire and patrols, seal it end to end. Finally finish the job of the Black Pig's Dyke.

I've seen many different figures claimed to be the border's length, 280 miles is most popular. The British army put it at 303 miles. That last three might inspire confidence;

surely they wouldn't insist on the extra three unless it was right. While stationed on the border, one officer jotted down what it would take to seal the whole length: 303 miles of mesh fencing set along a six-metre-wide ploughed and harrowed strip; a vehicle track along the entire length; a hinterland security fence; 360,000 explosive charges; 165 miles of vehicle hazards, such as ditches and steel spikes; a hundred pillboxes, a hundred concrete observation towers. The defence would also need command posts, bunkers, dogs, dog runs and thousands of arc lights. All of that before the boots on the ground are considered. Doable? Maybe, if the will was there. The will was not there, and the problem was as much ideological as practical. This was a different time, other conflicts and frontiers defined the era. Europe's east and west overrode Ireland's north and south. No British prime minister would build anything comparable to the Berlin Wall. Margaret Thatcher most certainly would not. Killings in the Fermanagh borderland did prompt one visit from Thatcher, a visit that would bring no obvious results. The ring of security around her was more intense than was necessary anywhere else in the United Kingdom. She viewed the border, but from the window of a high-speed helicopter. She was gone in half an hour.

*

Not me, I see the line close up. I don't want to miss a connection for my map. These are crossings that aren't on the Ordnance Survey and may never be – muddy byways roaming across the line, sneaky gates in hedgerows, stiles in border fences, all kinds of unofficial links. The connections aren't necessarily small. I found a set of substantial stepping stones on a river, each stone a one-ton boulder. They must have been there a long time but weren't on standard maps. So I've put them on mine, connection number thirty-eight. Other crossings are just a single plank laid across a border stream, called cross-sticks around here. On the side of Slieve Rushen, I found a slab of concrete laid down as a footbridge with a small brass plaque attached: 'The Fairy Bridge' – number fifty-three on my map. Many of the connections are links between northern and southern fields. Almost all the gates are tubular steel and have a clattering latch. I've found several connections made by children; toys lie scattered near these Saturday engineering projects. They use two breeze-blocks and a log to bridge a border stream, or loosen a plank in a fence to create a swinging door. Children know the shortcuts; they find the quick way to their pal's place or a shady brook. And if the route is not there they will make it, poking a hole in the border. Children are forever testing boundaries.

Today I find a bridge made from two sections of reinforced concrete, strong enough for a tractor and load, number fifty-eight. Then some stepping stones, fifty-nine. The tributary joins a more substantial river; I walk the wooded south bank, wading through ferns and brambles. I have to keep my hands aloft, like a jungle explorer who's lost his machete. I'm tempted to pull away from the border-line a while – I'd like to get free from this choked bank and I doubt there's anything to miss along here. There is nothing on the map and the river is too wide to be easily spanned. But just as I'm thinking of giving myself a break, I discover an intriguing connection. The steel footbridge is solid, both north and south ends resting on concrete bases. The foot-way is rippled so pedestrians won't slip and there are banisters and handrails at comfortable heights. Yet no paths lead to this bridge. It looks like the remnant of an abandoned civilisation. Number sixty is finely engineered but remote and, it seems, no longer used. Who built this? And for what? I've found plenty of uncharted footbridges on the border but this is the first with safety barriers and foundations. It would have taken time to build, and the materials would have been expensive, so surely a profit motive was at work. Perhaps the bridge was built by cattle smugglers, the barriers in place to stop cows falling in the river. The space between the handrails is narrow but with the tap of a stick a cow would squeeze through. But I doubt my own theory; smuggling would only explain a bridge sufficient for the job and this one goes beyond essentials: clean welds; seamless decking; the way the handrails angle down the steps at each end rather than being simply sheared off. Pride went into this bridge.

I walk to the nearest road and approach the nearest

house. I ask a man in the garden about the bridge. He says he doesn't live here, he is just visiting relatives. I think he says this because I am a stranger, asking questions about the border. When he grasps the innocuousness of my enquiry he relaxes, actually he does live here. I'd suspected this all along; you don't wear overalls when visiting relatives. He says the bridge has been there for decades and he doesn't know who built it. 'There used to be a shop across the way,' he says. 'We'd cross the bridge to go shopping the odd time.' This inspires a new theory: a shopkeeper built the bridge to tap the southern market.

From a giant couch in her conservatory, a woman talks to me through her open sliding door. She too mentions the shop and 'visiting friends and the like' but is surprised when I say steel. 'The bridge was wooden,' she says and pauses before adding, 'But then I haven't seen it in years.' She gives me the phone number of the man who owns the land south of the river. I return to the bridge and ring him on my mobile. 'That bridge has been there a long time,' he says. 'I'm not sure who built it. It might be from the sixties.'

'Could it have been for cattle smuggling?' I ask.

'There wasn't any cattle business in our area,' he says. 'And it was always a quiet area, we never saw any Troubles.'

I am struck by this hyperlocalism. Tommy Fletcher was killed close to here; confrontations between soldiers and borderbusters occurred only two miles away; two and a half miles along the border the village of Kiltyclogher saw a gunfight between the IRA and the British army, bullets zinging over the rooftops. What he means is there was no violence on his land or the adjoining land and perhaps a farm or two beyond. I wonder if this is a trait of border-landers, seeing the countryside in terms of small packages.

The border would encourage you to think in a subdivided way, and the violence even more so.

'Did you use the bridge yourself?' I ask.

'I used to go across to school with it,' he says. 'My school was in the north.'

A new theory: a collective of parents got together to build the bridge, a route to school that would keep their kids away from dangerous craters in the roads. This is a pleasing idea, probably too pleasing. I notice my own preference for explanations that contain characters or a hint of drama. The landowner says the bridge might have been built by an official body, like the south's Board of Works. That's rather dull but would explain its professional construction, though why they built it would remain a question.

I'm still unsatisfied but evening is upon me, it's time to move on. Maybe my mistake, the root of my dissatisfaction, is hunting for a single explanation. A family might have built the bridge for smuggling but also so their elderly relative could come across for Sunday dinners. The Board of Works might have built it, but due to pressure from a collective of parents. The archaeology of the recent might have something to teach the archaeology of the distant past: an attempt to categorise a construction by a single use will falter. So it goes with this bridge, so it goes with the Black Pig's Dyke. Anything we build will soon have a life of its own, hosting a thousand small events and journeys. Other life gets involved too; I see fox droppings on the steel footway.

6

27

38

53

miles   1   2   3

km   1   2   3   4   5

N

My direction of travel

Ballyshannon

62

The Battery
18th century

Belleek Pottery
19th century

Magheramenagh Castle
19th century

Donegal

Fermanagh

Leitrim

OB

Garrison

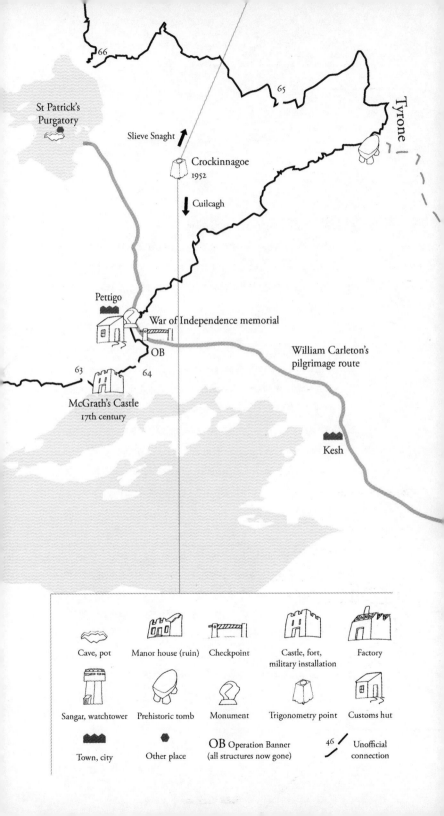

St Patrick's
Purgatory

66

65

Tyrone

Slieve Snaght

Crockinnagoe
1952

Cuilcagh

Pettigo

War of Independence memorial

OB

William Carleton's
pilgrimage route

63

64

McGrath's Castle
17th century

Kesh

Cave, pot   Manor house (ruin)   Checkpoint   Castle, fort,
military installation   Factory

Sangar, watchtower   Prehistoric tomb   Monument   Trigonometry point   Customs hut

Town, city   Other place   OB Operation Banner
(all structures now gone)   46 Unofficial
connection

Rejection, Perfection

The Atlantic is up ahead. The breeze has clarity – pollen-free and freshly landed. Lough Melvin's far end is only a few miles from the sea. With its grey ruffled surface, the lake looks like a fragment of the Atlantic thrown inland. Small waves break on the shore. Cottage gardens run down to the water but there are also patches of open country, headlands covered in gorse. I stop to ask a man if he knows any good camping spots along the lake. He has just mown his lawn and is in no hurry to do anything else. His retirement cottage is a comfortable size and right by the lake, his pansies have come up and his garden wall is freshly whitewashed, with capstones and gate painted the same bright green. Between grins he chats to me over his wall. 'Ah, you're like myself,' he says looking at my gear. 'You like to be off doing your own thing.'

'I guess I do.'

'I don't know about camping around here though,' he says. 'You'd be very exposed.'

'I don't mind that,' I say. 'I'd like to sleep where I can hear the lake.'

'You're like myself,' he says again. 'There's a campsite around in Garrison. Why don't you go there?'

'I'm not going to pay money to sleep in a field,' I say.

The man's grin is firmly in place. 'I don't know about pitching your tent along here,' he says. 'Someone mightn't like it. They might call the police.'

It takes me a moment to realise he is saying he will call the police if I try to camp nearby. I thought we were chatting but actually we were negotiating, and now I've lost. He does not want me to dent his idyll, does not want me to have for free what he has earned.

I'd like to camp directly on the borderline, confound the police by sleeping with my head in the north and feet in the south, but the border runs with a fast wide river, I'd need a raft. So I have to walk some more and check no one is watching before leaving the road, stepping through rushes to the shore. I find a clearing among banks of gorse, pitch my tent and set up my gas stove.

I am now at the border's south-west corner. It doesn't quite reach the ocean, the line angles back, keeping County Donegal attached to the rest of the south by a narrow neck. I won't dare call Donegal a polyp though, it balloons from the neck until it's the biggest county in Ulster, although not part of Northern Ireland. Donegal's links to the north are strong: on both sides of the boundary you can find the same taciturn nature and focus on practicalities; you'll meet the same dominating mammies; you'll hear the same accent, cadence and abrupt full stops. I feel qualified to comment as I grew up here.

In the decade leading to Ireland's partition, there was much debate within Unionism about what size the postulated state should be. Sometimes it was to be all nine counties of the province of Ulster, at other times just the four counties around Belfast. Many warned that the new state should not attempt to claim Donegal. It would become Northern Ireland's Afghanistan; difficult terrain, recalcitrant natives and mountains where rebels could slip away. More difficult to manage maybe, but the new state would have looked tidier on the map with Donegal included. Northern Ireland really would be the north of Ireland then, stretching from coast to coast and crowned with the island's northernmost point. But in the end Donegal was excluded. Unionist leaders were aware that wherever the line was drawn some of their followers would be left on the wrong side. In 1918 a Unionist MP had even won a majority in a Dublin district. The bordering process would leave those voters out in the cold, as well as Donegal's Unionists. They were there, but not in sufficient numbers. Irish independence was inevitable; Unionists had to rescue whom they could and not get sentimental about the rest. One politician put it bluntly: 'In a sinking ship, with life-boats sufficient for only two-thirds of the ship's company, were all to condemn themselves to death because not all could be saved?' That a Belfast MP was prepared to evoke the *Titanic*'s loss this way, only five years after the disaster, indicates how hardheaded the debate had become. It was painful, but Unionists had decided to fight only for six counties by the time negotiations between Britain and Ireland took place in London in 1921.

The north–south question was just one of many thrown up by the emergence of an independent Irish state, but, even so, the Irish delegation's lack of attention to partition during those weeks now appears remarkable. They were more concerned that they might be pressed to swear an oath to the king in a new Dublin parliament. The proposal was to use county boundaries to draw the new international frontier; British negotiators soothed any concerns with the promise of a Boundary Commission, a body that would later examine the north's topography and voting patterns and redraw the border with all that in mind. The Irish delegation hoped this would shrink Northern Ireland to something untenably small. They were putting a lot of faith in the Boundary Commission, a body whose description in the treaty was vague. When the Irish delegation accepted the Boundary Commission, they had accepted a border. The treaty was signed and suddenly there they were, Ireland north and Ireland south. Map publishers were busy. A couple of years later the commission was formed and came up with its recommendations. By not following county boundaries it offered a cleaner line, shortening the border by fifty miles, and transferring 286 square miles to the south and seventy-seven square miles to the north. But the commission had no real power and collapsed before its findings were published. The cabinet's Dominions Secretary concluded that 'the only alternative was to leave the boundary where it was, however unsatisfactory from many points of view'. In Ireland, both north and south, for one reason or another, this was every point of view.

*

On the edge of Donegal I can see, faintly, how comparisons with Afghanistan emerged. There are bleak highlands and blue mountains always in the distance. The population is thin, the soil thinner. The border is elevated now, passing through bogs rarely visited by anything else. For the next five or six days I'll meet fewer fields and green valleys, more heath, silent conifer plantations and big skies. The landscape becomes more demanding, there is no more *pretty*. Cavan/Fermanagh was Constable. Donegal/Tyrone is Rothko. The beauties will be desolate beauties and the ugly will be particularly brutal.

I've encountered flytipping before but here I find lots, beginning with a sack of VHS tapes dumped in a boggy depression, ten feet from a lane, five feet from the line. *The Lost Boys* stands out. Another day the border is marked by a refrigerator, spattered with shotgun pellets and laid lengthways in a ditch. I find rolled-up carpets; years alternating between sodden wet and sunbaked have transformed them into thick crusts, cracking and parting. Elsewhere, I find a record player and two sofas sitting together, the right way up and arranged to recreate the home that rejected them. I come across a washing machine lying on its back, its big circular mouth open to the sky in a fixed howl. How could you leave me like this? All this has been dumped covertly, the drivers glancing in their rearview mirror all the way from the turn-off. High open country makes flytipping easy. After dark headlights warn you someone is approaching minutes before they arrive. Even in daylight, witnesses are as rare as kingfishers up here. What happens on the border stays on the border. For some people dumping junk here is not just a practical solution, it's an almost instinctive urge. The border is a compromised place, so it's where people put the other flawed things in their life. The washing machine that coughs consumptively, the mattress with broken springs, the outdated wardrobe: bring them to the border, the unwanted place that is now the place for the unwanted.

*

People in need of repair end up on the border as well. There are church-run alcohol rehabilitation centres near both ends; I passed one on my third day and will see another on my second last. Both are large single-storey buildings with

lawns and saplings planted in rows. Inside recovering alco-
holics sleep, meditate, eat wholesome meals and partake of
group therapy. An atmosphere of hush descends as I walk
the perimeter fences, the understated buildings projecting
calm. I sense routine and whispered support. I see a gardener encouraging two young men to kneel by a vegetable
patch. They look like city boys, tracksuits, fidgety elbows.
They are unfamiliar with seedlings but begin to plant, taking too much care, using single fingers to dab compost down
around each shoot. They grin at each other, both starting to
enjoy themselves. When the gardener wanders off the two
young men light cigarettes but continue to plant. As they
bend over their work, the smoke gets in their eyes. They
blink and grimace but persevere. That is how I leave them,
knees in the open ground, smoking and planting.

Just past the George Mitchell bridge, I saw a group of log
cabins overlooking the river. Among them was a larger
building, a meeting hall perhaps. A CCTV camera looked
down from a mast. The only route in and out was gated and
locked. There were cars parked among the cabins but I saw
no movement. I took it to be a place of religious retreat, later
learning it was a weight loss camp.

Paddling Lough MacNean, Paddy and I saw a large
institution on the south shore, hidden from the road. It had
sprouted a few extensions but the original building had five
storeys, tall windows and grey pebbledash walls. This is the
look of Ireland's industrial schools, asylums and seminaries.
Nothing is painted and every surface is hard: tiled floors,
concrete yards, glass reinforced with wire mesh. It's as if the
corridors are designed to echo. My primary school was like
this too. The pronounced black drainpipes of the building
by the lake were enough to trigger a chill in me. It began as

a Catholic seminary in 1953. I imagine the priests-to-be hurrying along the halls to morning mass. They start buttoning their cassocks as they exit their dormitory and slip the last button home just in time to bless themselves and enter. In free time they gather around the windows that leak watery light into the corridors. They must talk about the border; every field they can see is in Northern Ireland. Some might come to an accommodation with it, believing a spiritual life is best lived at the periphery. Others might think the border was sent to test them.

The seminary was converted, fairly easily, into a prison. Now about 150 inmates gaze from the windows, contemplating the border and more immediate boundaries. Paddy and I were by the far shore but could see prisoners in the grounds. They were wearing fluorescent orange jumpsuits – to us they were eight bright dots floating in a dull background, like self-propelling specks of life in a petri dish. The prisoners moved towards each other, then came apart. Their movements seemed deliberate but we could not see their meaning. 'Are they gardening?' wondered Paddy. They might have been, or maybe institutional life had trained them to walk in formation. The prisoners moved towards each other, then came apart, came together, came apart. They might have been car thieves, muggers or tax evaders, it's a minimum-security prison. I bet it was harder for the student priests to slip away than it would be for them. In 2012 three prisoners made a spontaneous escape, they had only months to serve but someone left them alone by the perimeter fence and they just couldn't help themselves. Once the trio had dropped outside the fence, they realised they had nowhere to go but they started running anyway. A call went out that three men were 'unlawfully at large near the border'. Police officers from north and south gave chase. Like in a movie the escapees stayed together, not wishing to break up the classic unit of three. They ran back and forth over the fields, drawing a zigzag line into both jurisdictions, making an art project of breaking boundaries, a performance of transgression. The fence was irresistibly climbable, the border irresistibly crossable. Many of us, when standing at an international frontier, even if there's nothing for us over there, will place a foot over the line for a moment, just because . . . The three men were loose for hours but didn't leave the neighbourhood of the prison. They were caught in time for supper.

*

Around the border's western end, hiking towards a village called Belleek, I meet a strange tipping site: a mound the size of a small car made up of tiny white objects, each individual piece intricate. There are many thousands but they hit me as one impression: a mass of white against the dark wet grass. It's like a coral reef, fragile with a surface detail that I know perforates the whole mound. There are cups and broken side plates but most of the objects are short bars, hollow blocks and star-shaped spacers. I take them to be the pieces used to stack crockery for loading in a kiln, sometimes leaving tiny dents in the undersides of dishes. Each piece is of the same material; china clay. Momentarily, I imagine the china was not dumped here but bubbled up from under the ground, rising from a hidden reservoir of white geometric shapes. I dig a few inches into the mound. Unglazed, each object is bony and rough to the touch.

The process is not so immediate as in my daydream but

ceramics are drawn from this soil. It was John Caldwell Bloomfield who first discovered the land's potential when he inherited it in 1849. Still in his twenties, he came here looking for a life and livelihood. Almost as soon as Bloomfield – chubby, muttonchops, bowler hat – stepped off the coach he noticed the cottages were coated in a bright lime wash, glittering with flecks of a glassy mineral. He had the land surveyed and found fine kaolin and feldspar, the ingredients of china. Other elements were in place: enough people to create a staff and a river swift enough to power a waterwheel. He found investors with the capital he needed. He lobbied for a railway link to Belleek, a line to haul coal in and pottery out. He travelled to England and poached skilled potters from other factories. By 1857 his porcelain was in production. For any entrepreneur the biggest lesson here is to react to what you find instead of riding in with a preformed plan. Had Bloomfield found slate, he would have gone into roofing materials. Had the clay been heavier, he might have made bricks, like the Earl of Enniskillen was doing twenty miles away. But he found the makings of china, so china he would make. In retrospect, it seems the soil, the river and the people of Belleek were all waiting for Bloomfield and the synthesis he would bring. He wanted Belleek china to be among the world's finest, aimed for upper-class parlours and aspirant tables. Centrepieces, din-ing services, figurines and porcelain baskets were produced, each taking hours of fine finger work. After firing, every piece was carefully examined before being allowed to leave the factory; nothing was sold unless flawless. This dedica-tion to perfection continued after Bloomfield's death. Although dips in the market would force Belleek Pottery to make tiles or telephone insulators for a year or two, the ambition for fine porcelain always resurfaced. During the Second World War coal rationing forced Belleek into the production of earthenware, a crude material that didn't need such high temperatures to bake. Even then the potters learned the location of hotspots in the kilns, areas where the chance of convection produced temperatures high enough for fine china. They would craft elegant porcelain baskets and fire them among the bedpans and stewpots.

I walk across the border bridge to Belleek Pottery. The factory has a massive stone facade protecting kilns, turning wheels and sharp-eyed workers. China goods are still made here and there are still no Belleek seconds, anything with a flaw doesn't get beyond the gate. A tour bus arrives and I mingle with the group, retirees making gentle banter with each other. We enter the showroom on the ground floor. The tour group cluck at the work and grumble at the prices as they move around displays of tea sets, dishes and candle-holders. Background music is provided, elevator versions of 'The Rose of Tralee' and 'Danny Boy' lull us into a Hibernian trance until we desire nothing more than a delicate teacup decorated with pale green shamrocks. I pick one up, it has a buttery texture. I look at the cup's underside. Belleek's mark is a triptych of traditional Irish symbols, a wolfhound, a harp and a monastic round tower. Belleek pottery is still the pride of Ulster mantelpieces but critics have been hard on it, one writing that it is 'cloyingly glutinous in texture, senti-mental in design, fussy in detail, anaemic in its colouring, generally of a uselessness unparalleled in the annals of world pottery'.

We had one piece of Belleek china in our house when I was a child. It was a wedding present to my parents, a vase with a rippled surface. It was not displayed; it stayed in its box at the back of a wardrobe. My mother would say it was 'good', meaning it was special, too fine to be risked in the everyday. Other families had 'good' cutlery or even a 'good' room that children weren't allowed in. We just had this vase. My mother was protecting it from us but also from the mundane; it was to be kept rarefied, even looking at it too much could reduce it. Its box was an eight-inch cube of thick card with indented gold lettering. Inside, nestled in a silk holder, was the pearly globule. The lip was waved, you could run your finger around it to experience a hard undulating smoothness. It was like something that had spent a long time in the ocean. My mother let me take it out and hold it. 'They only sell Belleek if it's come out perfect,' she told me – I remember it now as a whisper.

I leave the tour group. I've been given directions to a spot in the car park, under a speed bump. The border river is before me and the china workshops a few steps behind me. Under here was another dumping ground, a landfill eventually covered over by the car park. For one hundred years, inside the nearest doors, porcelain inspectors worked with a magnifying glass and a hammer. Every piece of china the factory produced passed through their hands. By tradition, when they saw a fault, they would say, 'That's one for Ernie.' They smashed the object with the hammer and let the pieces fall into a wheelbarrow. When the wheelbarrow was full, the broken pieces were tipped into the pit by the river. Beneath where I stand is a mass of shattered porcelain, a century of flawed works. I imagine it, china dust and jagged shards, a jumble of teacup handles, shamrocks and cracked cherubs. It's all packed tight under the tarmac, any voids in the white conglomeration flooded with the border's groundwater.

Lost, Found

I don't know where I am. I can't find the border. The GPS wavers, won't commit, the satellites must be facing elsewhere. Conifers, silent and self-contained, make me feel like an idiot. I approach a bungalow, hoping for directions. A middle-aged man is sitting on his front step, radio playing through the open door. He greets me with a laugh. 'If you're here,' he says, 'you must be lost.'

He shows me the border and I follow it up across a moor. In the distance fir trees serrate the horizon. Under them I can see alternating dark and light stripes, the black trenches left by turf cutters and rows of bulging white sacks. Nearer are a few lakes and holly trees, their trunks curved by a decade of gusts. I pass where a digger has scraped away the peaty surface, exposing brown stones and leaving white scars across their crowns. A portacabin has collapsed into a heap of chipboard, the rain wearing down any jagged points and slowly melting the building into a single mound of pulp. *Desolate*: a description of both a place and a state of mind. I might be the first person to walk this way in weeks but this does not make it an adventure, I just feel I'm making a mistake. I don't mean I've misread the map, it takes a deeper kind of failure to end up on this barren bog – cold, unsure and far from society. I must have gone wrong repeatedly, compounding many errors to come to this.

The fence I am following ends and for the first time on

[227]

land the border is not attached to anything, it is invisible. I recall the words of a comedian wondering what will happen if Northern Ireland leaves the European Union. 'We're going to need the border again,' he wrote, 'if anyone can remember where we left it.' At first the border was charted only hazily across this highland but digital technology has now pinned it down, the line has been 'striped'. It cannot be seen but is here as a set of vectors, straight as laser beams, shooting between the only features, boggy rises and cold lakes.

*

After a couple of miles I descend again to fields and I see a mobile library parked near a bungalow. Too big for the lane, its side pressing into the hawthorns. The librarian is just about to leave when I happen by and we get talking. Ken has a long grey beard; he could be taken for a biker or professor of mathematics. He invites me to ride with him for a while. I buckle myself into the passenger seat – it's high, like a throne. 'I bring the library to people across the border sometimes,' Ken tells me as he starts the engine. 'But not today.' He turns the library's flat face around, pointing the behemoth back into Northern Ireland. It's a box on wheels. Branches slap the roof as we swing gracelessly around bends. We call to Ken's regulars, hill dwellers with particular interests – Tudor history, Cathy Kelly, LA noir. If the theme or author is right, then the borderlanders accept books based on titles alone, anything is fine as long as they haven't read it before. They do not flick through them or hover a while to read a random page. I feel like I've tagged along with a fuel supplier, distributing home heating oil or coal. The books are treated as consumables. Dimensions are a factor in the reader's selection too, thickness specifically. Borderlanders like big books, the evenings are long.

We park in a primary-school playground. The youngsters are released for ten minutes whenever the mobile library calls. As well as his beard, Ken has an English accent and the habit of looking out over the top of his glasses. It must be like a visit from Dumbledore. Kids tumble out of the school and run to us. Ken revolves his driver's seat and is instantly at his librarian's desk. I'm his assistant.

'What do you want to find out about?' I ask an eight-year-old boy. I kneel on the ground to be on the same level as the fact books and the boy is looking down on me.

'Racing cars.' He is unsmiling, examining me, trying to ascertain if I'm any use to him. I can imagine his father, at a cattle mart perhaps, exactly the same posture and manner rendered on a larger scale. I finger my way through the hardbacks. There are none about racing cars. 'How about space ships?'

'Racing cars.'

I look again. 'Steam trains?'

'Racing cars.'

'Tanks?'

He eyes me like I've tried to sell him a mastitic cow. 'Racing cars.'

The last call Ken and I make is to a tiny hamlet. A stiff breeze carries the smell of manure from surrounding fields. There is nothing here but half a dozen bungalows, a bus shelter and a phone box where you could call for help. A man aged about nineteen or twenty emerges from a house, steps aboard the library and says hello to Ken. They obviously chat whenever the library stops here. I think the young man is interested in Ken because he is an outsider and sees Ken as an outsider too. In an area where it seems a requirement for young people to wear tracksuits, he is dressed in black jeans and a black pullover. His eyes drift, he does not seem as firmly on the ground as most borderlanders, even the children project greater solidity. Ken asks his visitor questions in a probing way. Has he applied for this course or that, what are his plans? Ken is not satisfied with the answers. 'Look at this fellow,' he says, indicating me. 'He's travelling the border from end to end.'

The young man glances in my direction but does not engage with me. It's Ken he wants to talk to, my presence is ruining his few minutes with him. He mumbles about a book he is reading. Later in my notebook I write 'makes obscure references'. Too obscure for me to note it seems. I do not capture a single thing he says. All I remember are vague, open-ended sentences, each drifting away before finding definition. I sense a quiver of frustration from Ken.

'You're making a map, aren't you?' Ken says to me.

'I am, of the things I find along the way, the points that make the borderline.'

'It's a project, isn't it?' says Ken, turning back to his visitor. 'You could do something like that, couldn't you?'

His visitor is going through an aimless phase and Ken is exasperated with him. However, it is not unusual for someone his age. I've been there, but now I am walking the border and I suppose I seem like a man of commitment. Suddenly I realise that Ken has brought me with him specifically so this young man will meet me; so I can be a role model. I am not a natural role model. 'You just keep putting one foot in front of the other,' I tell him.

Lost, Found

*

Ken drops me near where he picked me up, on the border approach to Pettigo. 'Would have been better off in the north,' is Ken's assessment of the village. I walk on the trail left when the railway track was lifted. The station platforms remain, looking at each other across a strip of moss and rushes. For a century this village was the traditional last stop for pilgrims on their way to the Catholic retreat at Lough Derg, a few miles away. The pilgrimage involved fasting and vigils, so this was where they enjoyed a night on a soft bed and their last pork stew for three days. In 1813, many years before *The Black Baronet*, William Carleton came through here as a pilgrim. He found a snug little town, with crowded lodging houses and streets busy yet quiet, full with a kind of solemn bustle. Lough Derg is still a pilgrimage site but few pilgrims stop in this village any more. The pavements are empty and many buildings vacant. Across the border from Pettigo are farms and other villages but on this side the road rises to cross a marshy, wind-whipped plateau. Rhododendrons thrive in the acidic soil but there are few houses. The border cut Pettigo from the north's people and businesses, leaving it alone with this unpopulated expanse. I go into the village shop. There are many gaps on shelves. The chocolate bars are kept behind the counter, which is so old-fashioned as to be almost picturesque. I want milk but all they have is full fat in two-litre jugs. This is too much of everything.

'Are you on the pilgrimage?' the shopkeeper asks.

'Just one of my own,' I say.

'I wish you all the best with it,' she says.

I set off again. I want to camp by Lough Derg tonight;

[231]

I'm not going to fast or keep vigil but I would like to soak my feet in the water. On the edge of the village is a garage with two plain pumps. Beyond the range of brands and conglomerates, it doesn't have a name. A man is filling his tractor with diesel. I ask him if he knows any good places to camp around Lough Derg. We can't see it, but he looks in the direction of the lake, thinking. He thinks some more. He must be doing a circuit of the lake in his mind. The tractor's tank seems bottomless, the diesel continues to pour and slosh. Eventually he looks back at me. 'No,' he says.

Later, emerging from a conifer plantation, I see Lough Derg for the first time: three and a half square miles of grey water in an amphitheatre of fir-planted hills. The border doesn't quite touch the lake, it comes to within a fallen tree's length of the shore before swinging back into the plantation. I pick my way to the waterside. Out on the lake is what I think is the border's most astonishing construction, an octagonal basilica that can hold a thousand people: angular, monumental, capped with a copper roof and crucifix one hundred feet above the water. Other buildings crowd around the basilica, each substantial in themselves, four-storey blocks with slate roofs. There is an island underneath them but I can't see it from where I'm standing, just the grey citadel, walls plunging straight into the water. In the sixth century there were no buildings on the island, but there was a cave where the basilica now stands. If you'd come here then, canoed to the island and looked into that cave, you might have found a monk in it, stiff with hunger and hours of prayer. You would have needed to be careful what you said. He might have taken you as an emissary from God.

The island was shaped like a figure of eight, just a couple

of minutes' walk from top to bottom. The monk would have paddled over from a nearby monastery, now vanished. The word of Christ had reached the edge of Europe and with it came the example of men like St Anthony, who had passed decades of isolation in the desert to get close to God. This was Christian monasticism; to achieve union with God you had to withdraw, find a challenging outpost and call it home. Life by Lough Derg was frugal: pray, work, pray, work, pray, sleep. Toiling summers, brutal winters. Monks who wanted harsher penance went alone to the island cave and spent days reciting long litanies, kneeling on the rocky floor, arms extended, until they collapsed in agony/ecstasy. Self-mortification seeped into the rocks, all that lay ahead would be built on it. The cave became associated with purgatory, the place where you cold-sweated your sins after death, achieving the holiness needed to enter the joy of heaven. Admittedly, I can see a border in many things but I can see a border in this; purgatory is after death but before afterlife. It is the intermediary place, like the border checkpoints where my father and I waited, parked between blast walls, to be waved on.

The cave became known as St Patrick's Purgatory. It was not just some metaphor for the post-life experience; by the thirteenth century Lough Derg was believed to be the mouth of the real place. The remote location helped make this seem credible. Purgatory was under a cave, on an island, on a lake, on a bigger island, in the sea at the western rim of the world.

The *Sancti Patricii purgatorium* helped make Lough Derg famous. It was a description of a journey into the cave, written by a monk who signed off only as 'H'. He composed the work around the year 1200 and it was reproduced and translated many times; there are still about 150 manuscripts in existence, an unusually high number, suggesting that an unusually high quantity of copies were made. In the story, a sinner named Owein lowers himself into the cave and journeys into purgatory. He sees men and women going through all sorts of tortures, getting nailed to the ground, dipped in molten metal, hung from hooks, turned on spits. Owein is assaulted by demons who taunt him and attempt to set him alight but he escapes by invoking the name of Jesus. Imaginative grotesqueries and differently themed areas, all in interconnecting worlds – it is easy to see how the *Sancti Patricii purgatorium* influenced Dante. Owein glimpses the gates of heaven before going back the way he came, re-emerging on the island with his sins purged.

As the island's fame increased, a chapel was built around the cave, with a locked gate. You needed permission from the monastery to enter. Many pilgrims came and eyewitness reports from purgatory kept circulating. The monk care-takers forced pilgrims to fast many days before descending into the cave, so witnesses may have been starved into delu-sional states. Or they had come a thousand miles and weren't going to tell everyone back home all they'd done was sit in a dank cave in Donegal. But towards the end of the fifteenth century, complaints were lodged with the pope – Lough Derg's purgatory was just a mossy hole, a money-spinner for the monks. The pope condemned it and the cave was filled in. Yet pilgrims kept coming to the island. In 1632, the anti-Catholic zeal of a local Lord Justice saw everything else on the island erased and the monks driven away, but even then, pilgrims kept coming. Rituals and prayer cycles devel-oped, rocks were arranged into formations that soon became sacred. The faithful weren't seeing purgatory but some need was being satisfied. Cottages were built on the island, places for pilgrims to sleep between bouts of prayer. Assembly at Lough Derg was criminalised by the Penal Laws, but the pilgrims kept coming. Technically, it was still illegal to gather at St Patrick's Purgatory when William Carleton made his pilgrimage in 1813.

He walked over twenty miles to get to Lough Derg. Blisters rose on his feet so he took off his shoes, stowing one in a pocket and the other under his hat. Carleton gives us a picture of himself on the road, a 'tall, gaunt, gawkish young man, dressed in a good suit of black cloth, with shirt and cravat like snow, striding solemnly along, without shoe or stocking'. Carleton was nineteen years old, a devout Catholic, student of Latin and candidate for the priesthood. His manner of dress meant he was sometimes mistaken for a priest already, an error he did not always correct. Where the road rose Carleton saw Lough Derg and its famed island for the first time, 'with two or three slated houses on it, naked, and unplastered, as desolate-looking almost as the mountains. A little range of exceeding low hovels, which a dwarf could scarcely enter without stooping, appeared to the left; and the eye could rest on nothing more, except a living mass of people crawling about.'

It's already a let-down, and on the island he will have coins weaselled from him by other pilgrims and witness a priest's officious cruelty. It will be the beginning of the end of his Catholic faith. Carleton will forget the priesthood and convert to Protestantism. Recalling his pilgrimage, he refers to his younger self's commitment as fanatical, but under-stands the emotions that moved him. The island on the lake was a portal between here and the world beyond, a link to God's realm. 'Such then were my feelings, when all the faculties which exist in the mind were aroused and concentrated upon one object. In such a case, the pilgrim stands, as it were, between life and death.'

I sit in the flap of my tent and unlace my boots. I can see tiny figures on the island, pilgrims milling around the dock and on the lawn beyond. They are praying but I can hear nothing from here. Some move in circles, others in lines.

Evening draws in and midges rise around my tent, hatched in moss and mires. Hundreds come for me, wanting my blood, and their bites are maddening. I retreat and zip up the tent's insect net. The midges are stopped by the fine mesh. I watch them feel their way up and down, a single-synapse frustration firing in their tiny brains. Midges fill the air outside, black dots against the dull sky, perhaps one to every cubic foot in a band that extends high above the tree-tops. It's hard to tell if they're roving much, it might be an optical illusion but it looks as if each nips back and forth in

an area the size of a shoebox. Nothing with skin could move among them and not be driven crazy. Across the lake the pilgrims seem unaffected, maybe there is a breeze where they are, but I'm stuck in my tent for a couple of hours. Lough Derg has outsmarted me, sent a little purgatory my way.

At least I've positioned my tent for a view of the island. The buildings and basilica all arrived in successive redevelopments but do not look like that; it's easier to imagine they all appeared at once, lowered from the heavens. The basilica seems to sit directly on the water, giving it a supernatural quality; 123 pillars were driven into the lakebed to support it. The lake's harsh quality, what attracted the monks in the first place, has been dominated and subdued. The original island has vanished under walls, roofs, lawns and a tendency towards control and formalisation. Perhaps the naked landscape was too pagan, it needed to be tamed. The original cave is long gone, buried with the foundations and plumbing. But the pilgrims keep coming, there is still something to be found here. On the island – tired, hungry but full of prayer – you might glimpse the other side. I watch the faithful performing prayer stations. Some will have been awake for twenty-four hours, most will have not eaten today but for a slice of dry bread or an oatcake, all will be barefoot. They are circling sacred stones, kneeling, circling again, walking in patterns established over the centuries.

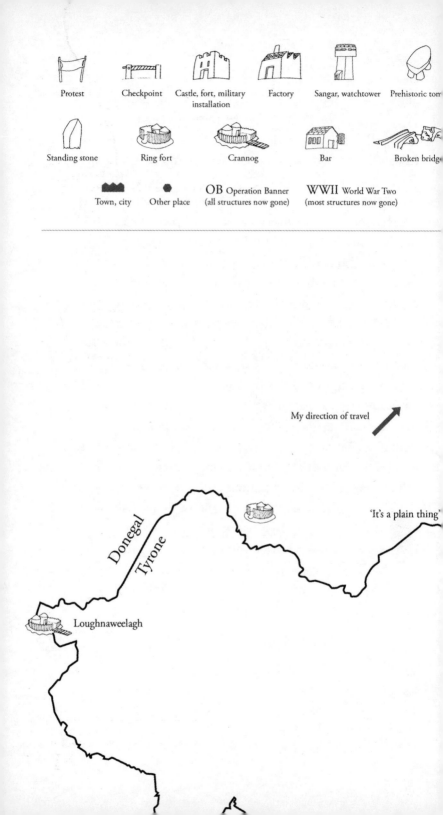

Protest

Checkpoint

Castle, fort, military installation

Factory

Sangar, watchtower

Prehistoric tomb

Standing stone

Ring fort

Crannog

Bar

Broken bridge

Town, city

Other place

OB Operation Banner (all structures now gone)

WWII World War Two (most structures now gone)

My direction of travel

Donegal

Tyrone

'It's a plain thing'

Loughnaweelagh

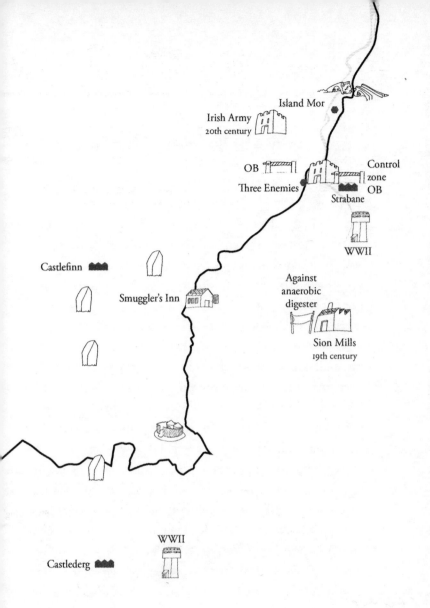

Island Mor

Irish Army
20th century

OB

Three Enemies

Control
zone
OB

Strabane

WWII

Castlefinn

Smuggler's Inn

Against
anaerobic
digester

Sion Mills
19th century

Castlederg

WWII

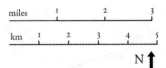

miles   1   2   3

km   1   2   3   4   5

N

Forgetting, Remembering

Beyond Lough Derg stretches a tree plantation twelve miles square. Most are the conical Sitka spruce, a hardy species able for heavy rain and poor soil. Spines along its fingers are upright and little more flexible than teeth on a plastic comb. Plantations are put on hilly terrain and highlands, marginal zones, places with low land value, so there are lots of plantations on the border. I've passed them to my north, then to my south and now here, on both sides at the same time. The border travels in a ditch, running below clashing branches. I follow from close by on a service track; the going is easy but it will still take a day to cross the plantation. The air is warm and still. There is the smell of dry wood and sap. The trees roll by like a picture on a cylinder, the same ones coming around again and again. I'm bored. I run out of water. Just as the bottlebrush fingers of the Sitka spruce repulse birds, my attention can find no perch here; it's an impervious landscape. I miss *desolate*. I didn't know how good I had it when things were desolate, wind-blasted and marsh-bound but able to see for miles, landmarks ahead giving me something to aim for. Here trees crowd my view. The closest thing to a landmark is a black rubbish sack in a ditch, and it is only ever minutes away. I see an irregularity in shadows between trees and go to investigate, finding rocks stacked in a line, a thick crust of pine needles along the top. It is a section of dry-stone wall, a reminder of the farms once here – potato crops, pigsties and single-room cabins where oil lamps burned at night. Around the table the talk would have been of one-way tickets to Glasgow or New York.

Some border plantations are semi-wild, brambles growing around the tree trunks, but not this one. Even if enough light reached the ground, years of fallen pine needles have smothered it, a thick blanket that keeps all other life down. I don't see a blackberry all morning. The track is silent, not even a birdcall. As surely as any port or coal pit, this landscape has been industrialised. It is an enormous factory producing floorboards and paper.

I get a break from the monotony when the land rises under me and I see light between trees. The border escapes the plantation for half a mile, climbing a trickle of water up into open bogland. I leap from one side of the stream to the other, seeking the easiest way, but my boots are soon claggy, sucking mud every time I raise them. The stream leads to a small lake. It has no shore, the bogland just ends at a rim and a ten-inch drop to the water. I drink palmfuls of lake water, though I won't recommend it. Compared to plantations, the bogs are saturated with life. I sit and watch a family of dragonflies zip about the lake surface, little blue lightning bolts. My arms are soon host to tiny crawling gnats, nipping at me, harvesting nutrients. It won't take long for sphagnum tendrils to begin wrapping around my ankles. Ireland's bogs also preserve life gone by. An abandoned cottage has been sitting here for a century – no roof but four walls, potato drills faintly visible as parallel ripples in the land. A small hump sits out of the lake in front of me, marking a ninety-degree turn in the border. It is a crannog, a human-made island, homestead to a medieval family. Once it would have had a hut on it and a palisade wall around the edge. It is at least a thousand years old.

To the poet Seamus Heaney, bogs were Ireland's memory. In 'Bogland' he represented the moist depths as an archive and store.

> Butter sunk under
> More than a hundred years
> Was recovered salty and white.

Peat's preservative ability often astounds. In a very real way the bog records. Butter, shoes, spear shafts, wooden cutlery, logboats, leather shields and the Dorsey palisades are just a few things held in boglands for up to twenty centuries or more. It may be thanks to a lack of oxygen, low temperatures and high levels of acidity, but Heaney's poem is not concerned with chemistry. In it the bog preserves because it is forever wet and soft, never moving on to another phase. It is outside of time, so whatever sinks into it becomes held outside of time too.

> Melting and opening underfoot,
> Missing its last definition
> By millions of years.

The bog doesn't dry out, it is never *done*. And it is a deep facility, 'Bogland' concludes: 'The wet centre is bottomless.'

If boglands are the border's memory, then spruce plantations are its forgetting. Farms, paths, tombs, mass rocks and much else will have vanished under rows of trees. Like a computer's memory, the land has been blanked and reformatted. All that was here has been wiped away.

Yet, to my surprise, as I leave the plantation, a memory of

my own appears. I suppose blanking the land also readies it for new information, new memories. Nobody lives here any more but there are visitors; at least one border walker, fly-tippers, Christmas tree poachers and others on clandestine business, here to take advantage of the plantation's ability to conceal. It is the red of the dirt track that brings back a bit of personal history that I haven't thought of in years. This might be the exact spot it happened, although these are not the same trees. The trees from that day are now supporting someone's plasterboard wall, and there have been at least two replantings since. It is thirty years since my father brought me here.

'Are you on for a spin?' he would have asked me. I was always happy to go, I liked having him to myself. The trips were called *spins* as if they were jollies but this was never the case, he was always going to see someone about something: a minor deal, an exchange, buying, selling – trying to piece together next month's mortgage repayment, or last month's. I was a chirpy youngster, good company for a man with a lot on his mind. I would talk all the way. He would be think-ing, driving was a kind of pacing for him, sometimes his lips would move soundlessly. Our destinations were workshops, scrap yards, prefab offices with taped-up windows. The men we met there were cheery. They knew the best way to talk to a young boy was to pretend to talk to him like an adult, and give him fifty pence. I felt grown-up just being there. I knew how to wait for my father's business to get done, how to sit on a chair and not be a nuisance. I remem-ber calendars illustrated with naked women pinned up above workbenches. I remember mince pies eaten straight from the packet. I remember a man with a missing hand, using the stump to hold a stack of ten-pound notes against his chest. Sometimes our spin was to find a replacement car. We had a succession of unreliable cars in my childhood, none lasting more than a year. This was the 1980s but the cars were from the seventies and in seventies colours: brown, orange and curious semi-matt silvers and bronzes no longer seen. We went through a lot of Ford Escorts, their doors failing one by one until the entire family had to get in through the only one that worked. The spin I recall now was the last outing of a brown Escort. My father had lined up a replacement but the exchange was unique, we weren't going to meet anybody.

I don't remember crossing the border this particular time but it was always the same: past the customs hut, over the frontier then stopped by the army a few hundred feet inside Northern Ireland. My father put the car in neutral and put himself in neutral too, gazing ahead silently until we were through. There was the sense of being furniture in somebody else's workplace. Over the car roof, soldiers talked about the things they would have talked about had we not been there. Inside Northern Ireland we took a turn-off, then another. Roads started as minor then became unsurfaced tracks, leading up into the plantation. My father would have cast the whole thing as an adventure, he always did that. 'Watch out now,' he liked to say, peering right and left. 'This is bandit country.' I doubt I asked where we were going, I don't think I ever did. He stopped the car. We got out and walked along the muddy track, I remember the dirt's redness. A Volkswagen Polo was parked up ahead. There was something eerie about the car, sitting there alone before a curtain of trees. The disconcerting feel of the moment is why I remember it with such clarity. My father got in the driver's seat and I got in beside him. I can't remember if the key was hidden somewhere or if he brought it, but he had it in his hand now. We drove off, leaving the Escort behind, never to be seen again.

All this was to get a cheaper car. A northern car could save you hundreds of pounds, but not if you had to pay import duty. Next we visited a back-road garage where a young man in overalls pressed out a set of southern number plates, I remember the *chunk chunk* as he operated the machine with its long handle. With new plates fitted we drove back towards home. My father probably didn't take the long detour necessary to cross the border at a different place; he was cocky like that. He would have enjoyed pulling in at the customs hut. The official would have looked in the boot, found it empty and been satisfied; no smuggling here.

My father died a few years later so I can't ask him about that day or anything else. I can't ask him what he thought of the border but I suspect to him it was just another hard edge in a world of hard edges, no better or worse than most. Impersonal and unavoidable, it was like mortgage interest rates, Atlantic storms, cancer. The border had beaten him by being there before he was born but he claimed some vitality for himself by outsmarting it in small ways. One man wanted to sell a car, another wanted to buy it, there was a deal to be done and technocrats weren't going to stop them. The Volkswagen Polo was our new transportation. It had fake leather seats and a small sporty steering wheel. 'It's going great,' my father would insist during spins, leaning into the wheel, willing us up a hill. It lasted about a year.

*

Dawn. From inside my tent I listen to the cries of sheep. A lamb's bleat sounds like an objection in the House of Commons. Another cry sounds like that of an older sheep, throaty, panicked, like a grandmother might produce when reaching for her personal alarm. There is also a drawn-out, boorish call that repeats again and again, like a man heckling football players from the couch in his living room. Then I hear a new sound, a distinctive knocking, coming from close by. It is a flat, hollow *tunk*. I remember the gorse bushes near my tent. *Tunk, tunk*. I think of their branches, gnarled and ribbed, like old cracked hosepipes. Two branches could be knocking together in the breeze but that would not explain the hollowness of the sound, the regularity. I slide out of my tent. A feral goat looks up from among the gorse. He has a long brown coat and curved horns. He projects a sharper, smarter impression than a sheep. The goat seems to have *character*, looking at me steadily, letting me know this is his patch. Then he lowers his head to tear at the grass under the bushes, his horns striking a branch as he does so.

I'd like muesli and a croissant, but only have bread, cheese and sardines. Prepared in the same pot, my tea tastes of last night's beans. I am on bare open country. From here I can see large bales of silage fermenting in black plastic wraps and rivers that are clear and cold, they could be glacial runoff. Round rocks sit out of the grey water. There is no distinct riverbank environment; heath suddenly gives way to the flowing channel, reverting sharply to heath again on the other side. The fields aren't really fields, they are wide expanses cut only rarely with a barbed-wire fence. A lane crosses the border. A speed limit sign has taken a blast from a shotgun, the '80' spattered with dents. A rowan tree's

red berries are the strongest points of colour in the landscape. Rowans are the only trees I can see although once this
area was a forest of oak and hazel – we know this because
the bog has preserved their stumps and roots.

As I walk, I scan the ground for remains; this area used
to be scattered with large lumps of bog oak but now the biggest pieces have been taken away, people like to make ornaments from them. I find a few shards jutting from the turf,
ossified wood, hard as rock and black as night. They have a
coarse texture, especially around the swirling knots. It is
possible the shards I hold were alive when the first Irelanders
arrived about ten thousand years ago, a time now known as
the Middle Stone Age, making Ireland one of the last lands
in Europe to be settled. The new arrivals were faced with
screen after screen of trees. Preserved trunks tell us they
could be massive, far bigger than trees growing in Ireland
today. To move inland, people probably stuck to rivers,
dense woods crowding them from both sides. They made
few marks and have left little trace, just fire pits with frag-
ments of fish bones and stone flakes chipped into spearheads. They foraged, hunted and fished, always in the
shadow of trees. They either did not have the ambition or
lacked the tools to clear land, although the endless forest
must have held anxiety for them. I imagine a hunter pushing into the woods. He treads lightly, listening for a wood
pigeon's coo or wild pig's snort; both creatures are his prey.
His dog sniffs around roots but finds nothing. Bad luck
forces the hunter further and further into the forest, perhaps a day's walk from his family. I wonder if he ever
encountered another hunter, an unknown one, roaming
from another direction. It is possible: although Ireland's
population was only in the hundreds or low thousands, relic

finds tend to be focused in the north. The two hunters might stand still, observing each other, both faces full of apprehension. Then they pull back, no sounds exchanged, and move off in opposite directions.

The Middle Stone Age gave way to the New Stone Age, meaning farming and social organisation. Hunter-gathers started to settle down. Now they had axes in their hands and land clearance began. When a clearing has been cut, something profound has happened: the land has been worked, it has been invested in, and a sense of possession begins to take shape. Other advances followed: domestication of animals, sowing crops and building permanent structures. All this meant committing to specific areas, a process that transforms land into territory. Territory needs markers, and the most elemental markers were standing stones.

I've been visiting standing stones since the beginning, there are many close to the border. They are oblong boulders or slabs that have been stood on end. Some are small enough to sit on, others tower above your head. The question of when a particular stone was set standing is always debatable. They shrug off the archaeologists, there is nothing to excavate. Most aren't scored or chiselled, they offer no clue to their origins other than the massive clue of themselves. Some standing stones are as recent as the nineteenth century, set up by farmers as scratching posts for cattle. Others are probably the most ancient marks in Ireland, standing for six thousand years. It is hard to know which is which, but among them are the longest memories on the border. One of the most impressive standing stones is back at the Dorsey, a wedge-shaped boulder standing over six feet tall. It is called the Watching Stone or the White Stone

– lore says it used to be painted white, guiding travellers to Ulster's doorway. I've heard that the tradition of white-washing the stone was maintained into the twentieth century, the job redone every spring.

The border's standing stones are marked on the 1:50 scale Ordnance Survey maps I carry, so I always know where to look. A hunt sent me into a border forest back in Armagh where I found not just one but a whole set of standing stones, the biggest four feet tall. I was suspicious of these stones though, there were too many of them, too close together. Later I discovered the 1837 Ordnance Survey did not record them so this was a fresher arrangement, perhaps set up by the landlord, Lord Clermont, later in the nine-teenth century to go along with the pretty grottoes and bridges he built elsewhere in the forest. But even those standing stones had cast a certain spell. I found other visitors had come away from them inspired to use stones for their own messages. Nearby a boulder in a glade was scraped with 'Jonny ♥ Olivia'. An empty can of Tennent's lay inches away, nectar of this lovers' ritual. Further along, a brass plaque was attached to a large boulder lying in the grass. It commemorated two young men, Joseph and Anthony, who died in a car accident on the nearest road. The power of stones had been appropriated, their long memories put to use, so people in the future would understand important things: Joseph and Anthony lived, Jonny and Olivia loved.

This morning I seek another standing stone, close to the area of the bog oaks. I cross open land, buffeted by the gusts dragging across the surface, loaded with the smell of sheep droppings and damp wool. A silver four-wheel drive is moving along the nearest lane. The driver sees me and stops. I often get this kind of attention, farmers in their cars pausing to observe me, using their stop to tell me my presence is noted. This would not happen in Ireland's west, a hiker could appear anywhere in Connemara, at any date, and not be unusual, but hiking is foreign to borderlanders and loose strangers are watched. The four-wheel drive does not pull in. There is no need to clear the road; one car coming this way is unlikely enough, two in the same five minutes would be freakish. They are close enough for me to see questioning expressions on faces of the driver and passenger. I approach them, waving with the hand that holds my Ordnance Survey map, this always helps. 'I'm looking for a standing stone,' I say.

Probably father and son – the older man is wearing a flat cap, the younger is at the wheel. He has rolled down his window. 'Aye, it's in there. Go on,' he says, giving permission and adding, 'It's a plain thing.'

This is a wonderful turn of phrase, *plain*, not meaning dowdy but straightforward, manifest. A standing stone's first quality is its undiluted there-ness. A standing stone is plain.

'Off the track, is it?' I ask.

'About twenty paces up,' says the father, 'fornenst the border.'

I'm not sure what he is saying and my face must show it.

'You can't miss it,' he says, 'for it's standing up.'

They drive off and I do find the stone easily. Tall and triangular, it's like a pie slice standing with its crust buried in the ground. Rushes grow around the base and it is tipped with yellow lichen. I can't know for sure but I accept this stone as an extremely old statement, put up when this land was a forest. Parts of it are very smooth; I imagine this might have appealed to a people touched by the power of stones, a prehistoric people. But the rock's distinction is mainly drawn from its pie-slice shape. Unlike everything else in the receding landscape, this standing stone comes to a clear point. It looks like something to contend with. About six thousand years ago a small group of people, probably members of an extended family, examined all the big stones around here, seeking the one that would make the best impression when stood on end. I can see why they selected this stone; I would have selected it too. Handle the rock to the site, dig a hole to accept it, raise it in; it might have been a morning's work to erect this marker.

We surmise things about Ireland's vanished religions by looking at passage graves and tombs. Tombs often face west, for example, indicating a spiritual relationship with the setting sun, but a standing stone is composed of just one uncarved block, it has no orientation and its plainness defies analysis. It tells us almost nothing apart from one thing, one important thing. It says: This Is Ours. The stone could not have stood up by itself, it marks commitment, the right to be somewhere. The stone's single message, This Is Ours, is so simple that it never erodes. Thousands of years later it is still broadcast as clearly as ever.

The co-ordinates of a standing stone are particularly weighty. The stone becomes a fixed point in the organisation of society around it. Early Irelanders say, *This is ours as far as that stone, then yours begins*. Ideas of homeland, territory and possession accrue around standing stones and over time the boundaries thicken up. The line between two family units becomes the line between clans or tribes. Even if other peoples move into the area, displacing former residents, traditional boundaries often remain in use. The stone comes to mark the edge of a *triúcha céad*, then a Norman cantred, then an earldom perhaps, then a barony. Power structures transform into new ones but find the old markers are still relevant to their outer limits. In the nineteenth century the county boundaries were officially defined and they too fell in with older lines on the land. For all of history this stone has been standing here, marking a boundary. And more, it has helped set the boundary, a boundary that may no longer be just Ireland's but also Europe's, the most westerly land frontier of a union populated by over four hundred million people. As the older man in the four-wheel drive said, and as I later translate, *fornenst*, meaning next to or up against. I touch the smooth stone and it does amaze me. The border is here rather than there or a mile away because six thousand years ago some people decided to stand a stone here rather than there or a mile away. The stone marked a presence and a demand for recognition. History has fallen in line with it.

This World, the Next

An inordinate number of rooks are wheeling above the village of Sion Mills. They nest in a ruin a few minutes' walk from the village green. For over 150 years the mill spun flax to produce linen. Now the tall windows are vacant and the roof has collapsed. The walls could stand centuries more though, they are solid masonry and brick all the way up. The floors are of stone slabs, strong enough to support hulking flax machines. For rooks the building is a five-storey hotel, hand-built cliffs with openings into wide shadowy chambers.

The mill was founded, along with the village, in 1835, by three brothers, James, John and George Herdman. Portraits

show three sincere gazes. They came here to build not just a business but a society, a human beehive of order, morality and productivity. In the village are rows of workers' terraced housing. It is still in use, as is the village's old gate lodge, church and school. The Herdmans' vision included the physical wellbeing of their people. They laid out a cricket ground, a bowling green, a football pitch and paths for Sunday strolls to the river. The Herdmans believed in education and temperance – you could go to evening classes but couldn't get a drink. The name Sion evolved from the local *Sían*, meaning *fairy-fort*, but the Herdmans surely allowed it to drift to Sion for the word's associations: biblical, utopian. On Sunday mornings James Herdman would beat a drum to call the people to service.

I walk down the main street. There are benches, flowers in planters and handsome blue bus shelters. Rows of tiny cottages with their terracotta chimney pots have something of the fairytale about them. The Mock Tudor style is rare in Ireland but plentiful here; Sion Mills feels more like an English village than a Northern Irish one, and a quaint one at that – a dream of Middle England here at the kingdom's furthest and most conflicted edge. I walk to the ruined mill. A few surviving ventilation fans turn lazily in their window panels. A rook hops along an exposed steel rafter. The brick chimney is 150 feet tall, tapering out at the lip, the closest thing to a flourish this building has. The rest is Victorian solidity; any beauty is in its generosity of scale, yellow sandstone and in the balance struck between masonry and open spaces. A modern single-floor extension has been made habitable and set up as a suite of offices. There I meet Margaret Loughrey. I had not expected her to receive me but after a few phone calls she has granted me time. Her office is as spacious as an empty warehouse, because it almost is an empty warehouse. The walls are bare but there is a desk and several new sofas. There is the sense of things beginning, still unshaped. Until next week the electricity is coming from a generator. Phone lines are getting installed today. 'Is it stressful,' I ask, 'suddenly owning this huge building?'

'The thing is to keep good people around you,' says Margaret. 'Then you just have to run with it, just keep going.'

Margaret is in her late forties. A couple of years ago she was unemployed and living on benefits. Returning from the Jobcentre one morning she spent £2 on a lottery ticket. 'Two pounds and that was it,' she says, 'my five numbers and two stars came up. Happy days.' Margaret won £27 million. The headline in the local newspaper was 'Mags to Riches'.

Meanwhile people in Sion Mills were protesting against the installation of an anaerobic digester in the ruined mill, a farm waste management plant that, it was feared, would bring queues of trucks through the village and produce a stench. Perhaps the campaign did trouble the investors because when Margaret offered to buy the site they accepted. She now owns about one hundred acres of industrial history and open spaces: the original mill, the warehouses. In addition, various sports clubs and a couple of houses pay rent to her.

Margaret offers me lunch. She makes soup every day for her employees; I'm surprised to discover she only has two, a manager and a gardener. The manager is a young man who is on the phone a lot. The gardener came with the site; he has maintained the sports grounds around the mill for years. He looks dazed at the changes around him. I ladle out the vegetable soup; an extra place was accidentally set and I fill this fifth bowl too.

'That's for the ghost,' Margaret laughs.

Margaret tells me that the mill is haunted. She seems convinced. Somebody photographed the ghost, she tells me, it appeared as dozens of white orbs floating in the shadows. The gardener says there might indeed be a ghost but I think he's just being polite. We eat our soup for a while. I ask Margaret about her plans for the mill. 'The money's not changing me,' she says, 'I'm changing things with it.' Margaret has a long list of ideas for the building: a museum, a cafe, a go-karting track, a bowling alley, a wedding venue. So far the plans seem to be limited to a few sheets of paper, ideas and shopping lists. 'I'll be in my office here, overlooking it all,' she says.

Margaret offers to take me into the old mill. We pass up through enormous empty workshops. Yellow paint is peeling and blistering on the stairwell walls, revealing the layers of decades. There is the smell of sodden plaster. Asbestos lingers in one large hall where the ceilings are as black as soot. Rows of round iron pillars support the roofs; I am reminded of peering into spruce plantations. The mill was built wider than most to accommodate longer machines, helping the Herdman company survive when most mills in Ireland were closing, although it too was eventually defeated by competition from Asia. Linen spun here was made into clothing, handkerchiefs, the skins of airships and the wings of First World War fighter planes. Generations of villagers worked for generations of Herdmans, the sharp smell of flax pervading their lives. Now flax spools litter the floor and empty linen barrels stand against walls. In one dark passage pigeons flutter out over our heads, escaping towards the light. 'This is where the ghost is seen,' Margaret tells me.

If anyone is haunting these passages and workshops, it's us. When the mill ran, flax dust was blamed for cases of lung disease among staff and there is still something dense about the darkness – it feels full of spores, from rotting wood and mortar perhaps. The halls are unsettling and inspire silence. I wonder about Margaret. Her stroke of luck has given her extraordinary freedom and while her desire to spread the wealth around is admirable, it's unclear why she has chained herself to this stranded lump of stone and iron. 'Do you ever feel like the heir to the Herdmans?' I ask.

Margaret shakes her head. 'I have my own family history to think about,' she says.

'But you have stepped into the Herdman shoes, haven't you?' I say. 'You have all these buildings, and tenants too.'

'I still live in my little terrace house,' she tells me. 'That keeps me grounded.'

We climb the last steps and emerge into daylight on the top floor. The roof is gone. Grass grows from the low walls. Margaret doesn't come to look at the view as she suffers from vertigo. Over the top I can see the river that powered the mill and, in the other direction, the houses of the village.

'I've fallen out with a lot of them,' says Margaret. When she bought the mill locals were pleased, they knew she was not going to build an anaerobic digester, but soon the villagers' sense of entitlement over the mill clashed with Margaret's actual ownership. 'They didn't give me the respect,' she says. Respect is something Margaret mentions quite often, accusing some people of snobbery towards her. She keeps a mental blacklist of locals she doesn't want to deal with. Conflict with Sion's sporting clubs led her to lock out the cricketers and then the bowlers for several weeks. 'I was up here one Sunday chasing out the dog walkers,' she tells me.

'Anglers are allowed?' I ask. I can see a man carrying waders and a rod, crossing her land to get to the river.

'Aye, I gave the anglers right of way,' says Margaret.

'They were the only ones who came and asked.'

Nests are clumped in the joints of the twisted steel rafters. As I walk about, broken slates crunch under my feet. 'I was quoted a million and a half just to put a roof on and windows in,' says Margaret. Even Margaret's entire fortune could not restore and bring life back to this mill. She is applying for grants and assistance but, having no business experience, it's hard to convince people she's a good investment. Margaret has gone straight from nothing to owning this immense landmark, skipping all the usual steps in between, the steps you might need to make in order to manage such a large lump of history, to be able to wrap your imagination around it.

'What if none of your plans work out?' I ask her. 'What if you can't make the mill into anything at all?'

'Then I'll have to remember that the ticket was only two pounds,' she says.

*

I walk back to where the border flows with a river, the Finn, which in fact is quite wide. I have arranged to meet Paddy Bloomer here and find him parked by a pub called the Smuggler's Inn, canoe strapped to the roof of his station wagon. It's late, we won't get far before dark but set off anyway. Cans crumple beneath our boots, but Paddy and I are hushed as we carry the canoe to the bank and lower it into the water. It might be the fading light or the increasing cold, but we only speak when necessary to keep us working in unison. Just before the Strabane–Lifford bridge the river brings us to Three Enemies. When I first heard this place-name, I imagined it was a battle site with a history of broken alliances and confused loyalties, but actually the enemies are three rivers meeting here in a Y. Ocean tide pushes back the Foyle to where the Finn and Moure pour in, so the three clash, knocking their eddies together. Paddy and I lurch between jutting stones and bicycle wrecks, black water breaking white. It is strange to be fighting currents while cars slip silently over the bridge ahead of us, their headlights exposing billboard advertisements. 'Liquidate Your Furniture', says one. I feel the drop to the river Foyle in the pit of my stomach, and we are pulled under the concrete span. The bridge's underside has deep square voids that echo. For a moment the river noise rebounds and we are in the epicentre of deafening white noise. Then we are out, beyond the bridge and away from the churning currents. We can hear our dipping paddles again.

In 2011 a young man called David Colhoun was arrested near here on a drunk and disorderly charge. He would not submit to due process but leapt from the police car and ran to the river. He could see the lights of his hometown, Lifford, on the other side. The police car had pulled up on the bridge, waiting for him. He must have felt like an Old West outlaw, sheriffs pursuing him to the border. The south was his Mexico, the Foyle his Rio Grande. He knew the river well, had fished it all his life and swum it before too, but the water was running high that night, rocks were invisible in the darkness and there was alcohol in his blood. He did not make it across. David's father spent days walking the riverbanks looking for his son's body. 'It's about finding him and giving him a proper burial,' he said. Search teams, divers and sniffer dogs were brought in but couldn't find him. Weeks went by, David's girlfriend hired a clairvoyant. But it was ten months before his body was found among reeds a few miles down river, by Island Mor.

Island Mor is unpopulated, flat, narrow and long, splitting

the river in two for a few miles. Paddy and I find a stretch of stony shore and drag up the canoe. While Paddy pitches the tent, I look for firewood, branches left on the stones by the flow. It is dark and I can see my breath in the torch beam. I pick up a branch that is disconcertingly light, I realise it's a cow bone. When I have enough logs, I lay them together. 'That'll do,' says Paddy, placing a burning firelighter under the wood while I stamp my feet against cold. As the fire builds, Paddy and I sip cups of wine. To warm it up Paddy heats a spoon in the flames and dips it in. Soon we are able to sit by the fire, content enough. We let the log ends burn before pushing them further in, sending up sparks. The night is silent and, when I leave the fire to pee, freezing. There is something Middle Stone Age about us, and pleasingly ritualistic: tending a fire on an island in a river. Something in the night has got me thinking of final crossings, maybe it's David Colhoun, or because I've just turned forty. It could be the border; unknown lands and the great unknown of death have often merged in the imagination. In Ireland the bodies of Iron Age men were deposited at frontiers, we know because the bogs preserved the bodies and history preserved the frontiers. After death, one man had spancel hoops – prop of the *Táin* – inserted into both his arms. During the seventeenth century the future border was a warzone, bodies piling up in the rivers in places like the Bloody Pass and here too in the Foyle. In the twentieth century the border was pierced by sniper fire and detonation signals and dug up for secret burials.

In this century crime writer Brian McGilloway sees the dramatic potential in the border. He has set all his novels here and uses the rich idea of crossing over. He took the very island Paddy and I are camped on tonight as a setting for *The Nameless Dead*. In this novel Island Mor isn't just on the political boundary, it hovers on the line between the living and the dead. The unmarked graves of children are uncovered by a team of investigators; it is a *cillin*, an old burial ground for babies who died before baptism. 'Wee limbo babies,' Inspector Devlin is told. Devlin is McGilloway's narrator-detective, guiding the reader through what is both a police procedural and something more meditative. When taking statements, Devlin seems to be officiating at memorials as much as solving crime. The subservience that created the need for *cillins* is explained to the inspector by another investigator: 'The Catholic Church would not allow babies that had died before baptism to be buried in consecrated ground, so families often selected somewhere either close to a church, or on a border or boundary between parishes. Or near a river.' All this is based on fact; there were many such graveyards in Ireland. Under this regime the bereaved had to create other holy grounds for their dead, and, like many things rejected by convention, they went to the periphery. Later in the novel the bodies of babies who died more recently are uncovered on Island Mor too. Devlin is pursuing this case but also a wider kind of justice, something more like closure. 'Those children deserve their story to be heard,' Devlin says, and it hardly matters which children he is referring to. Devlin hopes his discoveries mean that all the dead of Island Mor will find a place in the community's collective consciousness, will no longer be lost between this world and the next.

*

I crawl out of my warm sleeping bag and into a cold dawn. Hunched on the shore I wash last night's cups and dishes. Paddy and I fuel up on bread and jam. As we launch the canoe I mention the cow bone I found.

'Back on the Erne,' Paddy says, 'there's a tree growing on an island near the border. The tree is said to be carnivorous.'

'What does it eat?' I ask.

'Goats. It attracts them somehow and kills them. There's always a heap of goat bones around the trunk, caught up in the roots. Their bodies nourish the tree.'

I imagine a large oak with a dark green crown, each leaf heavy and glossy with protein.

'So it's said anyway,' says Paddy. 'I haven't seen the tree myself.'

'Who told you about it?'

Paddy tries to recall. 'It was either a man in a pub or a man by a campfire,' he says. After a short discussion, we agree that a man by a campfire is a more reliable source. 'At least you'd know he gets out occasionally,' says Paddy.

We pass the remains of a bridge that once carried the Great Northern Railway across Island Mor. Only the columns have survived, they march across the border in sets of three. The first set is on land and reaches a few feet above the ground. The next trio is taller, the next taller again, as if the fields are extruding them. By the time the columns are standing in the river each is a monster. This bridge obviously carried two lines, both wide-gauge. Paddy and I stop paddling and drift among the columns. I'm reminded of being under giant redwoods in California. Now the columns carry nothing and lead nowhere but I don't feel the melancholy of Sion Mills. Freeing the columns from the convention of usefulness has actually revealed their magnificence, they have more sculptural impact than anything I've seen in Tate Modern's Turbine Hall. It's a shame not many people see them. We are several fields from the nearest road and this is the border. Before

beginning this journey I enjoyed John Byrne's joke, imagining the border as a tourist attraction, but I don't think it's a joke any more. There are things here worth seeking out.

We are beyond Island Mor when a downriver breeze stings the backs of our ears. 'Good for sailing,' says Paddy. Laid inside the canoe is a pole wrapped around with a windsurfing sail that Paddy has adapted. A slot in the central bench holds the pole and makes it a mast. When it's up, Paddy unstrings the sail and it unfurls with a slap. It is bright pink and orange. I feel the canoe lift as it fills with the breeze; I stop paddling and we are still moving. I can relax. An otter swims across our bow, peeking above the water at intervals, leaving a trail of rings. I stretch out and let the river run through my fingers. Headway without effort, it's pleasant but I'd better not get used to it. To our right and left, north and south, are cattle fields. The cows that were ignoring us now raise their heads, made curious by the bright sail. They trot down to the shore and gaze as we pass up the line between them.

65

67

71

76

miles 1 2 3

km 1 2 3 4 5

N

O'Doherty Tower
14th century

Burt Castle
16th century

Grianán of Aileach
9th century

Raytheon
21st century

Agains
Raytheo

Against interr

74

72

71

73

70

17

69

WWII

Anthony Barrett's farm
21st century

Newtown Cunningham

OB

68

Donegal

67

Londo

Tyrone

Mongavlin Castle
17th century

My direction of travel

Island Mor

Irish Army
20th century

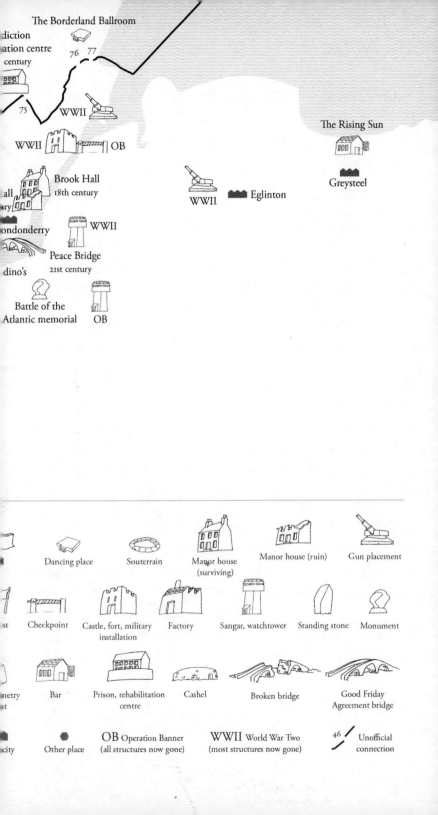

The Borderland Ballroom

diction
ation centre
century

76 77

75

WWII

WWII OB

all
ary

Brook Hall
18th century

ondonderry

WWII

The Rising Sun

Greysteel

WWII Eglinton

Peace Bridge
21st century

dino's

Battle of the
Atlantic memorial OB

Dancing place   Souterrain   Manor house
(surviving)   Manor house (ruin)   Gun placement

st   Checkpoint   Castle, fort, military
installation   Factory   Sangar, watchtower   Standing stone   Monument

netry
at   Bar   Prison, rehabilitation
centre   Cashel   Broken bridge   Good Friday
Agreement bridge

city   Other place   OB Operation Banner
(all structures now gone)   WWII World War Two
(most structures now gone)   46 Unofficial
connection

Home, Castle, Empire

The borderline climbs out of the river and up through farmland, letting the north take a nibble from Donegal and skirting the city of Derry/Londonderry. So I say goodbye to Paddy, until the border rejoins the water. Walking upland along fuchsia hedgerows, I see nothing to indicate I'm only a mile from city streets. It is quiet but for the *brum* of a tractor. Swallows zip and dive over fields. The border brings me straight to a chicken-wire fence and seems to insist I climb it. I have to remove my boots to get my toes between the wires. On the other side is an embankment that is unnaturally smooth and even, like a thirty-degree lawn. At the top I am faced with a water reservoir a quarter of a mile long, the border running up the middle. While I am wondering which way to go around, security arrives, a lone man wrangling four dogs. 'We can't have people visiting,' he says and he points between two hills. 'Creggan estate is just over there.' Young people from the city cut holes in the fence and sneak in to drink cider and take a dip. It is this man's job to chase them away.

The border takes up with a stream, against the flow, and climbs Holy Well Hill. It passes through a grove of sycamores and hidden among them I find a connection, number seventy-one, a new footbridge, constructed from the same treated planks used for garden decking. It is on brick foundations and has sturdy handrails. Hoping to find out about the bridge, I knock on the door of the nearest cottage and meet Albert and Margaret.

'This is Northern Ireland here and that's Donegal over there,' says Albert. Verification of position in relation to the frontier is a common opener among borderlanders, they like to make sure you know where you are. 'That house over the bridge belongs to a son of ours,' he goes on to explain. 'He married a girl from Donegal and we built the bridge to join the houses.'

'It's not finished yet mind you,' says Margaret. 'We're going to have it that you can step out our back door and straight onto the bridge.'

They tell me about other family members they have nearby and I am struck by how linked up they are, both sides of the border. Often as I walked the political line, I was passing through invisible networks of families like these, their love stories, marriages, children and grandchildren. 'It must be very satisfying,' I say, 'living here and having your family all around you. You're building your own empire, are you?'

'I won't call it an empire,' laughs Albert.

I move on. The holy well at the top of Holy Well Hill is a murky little pool. Albert told me that it was traditional to climb up here for a picnic at Easter, gathering around something called the Stone Man. I see nothing like a stone man, but perhaps it was a nickname for the Ordnance Survey trigonometry point. I look to a neighbouring peak, Greenan Mountain. On top of it is a stone fort, my next destination.

I walk down into the valley between the hills. I alarm two pheasants in the grass who fly away in a whirl of brown and scarlet. Up ahead a tractor is parked by a gate with a hay baler attached to the tow bar. The farmer is standing out by his machines and greets me enthusiastically.

'I love travelling too,' he says, 'you meet people, don't you?'

'You do.'

He pitches from his toes to his heels and back again as he talks to me, delighted that I have come wandering across his land.

'I love staying in the hostels. Do you ever do that?'

'I do,' I reply, 'but there aren't many along the border.'

'There can be great freedom in them,' he says. 'I've had some fabulous times in hostels.'

'I camp out mostly.'

'Fantastic. You must be having all sorts of interesting times, I'd say, are you?'

'I am. I'm also seeing lots of fields.'

'Meeting lots of people?'

'Yes, but more fields.'

'Where are you going now?'

'The fort on Greenan,' I say.

'Greenan, it's beautiful up there. The view's great. There'll be plenty of visitors up there at this time of day, but have you ever been up there at night?'

'I haven't.'

'There's one night a week,' he says, naming the day, 'when men meet up around the fort. I go up sometimes. You can meet all sorts up there, foreigners too sometimes. I met a couple of fellas one night . . . they weren't shy I can tell you.' He looks up towards Greenan and becomes suddenly thoughtful. 'I'm nearly sure they were Spanish.'

I thank him for the information and move on. A road goes to the top of Greenan and families have come for the afternoon. Five cars are parked at the top and there's a van selling ice cream. The fort is of a type called a cashel and this one is over a thousand years old. Its rock wall is nearly twenty feet high and the base almost as thick. It is circular and big enough to land a helicopter inside, if you were careful. Fuelled up on ice cream, children are racing each other around it, yelling and calling to each other. Before entering the stone cashel there are a few other things I want to find; it was built at the centre of three earthwork rings that are probably older and have bigger circumferences. They have almost vanished; people walk through them without knowing they are there. I step off the path and kick through the heather, sending hundreds of tiny black mites hopping away. I think I identify sections of the outer and middle circles, although I am too close to be sure. They are best seen in aerial photography, thin arcs of bare earth showing through the heather. I am more successful with the inner ring, the closest to the cashel, finding subtle but definite lips of raised earth. I walk the broken loop until I am back where I started.

Again the circle has primacy but here it means something different from the ritual building in Emain Macha. These outer rings – of earth, from before the stone cashel was built – were not a rite, they probably protected lives and property. When people lived here, the rings were topped with palisade walls, keeping thieves out and cows in. There was room enough for twenty or more dwellings inside, home and powerbase to an extended family, part of a dynasty called the Uí Néill, soon to be called the Northern Uí Néill. Squabbling children, squealing pigs, barking dogs, dunging cattle, it would have been lively in here. The wooden fort must have been an imposing sight and the head of the family ruled the neighbourhood. I imagine the chief bearded and, that rare thing, plump – full of honey, salted beef and entitlement. He claims to be great-great-grandson or perhaps great-great-great-grandson of Niall of the Nine Hostages, a semi-legendary king of Ireland. I picture him standing on a platform, looking out over the top of the palisade with his daughter. She peeks over the logs while he points things out to her. Her father is telling her where he plans to travel next. He leaves often for weeks at a time, raiding or warring. He is still celebrating a recent victory and wants to build something to mark it. There were no professional armies then, men of status lead from the front. Whenever he goes away he always brings back gifts; his daughter asks for new sewing needles.

Standing among these nested rings it is easy for them, and for me, to imagine bigger concentric circles, radiating out over the land. The round base of the hill carries the pattern another quarter of a mile. Further out, an imagined circle of a mile diameter takes in the closest relations of this nucleus, other families in smaller enclosures, homesteads generated through marriage. This is the day-to-day roaming territory of the girl. She is safe anywhere inside this circle and knows most of the people. All the families come together for celebrations and in times of trouble, to launch a raid or deflect one. These families inspire loyalty in her father but when he speaks of those living a little further out she detects a hardening in him. He probes her for information, asking who is building new dwellings and how many cows they lost in the last outbreak of murrain. It is summer and tributes may be owed to him. The girl is sometimes sent with a slave to fetch them, driving a gifted heifer back home with taps of a rod.

West, she can see mountains. It is the land of another northern kingdom. The hazy borderline between them is about two days away. The landscape was harder going than it is now, wide strips of fenland have since been drained. The girl has never travelled beyond this circle's rim although her father has. Looking that way her sense of belonging is stretched thin but at least they all belong to the north, she would be safe among them. She has a foster brother born of that family and has caught him looking west occasionally.

South-east are more distant mountains, the furthest rim she can project. Blue and unchanging, the ridge has the look of a frontier about it. They are a four- or five-day march away. It is the land of the Airgialla. They are inferior sorts, their name means *Those who give hostages*. The girl is in regular contact with Airgialla slaves, they muck out pigsties and collect firewood. Some of them are all right, once you get to know them. From where she is standing now the girl can see a line of Airgialla labouring up the hill towards the enclosure. Each is carrying a stone. They will offload it at the top and go down to get another. They've been at this for days. Beyond Airgialla country are the kingdoms of the midlands. They are too far for any landmark to be visible and are hard to place in her imagination. She has never met anyone from there, although she has heard the names of their kings. Even her father has not been that far, yet.

Somewhere among these concentric circles an idea is firming up, the idea of country. From this hilltop I think I can feel the tremors of nation building, rippling out from the homestead. Elsewhere other cultures project themselves too and where they clash a third thing is created: borderland.

[273]

In the following decades the country of the Northern Uí Néill expands and the heart consolidates. No wonder it hardens to stone; this hilltop becomes the axis point of something big. The stone cashel is called Grianán of Aileach. It was built in the late eighth or early ninth century. It is composed of irregular stones, only a few so large that one person couldn't lift them. I lower my head to pass through the entrance. Inside the ring is terraced, steps bring you up three levels before you can look out over the top. Children are running along the terraces, their parents shouting at them to slow down. I'd like to but can't call this the original ring; it is a modern reconstitution, put together from the original's scattered remains. I can see parts of the wall are a little touched by straightness, meeting at points like smoothed-down angles. This happened because in recent years workers stood on scaffolding to rebuild sections. When setting stones from a platform it takes concentration not to build in parallel with the platform. The result makes

it look as if Grianán's circle has been spliced with a few strands of octagon DNA. A lot of concrete has gone in between the stones, making it much more tidy than the original could have been, but this has stabilised the terraces and allowed children to climb up and run around and I like this place best with the children. Their unfiltered response to Grianán is to do circuits until they collapse, giggling and exhausted. No one appreciates the place more than they do.

This dynasty's expansion will absorb the other kingdoms of mid-Ulster. They will swallow up the Airgialla and eventually the Ulaid, dominating the island's north. The girl's great-grandchildren will centre themselves further east, and future generations will transfer east again. Some suggest Grianán was never intended to be lived in, but was left as a statement of dominance and site of Uí Néill inaugurations. An inauguration throne will certainly be created by the girl's descendants on a hill to the east called Tullyhogue. Her descendants will include Hugh O'Neill.

Grianán was destroyed in 1101, dismantled by a southern rival. The story goes that to make the destruction complete, each invading soldier was ordered to carry one stone away. They were supposed to march home with them but most stones were probably dropped at the base of Greenan, from where they came, and from where they would be taken yet again to produce the loose copy I'm visiting today.

From the rampart I can see acres of brown heather, miles of green and yellow fields and a scattering of magnolia houses. I can see an island and boats and where the border dissipates into the ocean. I examine the nearest hilltops, selecting my base for tonight.

*

It was a farmer named Anthony Barrett who told me how the use of scaffolding infected the rebuilt Grianán with straightness here and there. He would know, he has built a 1:5 scale version of Grianán fort on his farm a few miles away. I go to meet him in the morning. Anthony lives in the north but crosses the border every day to work his land, keeping cattle and growing barley. I find him with his employee, John, in the caravan he uses for breaks and sleepovers. Anthony is in his fifties. He has a firm and slow pace, looking off into the middle distance to deliver dead-pan remarks. John is older, missing a few teeth, and wears a woolly hat that I suspect he never takes off. We drink tea and eat apple turnovers straight from the packet.

'I used to have a driving range here,' Anthony explains, 'so in the evenings I'd be waiting around for the golfers. I started putting stones together to pass the time. I started with walls. Walls are handy after all. Then I had enough walls . . .'

Anthony and I walk over to his version of Grianán. It is in the middle of a field, cattle standing around it. It is about thirty-five feet in diameter and seven feet tall. It must have taken hundreds of hours to build. This Grianán is a dry-stone construction, no cement, held together by its own weight. John worked on the project too and I wonder how Anthony talked him into it. Anthony is himself unsure what came over them. 'We just built it,' he says. 'A hobby that went wrong.' A variety of stones have gone into the ring wall. Many are rounded, worn smooth by the tides that once ran in and out of this area until the land was drained and claimed in the nineteenth century. I see rectangular blocks in the wall too, blocks that circulated through other buildings before ending up here. A date is chiselled into one, 1764.

'There was a castle on the land,' explains Anthony. 'Later on the land became the Castleforward estate. They took the blocks from the castle and used them for the house. It was a big lump of a thing, forty rooms. The house was tossed in the sixties when the rates got to be too high. So now I'm using them.'

'You don't have to go far for stones,' I say.

'Nobody likes carrying a stone too far, myself included.'

The fort is not Anthony's only creation. Nearby is a stone model of the Sam Maguire Cup, a trophy awarded to Ireland's champion Gaelic football team. It is the traditional trophy shape, base, stem and wide bowl, but the stem is the size of a barrel and supports a cup that is twelve feet across. It is made of thin slabs and took three months to build. 'I could only put on an inch or so a day,' says Anthony. 'I was always afraid of the thing falling on me.'

I reach up and run my hand over the stones; all Anthony's creations seem to demand this. 'Is it like playing with giant Lego?' I ask.

Anthony does a sideways head tick, acknowledging the possibility. 'You'd want to be a bit of a child to do this kind of thing,' he says.

Considering how much commitment went into these creations, Anthony is shy, almost embarrassed about them. When he began work on the stone trophy he told his neighbours it was going to be a birdbath – as if that made more sense. Some locals are convinced he gets government grants to build these objects, not believing he does it for enjoyment. It's true that Anthony doesn't express much pleasure in the finished works; he looks at the results with bemusement, as if someone else put them here and he just tolerates them. This might be rooted in his natural restraint, or it might be that he is conflicted and doubtful about the work but feels driven to create it anyway. Which is a way of saying Anthony Barrett is an artist.

'The wife would ring looking for me,' he says, 'and I'd tell her I had to stay late because a cow was calving, when really I was putting one of these together.'

At the western end of the farm, overlooking a road, Anthony has built a scale model of a monastic round tower. It makes me laugh out loud, there is something comical about such self-importance in miniature. It stands overlooking a road, demanding to be noticed. Lastly we set off across a large field. A combine harvester has been in recently, cropping Anthony's barley down to tough stalks that crunch under our boots. We are visiting what might be his masterpiece, a castle over thirty feet tall. It has the classic medieval castle look, as a primary schoolchild might draw it: square in plan, a turret in each corner, chunky crenellations and a single centrally placed entrance. On a round hill a mile to the north we can see Burt Castle, a stronghold dating from the 1500s. If this was the television programme *Grand Designs* I'd say the two castles are in dialogue. Anthony's model castle could easily stand five centuries as well. It's the size of a two-storey house. He hired scaffolding to build it. We go inside and walk about between the walls, the towers looming overhead. Anthony does seem pleased with this, his most recent project.

'Every man's home is his castle, of course,' he says, 'but not every man has built a castle.'

We go back outside and I take a photograph of it. 'I think what you've done here is art,' I say.

'Aah, that's pushing it a wee bit,' says Anthony.

'It depends what you think art is, I suppose,' I say, 'but

anybody who has seen this won't forget it.'

Anthony looks up at the castle. 'It looks well,' he concedes. 'In the evenings too, when it's cooling and there's shade from the trees, it looks well.'

Dancing place

Gun placement

Protest

Lighthouse

Checkpoint

Castle, fort, military installation

Standing stone

Bar

Prison, rehabilitation centre

Monument

Trigonometry point

High cross

Town, city

OB Operation Banner (all structures now gone)

WWII World War Two (most structures now gone)

46 Unofficial connection

Slieve Snaght
1827

Cuilcagh

Crockinnagoe

Drung Point
1829

My direction of travel

Ardmore Gallen

The Borderland Ballroom

Addiction rehabilitation centre
21st century

76 77

75

WWII

OB

WWII

OB

The

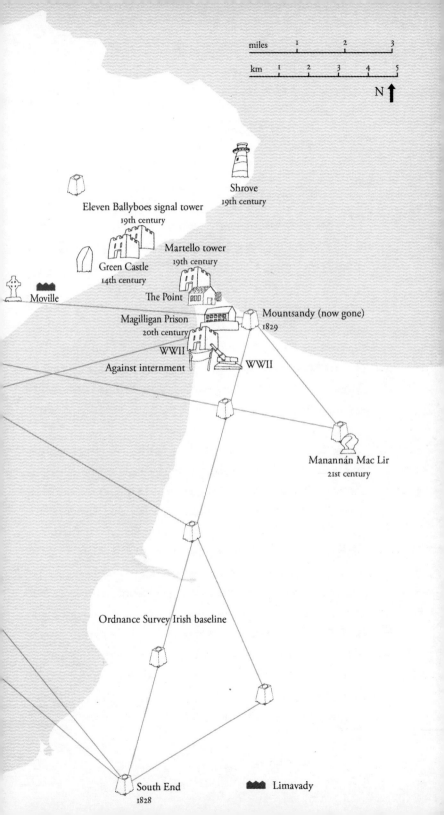

miles   1   2   3

km   1   2   3   4   5

N

Shrove
19th century

Eleven Ballyboes signal tower
19th century

Green Castle
14th century

Martello tower
19th century

Moville

The Point

Magilligan Prison
20th century

Mountsandy (now gone)
1829

WWII

Against internment

WWII

Manannán Mac Lir
21st century

Ordnance Survey Irish baseline

South End
1828

Limavady

Bars

The Foyle flows through Derry/Londonderry reflecting and reinforcing the city's double personality, dividing it roughly between Catholic and Protestant clusters. Very roughly, but well enough that it was suggested now and then that the border be rerouted along the water. This idea forgets the cultural importance of the old city on a hill on the western bank, the showpiece of Ulster's Plantation. The old city is walled with a great loop of stonework, crenellations, cannons and towers dating to 1618. The battlements can be walked; I set off at a brisk pace and am back where I started in about twenty minutes.

In a secondhand bookshop I look at the Local Interest shelf and buy a collection of poems written by inmates of Magilligan Prison. In another book I look at an old photograph taken in Derry/Londonderry. Two gents in suits and brogues are painting a line on the ground while soldiers watch from a short distance away. The line painters use a wooden stencil to get a clean line – white, three inches wide. This photograph is from 1969 and captures the making of a border; the line went across streets and along alleyways, marking off a neighbourhood that was called Free Derry, a new self-declared autonomous zone. Ireland had split from the United Kingdom, so Northern Ireland had split from Ireland and now in a similar process Free Derry was trying to get loose from Northern Ireland, although the line painters weren't seeking a tiny independent nation – they wanted political representation and, first of all, fair policing. Free Derry was declared and delineated during protests that were viciously put down by the authorities; the painted line was supposed to keep the police and army out and, at times, it worked. The enclave went on to exist in some form for several years.

Drawing a line is one way to make a state where we can belong, but a sense of belonging is often lost to borders too. Even a place as small as Free Derry would be big enough for some people to feel like they were in the wrong place. Within Free Derry I'm sure you could have found at least one family that did not want to be caught up in the enclave. They might have liked a further subdivision, a line painted around their house. And within that house a teenage son, or daughter would have stormed upstairs and locked their door.

When Free Derry melded back into its surroundings, the river was once again the border's strongest representative in the city. In 1982 Paul Theroux found 'Fuck the Pope' scrawled on one end of the city's only bridge, and 'Fuck the Queen' on the other. City planners, if there were any, didn't exploit the riversides; walking the banks you saw only lanes of traffic and the rear ends of shopping centres, both halves of the city cleaving apart along the seam of the river. It took until 2011 for a footbridge to be thrown across the divide, they've called it the Peace Bridge. The city is now beginning to creak around and look at itself. I walk across this new bridge, which curves this way and that over the water. City council workers are steam-blasting chewing gum from the decking. I stand in the centre for a while, watching people go by. There is a heightened glamour to the way some women dress here, a flamboyance you wouldn't quite see in Belfast or Dublin. A woman goes by in a slinky purple jumpsuit, diamond buttons, and on her arm a golden hand-bag that could hold four bowling balls.

Since this bridge was built, the river seems no longer the sharpest metaphor for the city's duality. Now the best way to experience it is to gaze upon the engineered name Derry/Londonderry. It is written this way on government publications but also by journalists and in many day-to-day communications. People even say it that way, 'Derry-stroke-Londonderry'; on the old city walls I heard tour guides use it like it was natural. It was designed to try to end an argument about the city's name. Some people insist on Londonderry, respecting the role the London guilds played in building the city. A person saying this to you might be indicating a commitment to the United Kingdom, or indi-cating they think you might have a commitment to the United Kingdom. Others refer to the city only as Derry, coming from the Irish for oak grove. A person saying this to you might be flagging up an allegiance to the south, although they might just like it because it's shorter. The compound name tries to close a cultural divide but it's hard to love Derry/Londonderry, it's full of awkwardness and insecur-ity, a bit like the border itself. With its self-conscious air of compromise, the '/' in Derry/Londonderry sits between identities just as Ireland's border runs up the middle of val-leys. As sure as the black line on my map, the slash between Derry and Londonderry represents the frontier.

Derry/Londonderry puts both identities side by side but keeps them partitioned, suggesting two peoples living in parallel but not together. So a more idealised form has now appeared. Derry~Londonderry is used in logos, govern-ment reports and grant applications, anything needing a positive spin. '~' throws the boundary on its side, using it to link rather than divide, and does so with a reassuring quiver, implying a healthy dash of flexibility. The new footbridge looks like a ~ from above. The symbol is also like the winding course of the Foyle travelling through the city.

Other names are available. There is the youthful Legenderry, but it's hard to imagine anyone writing it. There is the Maiden City, referencing the old city's unbreached defences, but it's hard to imagine anyone saying it. People do say Stroke City. London guilds and oak groves are mere clutter, dropped so the stroke between Derry and Londonderry can be better admired. Stroke City – a wise joke. Wise because it recognises that the city's character is its duality, hence the need to engineer labels in the first place. Stroke City makes the '/' the most important part of the name, suggesting it's the most important thing happening here. The act of encounter is the city's foundation. '/' is a place.

*

I am waiting for Paddy in a bar called Sandino's. Customers at the other end of the counter are discussing the European Single Market. There is consensus that the 'neo-liberal agenda' will not allow the free movement of labour to stop, even if Northern Ireland is carried out of the EU. 'And they won't stop people going shopping either,' one laughs. She points out that most politicians, both north and south, want the border to remain open so they will find ways to make sure it does.

'The current lot, sure,' worries her friend. 'But what about the next crowd, or the one after that?'

'And it won't be their decision anyway,' adds another.

'It'll be down to Brussels or London, people a long way from here.'

I look around. The walls of the bar are covered in posters expressing solidarity with Palestine, Gaza and Latin American socialists. A sign behind the taps says, '*No Pasaran*.' Hanging above my head is a drone missile made from cardboard and plywood and painted silver. 'Raytheon: Software for a Cleaner Kill' is painted across the fuselage. 'Raytheon make missile targeting systems,' explains Paddy when he arrives and takes the stool beside me. 'Like the programming in your GPS, except for bombs.'

Raytheon opened a base in Derry/Londonderry shortly after the Good Friday Agreement and software for the Patriot, Tomahawk and Sidewinder missiles was written behind the blue plate glass of its office block. So as the peace process advanced, Northern Ireland hosted a business making missiles aimed for lands with less luck. There were protests against Raytheon in the city and this bar was one of the movement's hubs, where petitions and vigils were organised. At a meeting upstairs in 2006, it was decided to take the protest further and occupy Raytheon's building. A group of men and women succeeded in breaking in, threw computers out of the windows and used a fire extinguisher to disable the mainframe. At the trial the jury was told £100,000 worth of damage had been done to the plant, but the protestors were acquitted. Apart from the odd fine, most people who hassled Raytheon in the following years were acquitted. The company was finally forced from the city in 2010.

'Raytheon make other things too,' Paddy tells me over our pints. 'Marine radars and the like. There was a time I was helping build a unit for washing seaweed. We got an old industrial washing machine from a hotel – I wanted the motor and the gearbox. It turned out that Raytheon had made the washing machine. I found their name stamped on the back.'

I wonder if Paddy has some sympathy for Raytheon, a maker's regard for other makers, although, of course, Raytheon is as easily described as a destroyer. It's hard to know what Paddy thinks: apart from general wariness and weariness I don't think I've ever heard him express a political position. He contributes to any political conversation but nothing sticks to him. This is a useful dexterity on the border.

We walk out of the bar, cross the road to the river and climb down a ladder to the canoe. We paddle out of the city to the border and make camp by a Second World War pillbox, built to defend the city from German U-boats. The pillbox was a liability during the Troubles so it was, as they'd say around here, tossed. Now it lies at an angle, half in the water and half on the bank. We unroll the tent and slot the poles together. A thick clump of dead plants restricts our campsite to a small patch of grass by the shore. The stalks of the plants are tall and hollow, with points like knuckles along their length; they are the dried-out corpses of another foreign invader, giant hogweed. Cold nights have killed the hogweed back but it will return next spring. I have to stamp down dozens of stalks to get tent pegs into the ground.

In the morning Paddy and I paddle out onto Lough Foyle. The sky is clear and there is no breeze for the sail. The water is a dead calm, a glassy stillness, only disrupted by poles standing out every few hundred yards to mark the shipping channel. The shorelines are softened by haze. One belongs to the north, the other to the south, but the borderline on the water is hazy too. It's here somewhere but nobody knows where and, so far, it doesn't matter. Officially both countries claim Lough Foyle but this argument is handled in the way many of us handle the irresolvable, by talking about something else instead.

Paddy and I are travelling in parallel with another invisible line today, although its co-ordinates are certain. The Ordnance Survey's first steps in Ireland were along the north shore. In 1827 a set of base points was erected in a straight line on the flat land near the water. Each was a stone pedestal with a notched wire embedded in the cap. The surveyors had created four pinpoints of an impressive fixity and the conceptual line running through them was to be their baseline. With ten-foot lengths of brass and iron, called compensation bars, and microscopes they worked over two years to measure the line, pausing for the winter and, as the line cut across farmland, for harvest. The baseline was measured with an accuracy never achieved before. This was important: any error in measuring the distance between the Foyle pedestals would be amplified across the entire island. The baseline was triangulated with points on mountaintops to produce new baselines and further triangulations. The mapping of Ireland had begun.

Paddy and I strike out for the heart of the blue void but are moving no faster than those surveyors did. The current is against us as it makes a slow turn through Lough Foyle. We are a speck on the surface of a warming cauldron, our paddles mean little against the heave under the hull. There is nothing ahead but sheets of blue, over and under us, meeting a diffuse horizon. A kind of sensory deprivation overcomes me. Sitting to stern, Paddy is always looking at my back but I, kneeling in the bow, am faced into a blue nothing. This, combined with the mindless action of paddling, makes me lose myself in long chains of thought and I'm soon muttering aloud. 'What?' says Paddy from stern.

'Nothing, nothing,' I reply, but minutes later I'm doing it again.

'What?' demands Paddy. 'What are you saying?'

We are in the middle of the lough, three miles from land, when we stop to eat lunch. We try to figure out our location by identifying features on both shores. Lough Foyle has a bit of everything, there's an example of almost every category of border landmark here, claims built with blocks and concrete, counter-claims and further claims. There are standing stones, megalithic tombs and the ruins of Norman castles. Hugh O'Neill had defences dug here against an invading force of Mountjoy's troops, trenches to protect his pikemen from naval cannon fire. No trace of them has been identified, but a Martello tower, an 1817 defence against the French, looks brand new. It is the last building in the north. The last building in the south is a lighthouse, designed by the same engineer responsible for Haulbowline. Three of the Ordnance Survey's baseline pedestals remain and there are a lot of remnants from the Second World War. Lough Foyle's role as border was at its clearest then. The south claimed neutral status while the north was a base in the fight for the Atlantic. The north shore was sprinkled with Royal Air Force runways, anti-aircraft guns, pillboxes and military Nissen huts, like half-buried cylinders peeking over the rushes. Paddy and I go by a ruined pier, a long row of black piles poking out of the water, where eight German U-boats surrendered at the end of the war. Folklore claims that five Nazi officers visited a bar in the town of Moville that week. They sat in a row at the counter, talking among themselves as their vessels were tugged out to sea and scuttled.

Military huts were later absorbed into a new prison to be

used as workshops. Magilligan Prison was built for all the convicts the Troubles were producing, and all the detainees getting scooped up. Nowadays creative writing classes take place behind the high wall; some of these students produced the book that I've got stowed in the canoe. Their surroundings edge into their writing. One poem is called 'Pater Noster':

> Take the Great Wall of China
> And the tumble-down crumble-down
> Wall of Roman Hadrian
> And the ivy-covered garden wall
> And the gas yard wall . . .
> The tall tower and the Long Tower
> The steel of the cannon the bronze of the bell
> The damning barbed wire that got higher

In 1993 three future prisoners were driving along Lough Foyle. They wanted to kill Catholics so they went to Greysteel, a mainly Catholic town, walked into a bar and fired into the crowd. Eight people died. It was a killing so indiscriminate it almost goes without saying that a couple of the victims were Protestant. Norman Hamill was a police officer who lived nearby and also happened to run the police press office. He felt it was time we saw what the aftermath of a massacre looked like. After the dead had been removed Hamill 'negotiated quite hard' with detectives to get television cameras inside the bar. In the broadcast we saw the kind of large, plain drinking barn familiar to many: lino floor, Formica tables, cigarette machine and branded ashtrays the size of dinner plates. Then we saw the blood wet on the seats and bullet holes in the upholstery, the death and injury made tangible. Hamill thinks the footage helped in the push towards the peace process. 'It was a turning point,' he said on the event's twentieth anniversary. 'I like to think that Greysteel was the beginning of the end of the Troubles.'

Gods have fought over Lough Foyle. In 2014 a statue of Manannán Mac Lir was commissioned and put on a hillside overlooking the water. Manannán was a sea god; old people like to attribute a storm on the Foyle to Manannán's rage. Portrayed in stainless steel and fibreglass, Manannán was the standard Celtic god type, with a beard, muscles and transfixed expression. On his wrists were bracelets decorated in spirals. One night a group of people – we don't know who but it would have taken a team – cut Manannán from his base with an angle grinder. They carried him to a cliff edge and threw him over. Then they replaced the statue with a large wooden crucifix chiselled with the words 'You shall have no other gods before me'.

Paddy and I go ashore in Moville, tying up at a small jetty. We have fish and chips in a cafe and darkness is falling when we return to the canoe. The spotlights of Magilligan Prison come on while the rest of the north disappears into the night. Paddy stands on the jetty, studying the water. 'The tide is running out the way, fast,' he says. We had planned to cross the channel tonight and finish our journey in the north but the tide is a problem. Going at about five knots it could carry us out to sea before we make the far shore. We discuss camping where we are and completing the journey in the morning. 'We don't want to end up in Scotland,' says Paddy.

'Sure it's only across the way,' says a ten-year-old boy who has invited himself into our deliberations, just walking right up and chipping in. 'You'll be there in no time.' I can tell he spends all his free time by the shore, talking to fishermen and developing an attunement to the tides that he'll probably have all his life.

'What do you think?' I ask Paddy. I want to be done, I realise, I want to be done tonight.

'We'd have to punch out into the current,' he says.

'Head for the light,' says the boy.

We paddle for the single tungsten light burning near the tip of the north. We're able for the current; it's the waves that challenge us. The big ocean is meeting the bay, the water shoaling against sandbars below and rolling at us steadily. Every ten seconds we are lifted up on a swell then sent sliding down the other side. Paddy and I are silent, focused on our tasks. Our small vessel could capsize if we aren't smartly angled to the swells but I love these few minutes, the sense of the ocean slapping against our port side, the puniness of the border and every other human effort when compared to it. Gradually the swells shrink. I notice something gritty between my teeth, sea salt.

'That's a pub ahead of us,' says Paddy.

Thanks to the tungsten light, I can make out the roof but all the windows are dark. 'There's nobody about,' I say. 'It's abandoned.'

'*A cold, uninhabited stretch*,' says Paddy, adopting the tone of a polar explorer. But when we round a breakwater we can see the ground-floor windows are bright and ten cars are parked out front. We pull the canoe up the beach, up above the tide line, and stamp about the sand to force life back into our legs. We then head for the bar. It's called the Point, which I like. Customers turn to look at us as we enter. We pull our wallets from ziplock bags. As if we were an entire football team, all three of the bar staff move into position as we approach the counter. Both Paddy and I have wet hair and grimy hands; everyone can see we've come a long way.

Acknowledgements

My thanks to Fabian Carr, Lorcan Carr, Caroline Sumpter, John Byrne, Alice Lyons, Joan Alexander, Neil Belton, David Park, Kathleen Jamie, J. P. Mallory, Barry McGuigan, Ian Sansom, Susan Lovell, Rachel Hooper, Paddy Bloomer, Georgina Capel, Walter Donohue, Sam Matthews, Moyra Haslett, Michael McAteer, Stephen Kelly, Stephen Royle, Steffi Lehner, David Brown, Lorraine Barry, Conor Graham, Colin Graham, Briege Magill, Susan Barrett, Eamonn Hughes, Feargal McNee, Garrett Sheehan, Emily DeDakis, Tom Clarke, Damian Smyth, the Arts Council of Northern Ireland, No Alibis Bookstore, my colleagues at the Seamus Heaney Centre, all the Sumpters, all the Carrs and all the Borderlanders.

Notes

With special thanks to Paddy Bloomer for joining me on the waterways of the border. The experts with whom I consulted are thanked in the notes for specific chapters; all errors are my own.

The Border Interpretive Centre

3 'something that unites': John Byrne quoting Kevin McAleer. *The Border Itself*. Exhibition, Temple Bar Gallery, Dublin, 2001.

Lighthouses, Vikings

9 relieved twice a week: Richard M. Taylor. *The Lighthouses of Ireland*. Cork: Collins Press, 2006. p. 155.

11 'He was above all things': Robert Louis Stevenson. *Records of a Family of Engineers*. London: Chatto & Windus, 1912. p. 82. *See also*: Bella Bathurst. *The Lighthouse Stevensons*. London: Harper Collins, 1999.

12 Carlingford truly is a fjord: H. E. Wilson. *Regional Geology of Northern Ireland*. Belfast: Her Majesty's Stationery Office, 1972. p. 3

13 on their behalf: 'Don't mention the pillage as academics explore the nice side of the Vikings'. *Irish Times*. 13 March 2009. p. 10.

15 this conjecture is now doubted: George Cunningham. 'Round Towers and Tall Tales'. *Irish Times*, 28 June 2014. p. 4.

15 American genealogists: Fiona Jones, Tom Cunningham, John Gattis, Barry Boecher and Brigitte Marmion. 'The Marmion Family of County Down'. Online www.marmionfamilytree. com/The_Marmion_Family_of_County_Down.html. Accessed July 2014.

16 'coaxing and wheedling': William Makepeace Thackeray. *Irish*

Sketchbook. London: Alan Sutton, 1990 (reprint of the 1843 text). p. 300. *See also*: Tony Canavan. *Frontier Town*. Belfast: Blackstaff, 1989.

Loving, Killing

22 lighthouses, out on the water, as a marker: Toby Harnden. *Bandit Country*. London: Hodder & Stoughton, 1999. p. 144.

23 'A survivor later recalled': quoted in Harnden. p. 144.

28 the Hewn Place: Thomas Kinsella (trans.). *The Táin*. Oxford: Oxford University Press, 1970. p. 71.

28 'Let us not make': Kinsella. p. 76. *See also*: L. Winifred Faraday (trans.). *The Cattle-Raid of Cooley*. London: Dodo, 2009 (reprint of the 1904 text); Ciaran Carson (trans.). *The Táin*. London: Penguin, 2008.

A Pass, a Chair, a Fort

Thanks to James O'Neill and S. J. Connolly for advice on this chapter.

36 'it is well-known': Edmund Spenser. 'A View of the present State of Ireland'. James P. Myers (ed.). *Elizabethan Ireland: A Selection of Writings by Elizabethan Writers on Ireland*. Connecticut: Archon, 1983. p. 111.

36 the Great Irishry: Jonathan Bardon. *The Plantation of Ulster*. London: Gill & Macmillan, 2012. p. 9.

36 educated among the English: S. J. Connolly. *Contested Island: Ireland 1460–1630*. Oxford: Oxford University Press, 2007. p. 230.

36 We have a sketch of the moment: reproduced in Elizabeth FitzPatrick. 'An Tulach Tinóil: Gathering-Sites and Meeting-Culture in Gaelic Lordships'. *History Ireland* 9.1 (Spring 2001). pp. 22–6 (p. 23).

37 Archtraitor: Ernest George Atkinson (ed.). *Calendar of the State Papers Relating to Ireland of the Reign of Elizabeth, 1 November 1600–31 July 1601*. London: His Majesty's Stationery Office, 1905. p. 22.

37 dainty, gentle and sensitive: Fynes Moryson. *A history of Ireland, from the year 1599 to 1603*. Dublin: George Ewing, 1735 reprint. p. 107.

38   a pious man, a defender: Peter Lombard. *The Irish War of Defence 1598–1600: Extracts from the De Hibernia Insula Commentarius of Peter Lombard, Archbishop of Armagh*. Trans. and ed. by Matthew J. Byrne. Cork: Cork University Press, 1930. p. 29.

38   'but each was joined to him': Lombard. p. 41.

38   'They really transform': Brian Friel. *Making History*. London: Faber & Faber, 1989. p. 2.

39   'Maguire is a fool': Friel. p. 30.

39   the safety of their wives and children: Atkinson. 1903. p. 465.

39   no task in Ireland more important: Atkinson. 1903. p. 473.

39   Dysentery broke out: Ernest George Atkinson (ed.). *Calendar of the State Papers Relating to Ireland of the Reign of Elizabeth, 1600, March–October*. London: His Majesty's Stationery Office, 1903. p. 531.

40   'villainous piece of work': quoted in James O'Neill. 'Half-Moons and Villainous Works'. *Archaeology Ireland*. 28.4 (Winter 2014). pp. 12–15 (p. 15).

40   kneeling before Mountjoy for an hour: Connolly. p. 254.

43   'keep the Irish in awe': Fynes Moryson. *The Commonwealth of Ireland*. Online: http://www.ucc.ie/celt/online/T100072.html. Trans. by Charles Hughes. Accessed August 2014. Manuscript: Oxford, Corpus Christi College Library, MS 94. *See also*: G. A. Hayes-McCoy (ed.). *Ulster and other Irish maps, c.1600*. Dublin: The Stationery Office for the Irish Manuscripts Commission, 1964.

Camera Mountains, Slieve Gullion

45   entered the army's lexicon: Donovan Wylie and Louise Purbrick. *British Watchtowers*. Göttingen: Steidl, 2007. p. 64

46   'It is an argument': Peter Morton. *Emergency Tour, 3rd PARA in South Armagh*. London: William Kimber & Co., 1989. p. 53.

46   'group of lawbreakers': Morton. p. 50.

47   towers came in preset elevations: Wylie and Purbrick. p. 63.

47   functioning in less than three hours: Wylie and Purbrick. p. 63.

47   'being in prison': Morton. p. 92.

51   a nationalist politician argued: Jonathan Olley. *Castles of Ulster*. Belfast: Factotum, 2007. (The politician interviewed is Davy Hyland.)

52   to tell Tóibín: Colm Tóibín. *Walking Along the Border*. London: Queen Anne Press, 1987 (reprinted as *Bad Blood* in 2010). p. 150.

56   'Slievegullion of a son': William Makepeace Thackeray. *Irish Sketchbook*. London: Alan Sutton, 1990 (reprint of the 1843 text). p. 298.

56   sent surges of magma radiating out: W. I. Mitchell (ed.). *The Geology of Northern Ireland: Our Natural Foundation*. Belfast: Geological Survey of Northern Ireland, 2004. p. 187.

56   Slieve Gullion's greatest distinction is hidden: Mitchell. p. 236.

Farmers

Many thanks to all the farmers I met on the border.

Checkpoints, Customs

Thanks to David Brown of Queen's University, Belfast, for showing me the oak samples from the Dorsey and explaining the process of dendrochronology, and to J. P. Mallory of Queen's University for his advice on this chapter.

71   In 1940 a gang of smugglers: 'Donkey Serenade'. *Fermanagh Herald*, 6 April 1940. p. 5.

76   one other source: bbc.co.uk. 'WW2 People's War – Living on the Border Between Derry and Donegal'. 2006. Online: www.bbc.co.uk/history/ww2peopleswar/stories/04/a8976504.shtml. Accessed June 2016. *See also*: House of Commons, Northern Ireland Affairs Committee. *Fuel Laundering and Smuggling in Northern Ireland*. London: The Stationery Office Limited, 2012.

80   Archaeological excavations have dug up palisade walls: Chris Lynn, 'Excavations at the Dorsey, County Armagh, 1977'. *Ulster Journal of Archaeology*, Third Series, 54/55 (1991/2). pp. 61–77.

81   impression of concentricity: Chris Lynn, Cormac McSparron and Peter Moore. 'Data Structure Report, Navan Fort, Co. Armagh'. 2002. Online: www.qub.ac.uk/schools/Centrefor ArchaeologicalFieldworkCAF/PDFFileStore/Filetoupload, 180972,en.pdf. Accessed August 2014.

82   mound of stones emerged: Chris Lynn. 'The Iron Age Mound In Navan Fort: A Physical Realization of Celtic Religious

Beliefs?'. *Eamnia, the Bulletin of the Navan Research Group* 10 (1992). p. 40.

82   twenty-one distinct types of soil: Lynn, McSparron and Moore. p. 10. *See also*: Chris Lynn. 'Navan Fort – Legendary Capital of Prehistoric Ulster'. *Archaeology Ireland Heritage Guide No. 40* (2015). pp. 1–6; Chris Lynn. 'Navan Fort: Home of Gods and Goddesses?'. *Archaeology Ireland* 7 (Spring 1993). pp. 17–21.

84   Archaeologists stripped away the topsoil: Declan P. Hurl, Cormac McSparron and Gill Plunkett. 'Excavations at the Dorsey, County Armagh'. *Ulster Journal of Archaeology*, Third Series, 63 (2004). pp. 41–51. *See also*: Declan Hurl, Cormac McSparron and Peter Moore. 'Data Structure Report, Dorsey, Dorsy, Co. Armagh'. 2002. Online: www.qub.ac.uk/schools/ CentreforArchaeologicalFieldworkCAF/PDFFileStore/ Filetoupload,180961,en.pdf.

Landlords, Tenants

Thanks to Yvonne Kelly, Cultural Heritage Manager at the Castle Leslie Archives, for additional information on the Leslie family.

88   'shamrock pattern': Richard Hayward. *Border Foray*. London: Arthur Barker Limited, 1957. p. 105.

89   Lieutenant C. Bailey surveyed these hills: Angélique Day and Patrick McWilliams (eds). *Ordnance Survey Memoirs of Ireland, Vol 20: County Tyrone II, 1825, 1833–35, 1840*. Belfast: The Institute of Irish Studies, Queen's University, 1993. p. 142.

90   'fine specimen of a bastard': George Petrie quoted in William Stokes. *The Life and Labours in Art and Archaeology of George Petrie*. London: Longman Green & Co., 1868. p. 123.

91   back to Attila the Hun: The Leslie Family. 'History of Castle Leslie – Castle Leslie Estate Monaghan'. Castle Leslie Estate. Online: www.castleleslie.com/historical-castle-ireland.html. Accessed June 2016.

92   'symbols of hated unionism': quoted in Neil C. Fleming. 'Aristocratic Rule? Unionism and Northern Ireland', *History Ireland* 15.6 (Nov./Dec. 2007). p. 26.

92   had played an active role in politics: Fleming. p. 26.

96   '20 Protestants, 20 Catholics': Day and McWilliams. p. 142.

98   'behind our demesne walls': Shane Leslie. *The Landlords of Ireland at the Cross-Roads*. Dublin: James Duffy, 1908. p. 5.

98   'magnificent red-bearded Celt': Shane Leslie. *Long Shadows*. London: John Murray, 1966. p. 35.

99   'maze twisting between bogs and rivers': Leslie. *Long Shadows*. p. 144.

99   'men bearing mysterious bags': Leslie. *Long Shadows*. p. 11.

100   'they exemplified how': Shane Leslie. 'Conversion in Ireland', *The Furrow* 4.3 (March 1953), pp. 132–5 (p. 134).

102   'The convert is impeded and discouraged': Leslie. 'Conversion in Ireland'. p. 133. *See also*: Shane Leslie. *The End of a Chapter*. New York: Charles Scribner, 1916; Otto Rauchbauer. Shane Leslie: *Sublime Failure*. Dublin: The Lilliput Press, 2009.

105   'a right to change my name': William Carleton. *The Black Baronet*. Dublin: James Duffy & Sons, 1875. p. 84.

106   'both slave and tyrant': Carleton. p. 277.

106   'Crackenfudge must get to the bench': Carleton. p. 279.

Highs, Lows

108   endless rollercoaster: Carlo Gébler. *The Glass Curtain*. London: Hamish Hamilton, 1991. p. 196.

110   'necklace of beads': Estyn Evans. *The Personality of Ireland*. Cambridge: Cambridge University Press, 1973. p. 27.

110   'One might think of the moulded drumlins': Estyn Evans. *Ulster: The Common Ground* (lecture published as pamphlet). Dublin: Lilliput Press, 1984.

110   'culturally productive borderland': Evans. *The Personality of Ireland*. p. 75. *See also*: Brian Graham. 'The Search for the Common Ground: Estyn Evan's Ireland', *Transactions of the Institute of British Geographers* 19.2 (1994). pp. 183–201.

113   'Imagine your final steps': 'Digging for the IRA Disappeared: Moors Murders police officer searching peat bog for victims'. *Mirror*, 8 June 2013. p. 4.

113   'He was a big child': 'Mother Prays Bog Will Yield Grisly Secret'. *Guardian*, 12 September 2013. p. 7.

114   Anonymous tip-offs: 'Search for Disappeared Victim Resumes'.

BBC News Northern Ireland, 17 September 2012. Online: www.bbc.co.uk/news/uk-northern-ireland-19622787. Accessed June 2016.

114   'We know how he died': 'The Disappeared: Sister of Murdered Columba McVeigh Talks to BBC'. BBC News Northern Ireland, 2 May 2014. Online: www.bbc.co.uk/news/uk-northern-ireland-27251094. Accessed June 2016.

300   'I refused to go': 'The Disappeared'. BBC TV documentary, 2013.

A Boy Racer, a Buster, a Boxer

128   Concrete pipes were too expensive: 'The Border-Busters'. *An Phoblacht*, 18 October 2007. Online: www.anphoblacht.com/contents/17606. Accessed February 2015. The wording on the plaque is available online: www.geograph.org.uk/photo/1054582

129   In 1972 two men were killed: Martin Dillon. *The Dirty War*. London: Arrow, 1991. p. 126

130   'I'd just belt away at the bag': Barry McGuigan, Gerry Callan and Harry Mullan. *Barry McGuigan: The Untold Story*. London: Robson, 1991. p. 4.

131   'Go out and give it everything': McGuigan, Callan and Mullan. p. 124.

131   'You'll be a good champion': McGuigan, Callan and Mullan. p. 124.

132   'BOX 1T': McGuigan, Callan and Mullan. p. 125. *See also*: Barry McGuigan. *Cyclone: My Story*. London: Virgin, 2011.

Bridges, Dead Ends

137   'No Popery': Jonathan Bardon. *A History of Ulster*. Belfast: Blackstaff, 1992. p. 159.

137   one description claims the slaughter: John Henry Crichton, Earl of Erne. 'An Account of Some Plantation Castles on the Estates of the Earl of Erne in the County of Fermanagh'. *Ulster Journal of Archaeology* 2 (1896). p. 15

137   one Jacobite soldier made it across: Bardon. *A History of Ulster*. p. 159.

138 'You're wasting your time': Council on Foreign Relations. Video interview, HBO History Makers Series with George J. Mitchell. 2013. Online: www.cfr.org/united-states/hbo-history-makers-series-george-j-mitchell/p35429. Accessed June 2016.

138 'contentious people to their feud': George Mitchell. *Making Peace*. Oakland: University of California Press, 2000. p. 50.

141 'I made certain that every single word': Council on Foreign Relations.

A Tomb, a House, a Hotel

144 Irelanders: a term coined by J. P. Mallory. *The Origins of the Irish*. London: Thames & Hudson. p. 42.

146 'Dozens come across': Dervla Murphy. *A Place Apart*. London: John Murray, 1978. p. 43

146 told Tóibín about the cement factory: Colm Tóibín. *Walking Along the Border*. London: Queen Anne Press, 1987 (reprinted as *Bad Blood* in 2010). p. 87.

147 'a bit Quinny': Gavin Daly and Ian Kehoe. *Citizen Quinn*. Dublin: Penguin Ireland, 2013. p. 50.

147 Gébler travelled in a Quinn truck: Carlo Gébler. *The Glass Curtain*. London: Hamish Hamilton, 1991. p. 191.

152 actions of a gambling addict: Daly and Kehoe. p. 48.

153 Sean Quinn in an interview: *Tonight with Vincent Browne*. TV3, Raidió Teilifís Éireann, 1 August 2012.

153 'blatant, dishonest and deceitful': Quoted in Fintan O'Toole. 'Irish State Means Little to Many of Its Citizens'. *Irish Times*, 7 August 2012. p. 14.

154 alone and resentful: 'End to Seán Quinn's latest saga a bitter pill to swallow'. *Irish Times*, 21 May 2016. p. 10.

154 'Jesus Christ hotel': Daly and Kehoe. p. 5.

157 didn't fight existing land systems: *Making Sense of the Molly Maguires*. Kevin Kenny. New York: Oxford University Press, 1998. p. 22.

123 who the original Molly was: Kenny. p. 19.

158 'The Mighty Quinn from Derrylin': Tony Bannon. 2012. Available online: www.youtube.com/watch?v=daHe4tBvapc. Accessed June 2016.

159 'There is, however, a historical meaning': 'Letters to the Editor'. *Irish Examiner*, 2 August 2012. p. 12.

159 'good Cavan people, good Fermanagh people': O'Toole. p. 14.

A Peak, a Pot, a Tunnel

Thanks to Stephen, Jock and Rocky for telling me about the exploration of the Cuilcagh Mountain system.

164 'Exploration was terminated': Gareth Llwyd Jones. *The Caves of Fermanagh and Cavan*. Enniskillen: Watergate, 1974. p. 46.

166 'mighty fountain': W. F. Wakeman. *Lough Erne, Enniskillen, Belleek, Ballyshannon and Bundoran with Routes from Dublin to Enniskillen and Bundoran, by Rail or Steamboat*. Dublin: John Mullany, 1876. p. 133.

167 'like inside a washing machine': Paul Doig and Al Kennedy. 'Log na Sionna / Shannon Pot'. 2009. Online: wiki.technical-diving.ie/index.php/Log_na_Sionna_/_Shannon_Pot. Accessed May 2015.

167 'Bend ye hills, on either side': Gerald Griffin. *The Poetical Works*. Dublin: James Duffy, 1854. p. 124. *See also*: Gareth Ll. Jones, Gaby Burns, Tim Fogg and John G. Kelly. *The Caves of Fermanagh and Cavan*. Florencecourt: The Lough Nilly Press, 1997.

Relics

Thanks to Séamus Ó hUltacháin for information about the Cavan Burren. *See also*: www.cavanburren.ie. Accessed February 2015; Ll. Jones, Burns, Fogg and Kelly. *The Caves of Fermanagh and Cavan*.

Romance, Break-ups

Thanks to Jerry Finneran and Michael McLoughlin for sharing their memories of the Rainbow Ballroom.

188 'ingenuity of the builders': 'Old Railway Bridge Destroyed'. *Fermanagh Herald*, 12 June 1976. p. 1.

191 'It wasn't a time for conversation': William Trevor. 'The Hill Bachelors'. *The Hill Bachelors*. London: Viking, 2000. p. 226.

191   'His mother didn't ask why': Trevor. 'The Hill Bachelors'. p. 241.

191   'Enduring, unchanging': Trevor. 'The Hill Bachelors'. p. 245.

192   'scant acres': William Trevor. 'The Ballroom of Romance'. *The Ballroom of Romance and Other Stories*. London: Viking, 1972. p. 51.

192   'miles from anywhere': Trevor. 'The Ballroom of Romance'. p. 52.

192   'People came on bicycles': Trevor. 'The Ballroom of Romance'. p. 53.

Walls, Ways

Thanks to J. P. Mallory of Queen's University, Belfast.

200   O'Donovan was among the first: Aidan Walsh. 'Excavation at the Black Pig's Dyke'. *Clogher Record* 14.1 (1991). pp. 9–26 (p. 9).

201   'The young lad says': R. S. Rogers. 'The Folklore of the Black Pig's Dyke'. *Ulster Folklife* 3.1 (1957). pp. 29–36 (p. 30).

203   Little White Lane and the Great Man's Track: William Francis de Vismes Kane. 'The Black Pig's Dyke: The Ancient Boundary Fortification of Uladh'. *Proceedings of the Royal Irish Academy. Section C: Archaeology, Celtic Studies, History, Linguistics, Literature,* Vol. 27 (1908/9). pp. 301–28 (p. 321).

204   Some archaeologists reckon: Cóilín Ó Drisceoil and Emer Condit. *Archaeology Ireland, Heritage Guide No. 68. The Black Pig's Dyke – Power Lines in the Landscapes.* Dublin: Wordwell, 2015. *See also*: 'Trench Warfare'. BBC Radio 4, 19 April 2006, 11:00–11:30 a.m.

204   hit ten different targets: Ian S. Wood. 'The IRA's Border Campaign'. In Malcolm Anderson and Eberhard Bort (eds). *Irish Border: History, Politics, Culture.* Liverpool: Liverpool University Press, 1999. p.115.

205   two hundred connections: Henry Patterson. *Ireland's Violent Frontier.* London: Palgrave Macmillan, 2013. p. 11.

205   'They were like ponds': Border Roads to Memories and Reconciliation. 'Kiltyclogher Bridge' (video interview with Thomas Maguire). Online: www.borderroadmemories.com. 2012. Accessed July 2015.

205   Tommy Fletcher was stopped: David McKittrick, Seamus Kelters, Brian Feeney and Chris Thornton. *Lost Lives: The Stories of the Men, Women and Children Who Died as a Result of the Northern Ireland Troubles*. Edinburgh: Mainstream, 1999. p. 158.

205   The week Fletcher was killed: Border Roads to Memories and Reconciliation. 'Gilmartins Lane' (video interview with Kathleen Richey). Online: www.borderroadmemories.com. 2012. Accessed July 2015.

205   you couldn't even get across on a bicycle: Border Roads to Memories and Reconciliation (video interview with Thomas Maguire).

205   a well-known local storyteller: Border Roads to Memories and Reconciliation (video interview with Thomas Maguire). *See also*: Henry Patterson. 'War of National Liberation or Ethnic Cleansing? IRA Violence in Fermanagh during . In Brett Bowden and Michael T. Davis (eds). *Terror from Tyrannicide to Terrorism*. Brisbane: University of Queensland Press, 2008. pp. 230–42.

206   'The bark of a dog in the night': 'Where Protestant Families Fear for Their Lives'. *Irish Press*, 7 July 1980. p. 4.

206   dogs died from poisoning: 'Where Protestant Families Fear for Their Lives'.

206   The leader of the Unionist Party thought even bigger: 'Unionist Call to Seal the Border'. *Irish Press*, 29 July 1986. p. 4.

206   303 miles: Peter Morton. *Emergency Tour, 3rd PARA in South Armagh*. London: William Kimber & Co., 1989. p. 32.

207   window of a high-speed helicopter: *Irish Press*, 7 March 1981. p. 4.

Rejection, Perfection

Thanks to historian Joe O'Loughlin for further information on the history of Belleek.

218   'In a sinking ship': Thomas Moles quoted in Ged Martin. 'Origins of Partition'. In Anderson and Bort (eds). *Irish Border*. p. 78.

218   pressed to swear an oath: Michael Laffan. *The Partition of Ireland 1911–25*. The Historical Association of Ireland: Dublin, 1983. p. 86.

218 promise of a Boundary Commission: Martin. p. 70.

219 putting a lot of faith in: Laffan. p. 89.

219 vague: Laffan. p. 88.

219 286 square miles to the south: Martin. p. 96.

219 'however unsatisfactory from many points of view': Leo Amery quoted in Martin. p. 96.

222 'unlawfully at large': 'Arrests Follow Cavan Prison Escape'. BBC News Northern Ireland, 25 April 2012. Online: www.bbc.co.uk/news/uk-northern-ireland-17840926. Accessed July 2015.

225 potters learned the location of hotspots: Richard K. Degenhardt. *Belleek: The Complete Collector's Guide and Illustrated Reference*. New York: Portfolio Press, 1978. p. 15.

225 'cloyingly glutinous in texture': Bruce Arnold. 'Lovably Hideous and Still Popular'. *Irish Independent*, 2 June 1979. p. 6. *See also*: Tommy Campbell. 'The Story of the Belleek Pottery'. *Ulster Herald*, 16 April 1983. p. 16.

Lost, Found

Thanks to Ken for sharing his workday with me.

228 'We're going to need the border again': Kevin McAleer. 'Happy Brexmas from Kevin McAleer'. *Irish Times*, 28 June 2016. p. 10.

231 snug little town: William Carleton. 'The Lough Derg Pilgrim'. *Traits and Stories of the Irish Peasantry* Volume 1 (5th edition). London: William Tegg, 1864. p. 250.

233 helped make Lough Derg famous: Jacques Le Goff. *The Birth of Purgatory*. Aldershot: Scolar Press, 1984. p. 193.

234 150 manuscripts in existence: Joseph McGuiness. *Saint Patrick's Purgatory Lough Derg*. Dublin: Columba Press, 2000. p. 17.

234 influenced Dante: Le Goff. p. 200.

234 complaints were lodged with the pope: McGuiness. p. 22.

234 monks driven away: McGuiness. p. 23.

235 'tall, gaunt, gawkish': Carleton. p. 244.

235 'two or three slated houses': Carleton. p. 256.

236 'between life and death': Carleton. p. 255.

237 123 pillars: McGuiness. p. 41.

Forgetting, Remembering

Thanks to Isabella Mulhall, National Museum of Ireland, and J. P. Mallory of Queen's University, Belfast.

242   'Butter sunk under': Seamus Heaney. 'Bogland'. *Door into the Dark*. London: Faber & Faber, 1969. p. 41.

247   about ten thousand years ago: J. P. Mallory. *The Origins of the Irish*. London: Thames & Hudson, 2013. p. 40.

247   Preserved trunks tell us they could be massive: Frank Mitchell and Michael Ryan. *Reading the Irish Landscape*. Dublin: Townhouse, 2007. p. 144.

247   fish bones and stone flakes: Mallory. p. 40.

247   They either did not have the ambition: Mitchell and Ryan. p. 114.

247   wood pigeon's coo or wild pig's snort: Mallory. p. 45.

247   dog sniffs around: Mitchell and Ryan. p. 115.

247   only in the hundreds or low thousands: Mallory. p. 69.

248   Watching Stone or the White Stone: Hurl, McSparron and Moore. 'Data Structure Report'. p. 8.

252   traditional boundaries often remain in use: Paul MacCotter. 'Medieval Irish Political and Economic Divisions'. *History Ireland*, 15.5 (Sept.–Oct. 2007). pp. 17–21 (p. 18).

This World, the Next

Thanks to Isabella Mulhall for her expertise on bogs and the ancient objects found in them. Thanks also to Margaret Loughrey.

255   'Mags to Riches': 'Mags to Riches'. *Strabane Chronicle*, 5 December 2013. p. 1.

256   lung disease: 'Spotlight on Flax Byssinosis'. *Ulster Herald*, 16 April 1983. p. 16. *See also*: Sion Mills Buildings Preservation Trust. *Sion Mills: Historic Irish Linen Village*. Sion Mills, n.d.; www.sionmills.com. Accessed February 2015.

259   'giving him a proper burial': 'Father of David Colhoun Fears His Son Has Drowned'. BBC News Northern Ireland, 26 May 2011. Online: www.bbc.co.uk/news/uk-northern-ireland-13561016. Accessed August 2015.

259   by Island Mor: 'Body's identity confirmed as David Colhoun'.

Belfast Telegraph. Online: www.belfasttelegraph.co.uk/news/republic-of-ireland/bodys-identity-confirmed-as-david-colhoun-28720535.html. Accessed August 2015. *See also*: 'Family Fear Man (22) Drowned After He Fled Police'. *Irish Independent*, 26 May 2011. Online: www.independent.ie/irish-news/family-fear-man-22-drowned-after-he-fled-police-26736379.html. Accessed August 2015.

260   deposited at frontiers: Eamonn P. Kelly. 'Secrets of the Bog Bodies: The Enigma of the Iron Age Explained'. *Archaeology Ireland*, 20.1 (Spring 2006). pp. 26–30 (p. 26). *See also*: Isabella Mulhall. 'The Peat Men from Clonycavan and Oldcroghan'. *British Archaeology* 110 (Jan.–Feb. 2010). pp. 34–9 (p. 36).

261   'The Catholic Church would not allow': Brian McGilloway. *The Nameless Dead*. London: Pan Macmillan, 2012. p. 7.

261   'Those children deserve their story to be heard': McGilloway. p. 244.

Home, Castle, Empire

With thanks to Brian Lacey and Anthony Barrett.

273   *Those who give hostages*: Seán Duffy (ed.). *Medieval Ireland: An Encyclopedia*. London: Routledge, 2005. p. 23.

274   built in the late eighth or early ninth century: Brian Lacey. 'The Grianán of Aileach: A Note on Its Identification'. *The Journal of the Royal Society of Antiquaries of Ireland*. 131 (2001). pp. 145–9.

272   men of status lead from the front: T. M. Charles-Edwards. 'Irish Warfare before 1100'. In Thomas Bartlett and Keith Jeffery (eds). *A Military History of Ireland*. Cambridge: Cambridge University Press, 1996. p. 28

275   ordered to carry one stone away: Peter Harbison. *Guide to National and Historic Monuments of Ireland*. Dublin: Gill and Macmillan, 1992. p. 101.

Bars

Thanks to Anna Maria Hamilton for information on the statue of Manannán Mac Lir.

282   showpiece of Ulster's Plantation: S. J. Connolly. *Divided*

Kingdom: Ireland 1630–1800. Oxford: Oxford University Press, 2008. p. 182.

282   Two gents: Willie Carson. *Derry – Thru the Lens*. Ballyshannon: Donegal Democrat, 1976. p. 115. *See also*: Willie Carson. *Derry: Through the Lens – Refocus*. Derry: Guildhall Press, 2006.

283   protests that were viciously put down: Bardon. *A History of Ulster*. p. 659–61.

283   'Fuck the Pope': quoted in Paul Theroux. *The Kingdom by the Sea*. London: Penguin, 1983. p. 239.

286   upstairs in 2006: Eamonn McCann. *The Raytheon 9 – Resisting War Crimes Is Not a Crime*. Derry: Derry Anti War Coalition, 2008. p. 3.

286   occupy Raytheon's building: 'Defence Firm Protesters Arrested'. BBC News Northern Ireland, 9 August 2006. news.bbc.co.uk/1/hi/northern_ireland/4776051.stm. Accessed July 2016.

286   fire extinguisher to disable: McCann. p. 9.

286   forced from the city: 'Raytheon to Close Its Plant in Derry'. *Irish Times*, 14 January 2010. p. 9.

288   In 1827 a set of base points: Rachel Hewitt. *Map of a Nation: A Biography of the Ordnance Survey*. London: Granta, 2010. p. 254.

289   O'Neill had defences dug here: O'Neill. 'Half-Moons and Villainous Works'. *Archaeology Ireland*. 28.4 (Winter 2014). pp. 12–15 (p. 14).

290   'Take the Great Wall of China': Neil Hanna. 'Pater Noster'. *Magilligan Prison Writing: Writ, Judgment, Sentence, Parole* (ed. John Brown). Limavady: HMP Magilligan and The Prison Arts Foundation, 2007. p. 26.

290   they went to Greysteel: 'Greysteel "Trick or Treat" Massacre 20 Years On'. BBC News Northern Ireland, 30 October 2013. www.bbc.co.uk/news/uk-northern-ireland-24736060. Accessed June 2016.

290   'negotiated quite hard': Norman Hamill, quoted in 'It Was Watershed Moment'. *Belfast Newsletter*, 30 October 2013. p. 7.

Index

Numbers in *italics* refer to pages with illustrations.

Index

Index

Index